Benefit–Cost Analyses for Security Policies

Benefit–Cost Analyses for Security Policies

Does Increased Safety Have to Reduce Efficiency?

Edited by

Carol Mansfield

Senior Economist, RTI International, USA

V. Kerry Smith

Emeritus Regents' Professor and Emeritus University Professor, Arizona State University, USA

EE Edward Elgar PUBLISHING

Cheltenham, UK • Northampton, MA, USA

Published by
Edward Elgar Publishing Limited
The Lypiatts
15 Lansdown Road
Cheltenham
Glos GL50 2JA
UK

Edward Elgar Publishing, Inc.
William Pratt House
9 Dewey Court
Northampton
Massachusetts 01060
USA

A catalogue record for this book
is available from the British Library

Library of Congress Control Number: 2014950916

This book is available electronically in the **Elgar**online
Economics subject collection
DOI 10.4337/9781784711085

FSC www.fsc.org MIX Paper from responsible sources FSC® C013056

ISBN 978 1 78471 107 8 (cased)
ISBN 978 1 78471 108 5 (eBook)

Typeset by Servis Filmsetting Ltd, Stockport, Cheshire
Printed and bound in Great Britain by T.J. International Ltd, Padstow

Contents

List of contributors vii
Preface ix

PART I INTRODUCTION AND OBJECTIVES

1 Introducing the issues: meeting the challenges in evaluating homeland security policies 3
Carol Mansfield and V. Kerry Smith
2 The design of benefit–cost architecture for homeland security policy analysis 26
V. Kerry Smith and Carol Mansfield

PART II SECURITY POLICIES AND REDUCING RISKS

3 Lessons from risk assessment, economics, and risk management at EPA 63
Chris Dockins and William Wheeler
4 The heterogeneity of the value of statistical life: evidence and policy implications 78
W. Kip Viscusi
5 Dealing with safety in UK public sector project appraisal 117
Michael Jones-Lee
6 A comparison of key benefit estimation issues for natural hazards and terrorism: *ex ante/ex post* valuation and endogenous risk 140
Scott Farrow

PART III ADAPTATION AND ECONOMY-WIDE EFFECTS

7 Urban adaptation to low-probability shocks: contrasting terrorism and natural disaster risk 157
Matthew E. Kahn

8 Macroeconomic consequences of terrorist attacks: estimation for the analysis of policies and rules 172
Adam Rose

PART IV PRACTICAL IMPLEMENTATION OF POLICY EVALUATION

9 Valuing time for Department of Homeland Security projects and policies 203
Kenneth E. McConnell
10 Applicability of benefit transfers for evaluation of homeland security counterterrorism measures 225
Kevin Boyle, Sapna Kaul, Ali Hashemi and Xiaoshu Li
11 What we know and what we need to learn 254
Carol Mansfield and V. Kerry Smith

Index 267

Contributors

Kevin Boyle
Professor and Director, Program in Real Estate, Virginia Tech

Chris Dockins
Senior Economist, Research and Program Support Division, National Center for Environmental Economics, US Environmental Protection Agency

Scott Farrow
Professor, Department of Economics, University of Maryland Baltimore County

Ali Hashemi
Assistant Professor, Economics, Richard E. & Sandra J. Dauch College of Business & Economics, Ashland University

Michael Jones-Lee
Emeritus Professor, Business School, Newcastle University

Matthew E. Kahn
Professor, Institute of the Environment, Department of Economics, and Department of Public Policy, University of California Los Angeles

Sapna Kaul
Post-Doctoral Research Associate, Department of Pediatrics and Huntsman Cancer Institute, University of Utah

Xiaoshu Li
Post-doctoral Scholar, Department of Forestry, University of Kentucky

Carol Mansfield
Senior Economist, RTI International

Kenneth E. McConnell
Professor, Agricultural and Resource Economics, University of Maryland College Park

Adam Rose
Research Professor, Price School of Public Policy, and Faculty Affiliate, National Center for Risk and Economic Analysis of Terrorism Events (CREATE), University of Southern California (USC)

V. Kerry Smith
Emeritus Regents' Professor and Emeritus University Professor, Department of Economics, W. P. Carey School of Business, Arizona State University

W. Kip Viscusi
University Distinguished Professor of Law, Economics, and Management, Vanderbilt University Law School

William Wheeler
Economist, Benefits Assessment and Methods Development Division, National Center for Environmental Economics, US Environmental Protection Agency

Preface

As a rule, economists love markets and underappreciate lawyers. As we were completing the final preparation of chapters for this volume, David Brooks' March 24, 2014, column reminded us of the importance of the rule of law. His column devotes most of its attention to crime and unequal access to legal protection, but the lessons from his argument are more general. The legal structure of a nation conditions everything its citizens can do. One that is fair and reliable creates different outcomes than one that is not. Markets cannot function effectively without well-defined, or at least reasonably enforceable, property rights. Economic activities and the rule of law are intertwined. This point is so basic it can be underappreciated. Thus, when we consider the infrastructure that supports economic activity and the ability to sustain and enhance people's well-being we need to include recognition of the importance of the 'rule of law'. Terrorism poses threats to many dimensions of our infrastructure: physical, economic, political, social, and legal processes. Policies to protect homeland security are also not neutral interventions. Homeland security policies can threaten the freedoms people enjoy because the rights accorded citizens and residents of this country may be compromised in an effort to protect against terrorist attacks. Both the threat and the remedy can change this generalized concept of infrastructure and as a result the economic and social outcomes within our country. Thus, as part of the process of evaluating new policies to protect security an important dimension of the evaluation must begin with a clear definition of what these policies are intended to provide and how they will accomplish these objectives. This specification is important because the means used to enhance security may well diminish other 'rights'.

At one level, policies can mean more waiting time for security at airports and no access to the gates for non-passengers. Such changes can be represented as fairly straightforward modifications in the time required for travel and in the attributes of a visit to the airport to meet family or friends arriving for a visit. They can also mean fundamental changes in the privacy of communication, transactions, and ultimately each individual's private lives. While our focus in this volume is primarily on the changes that have direct economic implications, it is important to recognize the many ways the formulation and implementation of security policies can affect all aspects of our social interactions and well-being. Thus, the economic system that results and its performance in meeting people's needs can become very different depending on the policy decisions that are made.

Describing the intended outcomes of new policies and the mechanisms for implementation is not easy. Economic models use a shorthand to characterize the outcomes of policies and the mechanisms through which the outcomes are achieved as specifying a production process. In the case of security, however, it is not simply a plant or coordinated set of facilities producing a good or service. Instead, the production of the final outcomes can involve people, public and private institutions, and firms in diverse ways.

The same comment might have been made about environmental policies in the early days of conducting economic analysis to support environmental regulation. Faced with a requirement to conduct benefit-cost analysis of Federal regulations, environmental analysts from many disciplines worked together to create a framework to analyze the economic impacts of environmental regulations. This work has spanned many decades and has been supported by a large and ambitious body of research carried out by government scientists, academics, and all types of consultants and researchers in the nonprofit and for profit sectors. It was not easy, it took considerable time, and it required a concerted effort to develop, in this interdisciplinary setting, a framework for analysis. This is what we refer to as a 'platform' for policy analysts to use to organize the research activities necessary to conduct regulatory impact analyses. The goal of the workshop in 2010 and the subsequent research that produced this volume was to support this process in the US Department of Homeland Security.

The workshop and this book are outputs of our long term collaboration with CREATE (National Center for Risk and Economic Analysis of Terrorism Events), the US Department of Homeland Security university research center at the University of Southern California. Our participation was initiated by its first director, Detlof von Winterfeldt, and supported throughout by Isaac Maya and the director at the time this work was being finalized, Stephen Hora. We would never have been able to successfully organize the workshop or complete the research needed for this volume without their support as well as the support and research contributions of CREATE's Coordinator for Economics at the time, Adam Rose.

Many others contributed to this effort as well. Aaron Strong and H. Allen Klaiber were post-doctoral fellows at Arizona State University (ASU) during the time some of this research was undertaken and contributed to its success. Several undergraduates served as research fellows during our activities and contributed significantly to our research. They include Jacob Fishman, Michael Kaminsky, Eric Moore, Jesse Snook, Eric Stewart, and Carlos Valcarcel. At RTI International, the research and workshop were supported by Laurel Clayton and Paramita Sinha. In many different ways they all contributed to assuring our research was successfully completed.

Administrative management at ASU and RTI International were also essential to our ability to complete the work. We would like to especially acknowledge Natalie Cardita and Shauna Mortensen at ASU for assuring every dimension of the focus groups, conference planning, and manuscript preparation was successfully completed. At RTI, Sharon Barrell did much of the editing for this volume. At ASU, Kathryn Kyle helped us to complete the editing task quickly.

The official acknowledgment of support requires we note that research was supported by the US Department of Homeland Security through the Center for Risk and Economic Analysis of Terrorism Events (CREATE) under grant numbers 2007-ST-061–000001 and DE-AC05–76RL01830. However any opinions, findings, and conclusions or recommendations in this document are those of the authors and do not necessarily reflect views of the US Department of Homeland Security.

Finally, the volume would not have been possible without the contribution of our authors. Not only did they work to inform the research needs for regulatory impact analysis of homeland security policies but they also were very patient with us as we deliberately (but slowly) moved this volume to completion. Our families support all we do. Thank you to all those we mentioned and to many others who are not mentioned but contributed to this effort. In the end, the final judgments on the composition and content of the volume were ours, so errors and omissions fall on us.

Research is about promoting a better understanding of the world around us, including what we do to it and to each other. A book that takes stock of a set of research on the evaluation of security policy seeks to enhance this learning by promoting greater interaction among analysts and policy makers. This was our objective. Hopefully you will agree the efforts of all involved in this volume contribute to enhancing this process.

Carol Mansfield
V. Kerry Smith
April 17, 2014

PART I

Introduction and objectives

1. Introducing the issues: meeting the challenges in evaluating homeland security policies

Carol Mansfield and V. Kerry Smith

The task of evaluating the benefits and costs of public policies intended to enhance homeland security poses unique problems. After 9/11, the risks faced by the United States (US) population and policies needed to address them were seen in different terms. Prior to 9/11, national defense and security were often used as examples of 'pure public goods' in introductory economics texts. One of the earliest comprehensive texts, by Nobel laureate Paul Samuelson (1976), defined public goods using security as an example. He noted:

> Nothing is more vital to a threatened society than its security. But national defense, regarded as a commodity, differs completely from the case of a private commodity like bread. Ten loaves of bread can be divided up in many ways among individuals in a group; but national defense has to be provided *more or less automatically for all.* (pp. 159–160)

For the most part, discussions of national security as a public good were intended to illustrate the difficulty of measuring the 'amount' of the good and of substantiating the fact that no one is easily excluded from a defense program that protects the US population and the resources that sustain its well-being. For any such program each resident enjoys this umbrella of protection without infringing on others.

Shortly after the US Department of Homeland Security (DHS) was formed in 2002, analysts faced the challenge of developing measures for the amount of protection associated with any homeland security program and what people might be willing to give up to sustain or increase it in a way that conformed to the requirements for policy evaluations. The broad umbrella of security as a pure public good is an *ex ante* concept, and the reality of meeting threats can involve a complex array of new regulations that inevitably target specific types of activities associated with different types of threats. In many respects the challenge that analysts faced was unprecedented. However, there is hope that we can structure a systematic approach to evaluating security policy as an interconnected sequence of individual rules placing limits on private behavior.

Our goal here is to convince you that the issues are new but the task is do-able. To develop a platform for policy evaluation, we must acknowledge that we need to learn by doing the regulatory impact analyses assessing the major rules associated with the implementation of security policy. And in designing the preliminary template for analyses of rules, we need to identify strategies that are especially robust to surprises, as well as to complementarities among programs, which cannot be easily anticipated. For example, complementarities could arise with perceived safety. Suppose, for example, that the policies designed to reduce specific individual risks also reduced the 'feeling of being unsafe', or what we might refer to as the ambiguity of risk,[1] by assuring the public that some sources of risk were effectively 'off the table'. An individual analysis of each risk source might provide estimates that imply a relatively small positive value for the net benefits for each activity associated with an individual rule. That is, the margin of benefits over costs might be small enough so one could reasonably assert that when the estimation errors are considered, the net benefits could be negative. Nonetheless, analysts might want to point out that the overall impact of rules reducing the security risks people face also had the collective effect of enhancing 'feelings of safety'. Under these circumstances the set of rules would accomplish more as a composite than the sum of the net benefits estimated for each one of them. Of course, such claims are difficult to substantiate. The bottom line, then, is that to structure analysis strategies to overcome challenges, we need practical methods for the near term that recognize that security has many dimensions: risk reduction, less ambiguity or generalized uncertainty in daily activities, and greater assurance that the infrastructure supporting activities of daily living will not be disrupted. Security is embedded in all we do, so we should expect that it will be difficult to enumerate each component. Equally importantly, we cannot be expected to fully anticipate how people and institutions will adapt to these new threats and public actions to reduce them. Therefore, 'analysis sprinkled with caution' may be warranted.

Security policy evaluation poses special challenges for five reasons. Firstly, the 'outputs' of new rules are not easily connected to the risks they seek to address. Secondly, but equally importantly, there are few situations in which people make choices that unambiguously reveal the trade-offs they are willing to make to reduce risks. Thirdly, while security-related events can harm people and destroy assets, these effects are only a part of their impact. Fear is a public bad. Inability to quantify the risks of some actions (ambiguity in the risks) has negative effects that are distinct from events that lead to reasonably well-understood increases in the risks of bad outcomes. Fourthly, threats arise as a result of other people's decisions, so once any policy of the 'target economy' is recognized by the group that is initiating the threat, we should expect to encounter changes in the behavior of those seeking to do harm. In contrast to environmental policy, where concentration-response functions follow set patterns, risk assessment of terrorist threats must reflect strategic behavior on the part of the agents who are the source of the risk and the focus of policy. Fifthly, evaluations of security policies must be completed in a timely fashion, but with much less data and experience than is available for most of the other common areas of regulatory analysis. Policy delays in the case of security-related decisions can have especially significant impacts. For these five reasons, we conclude that the evaluation of homeland security policies, and the benefit–cost analysis of the regulations that stem from such policies, is new terrain.

In the fall of 2010, the National Center for Risk and Economic Analysis of Terrorist Events (CREATE) at the University of Southern California sponsored a workshop to take stock of what we knew for meeting the tasks associated with doing regulatory impact analyses for homeland security policies and to assess how experience in other areas might be adapted to the special requirements for evaluating these policies. Early versions of the chapters in this volume were discussed at that workshop, with academics and analysts from DHS. After the workshop, the papers were revised, new research was completed, and new papers were written. All of that work is reflected in this volume.

The chapters that comprise this volume share a problem context, which we discuss in two parts. We begin with a summary of the rapid development of DHS, and of the scale of the activities included in this relatively new, cabinet-level department. Then we comment on two of the DHS rules included in United States Office of Management and Budget (OMB)'s 2010 *Report to Congress on the Benefits and Costs of Federal Regulations and Unfunded Mandate on State, Local and Tribal Entities*. Finally, the last section of this chapter provides a short guide to the chapters that follow, explaining why they are here, and how they relate to our overall goal: developing a platform for the economic evaluation of security-related regulations.

DHS: THE BEGINNING, THE SCOPE, AND THE IMPACT ON ECONOMIC ACTIVITY

A little over a year after the 2001 attack on the World Trade Center, Congress passed the Homeland Security Act (2002) and DHS was established as a cabinet-level department. The primary mission of the department is to:

> prevent terrorist attacks within the United States;
> reduce the vulnerability of the United States to terrorism; and
> minimize the damage, and assist in the recovery from terrorist attacks that do occur within the United States. (Public Law 107–296, November 25, 2002; Section 101, 116 Stat. p. 2142)

DHS was given four areas of responsibility:

- chemical, biological and nuclear countermeasures;
- information analysis and infrastructure protection;
- border and transportation security; and
- emergency preparedness and response. (Pub. L. 107–296, November 25, 2002; Section 101, 116 Stat., p. 2)

Each area had a number of sub-areas. The President's 2003 budget anticipated that the department would have over 169 000 employees, measured as full-time equivalents (FTEs). A little over a decade later, the President's 2014 budget estimated an increase in FTEs of 35 percent, to nearly 229 000. Budgeted expenditures in nominal terms have increased 60 percent from $37.5 billion to $60.0 billion. Figure 1.1 provides an organization chart for the composition of the department as of 2013. As this diagram suggests, DHS has a number of responsibilities that are not directly related to security but could be viewed as complementary activities.

For both of the years we described, these budget figures do not include the resources associated with the Federal Bureau of Investigation, the Central Intelligence Agency, the National Security Agency, and other agencies that provide support to assist DHS in its mission. They also do not reflect the resources that US residents implicitly expend in the form of time spent waiting in lines to clear airport security or at US borders to enter the country.

Of course, many security activities were underway before 9/11, and some do not have a direct connection to homeland security. The President's 2014 budget allocates about 42 percent ($25 billion) to 'non-homeland security' functions. The Federal Emergency Management Agency (FEMA) and the

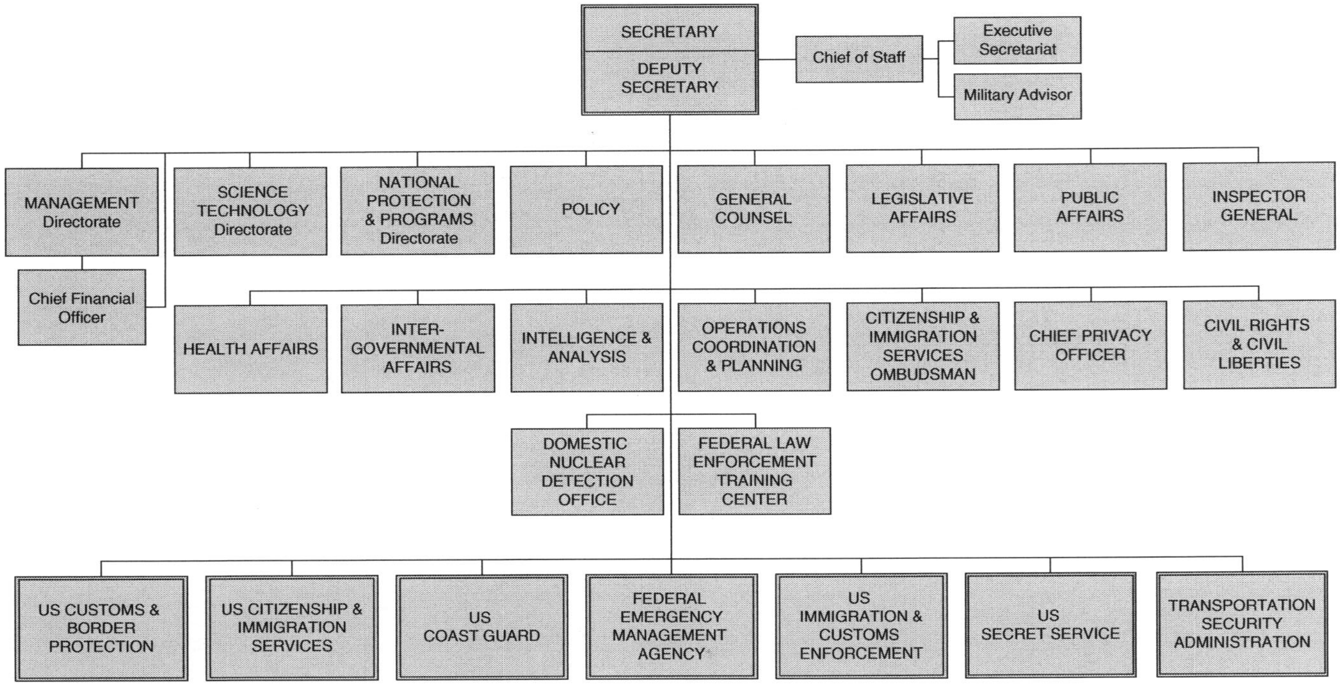

Figure 1.1 *US Department of Homeland Security*

Coast Guard operations that are not associated with homeland security account for half of this $25 billion. Nonetheless, $35 billion in annual expenditures for homeland security suggests that the agency engages in a large set of activities. Yet those activities are not the full story. Indirect costs are important as well. Immediately after 9/11, analysts examined the indirect effects of security measures. For example, Navarro and Spencer (2001) estimated that the bulk of the costs of increased aviation security would be due to waiting time. They estimated that if 550 million passengers each required 90 minutes of added time to complete their trips, with shadow values of time between $10 and $40 an hour, then the overall indirect costs of the requirement for passenger screening would be $8 billion to $32 billion annually. A year later, a separate assessment by Hobijn (2002) suggested lower aggregate costs of about $12 billion, using lower estimates of the opportunity costs of time. Regardless of the estimate used, these are large costs.

Examining the costs of homeland security from 2001 to 2005, Hobijn and Sager (2007) concluded that the costs had not led to a slowdown in economic activity. They based this conclusion on the growth rate in average labor productivity and the inventory-to-sales ratio from the business sector. They found that neither index was substantially affected. Since the costs of homeland security programs rose from about 0.5 percent of gross domestic product (GDP) in 2001 to nearly 1 percent in 2005, it seems reasonable to conclude that the programs did not markedly constrain economic activity during those years. Hobijn and Sager's (2007) conclusion might be used to suggest that the perception of safety is more important to economic activity than these relatively small additions to the costs of daily activities. With the dramatic downturn of the US economy in 2007, it is likely that sustained government spending, as well as the process of maintaining and increasing personnel and capital expenditures for these programs, helped to bolster private demand of other goods and services.

While the aggregate impact of homeland security programs on growth seems small, it is nonetheless important to consider the net benefits we realize from new rules and major modifications to existing programs. With federal programs that require commitments approaching 1 percent of GDP, it is important to consider ways that objectives might be achieved more efficiently. Executive Order 13563 did just that. It required each executive-branch agency to develop plans to periodically review the regulations associated with each agency's responsibilities and identify when the regulations should be 'modified, streamlined, expanded or repealed' (Executive Order 13563, issued 1/18/2011, Federal Register, Vol. 76, No. 14, p. 3822). The goal of the requirement is to ensure that the objectives of the rules can be achieved and to determine if the associated programs could be implemented in a less burdensome way.

DHS's final plan for reviewing significant regulations under the order is a three-step process involving rule selection, prioritization, and efficiency assessment (Department of Homeland Security, 2011). The document describing these steps outlines the process of meeting each component in very general terms, detailing the sources of input information to the task without explaining specific criteria. Therefore, it is difficult to comment on the issues considered in implementation. For example, in discussing rule selection, the plan identifies public feedback as a primary factor and the experience of public officials as a secondary factor. Under the primary factor the plan suggests that DHS is looking for new information and new economic data to support proposed changes. It does not identify an internal process to proactively evaluate performance metrics as part of its implementation.

Rules for retrospective evaluation are supposed to be prioritized according to measures of the net benefits of changes. More specifically, the regulation review plan states that:

> DHS will seek to measure net benefits against a baseline. The baseline is the best assessment of how the world will look in the future with the regulation in place. This will be compared to an estimate of how the world would look if the regulation were modified, streamlined, expanded, or removed. DHS will afford higher priority to those regulations that are likely to generate higher net benefits (greater reductions in net costs).[2]

Unfortunately, when the plan discusses benefit–cost analysis more specifically, it concludes: 'After reviewing the public comments received in response to our March 2011 *Federal Register* notice, IdeaScale webpage, and DHS Preliminary Plan, and after considering the discussions at the Department-wide Working Group on retrospective review, our preliminary analysis indicates that a significant number of retrospective analyses will not require extensive cost–benefit studies'.[3] Moreover, a key reason for this assessment, according to the plan, is the absence of 'high-quality' data to perform these analyses. This reaction to the comments DHS had received was widely recognized within DHS before the plan was finalized, and was also an important motivating factor for the 2010 CREATE workshop of which this book is an outcome. The DHS (2011) report on the plan for conducting retrospective analyses supports these efforts directly, noting an absence of the substantive information that would be required for retrospective benefit–cost analyses to be informative. This report observes that:

> The Department believes obtaining quality data could be a challenge for the retrospective analyses of its regulations. GAO [the Government Accountability Office] has reached similar conclusions, noting, in the past, that the inability to obtain the information and data needed to conduct retrospective analyses is a major barrier to such reviews. Thus far, there has been a lack of substantive benefit–cost data from the public. For example, in our March 2011 *Federal Register* notice, we specifically posed questions such as – 'What information, especially new or additional information or data, regarding the costs and benefits of these regulations are available?' – to help facilitate public comments in this area. We did not receive any substantive information or data from the public that would assist us in conducting retrospective benefit–cost analyses.[4]

Of course, the same comment about data needs could be noted for analyses undertaken as part of the regulatory impact analysis (RIA) process itself.

The goals of the Executive Order and the concerns stated in the plan for retrospective analyses are consistent with recent mandates from the Executive Branch. In July 2013 the director of OMB, along with the directors of the Domestic Policy Council, the Office of Science and Technology Policy, and the chairman of the President's Council of Economic Advisers, called for agencies to:

- harness data to improve agency results;
- conduct high-quality, low-cost evaluations and rapid interactive experimentation;
- use innovative, outcome-focused grant designs; and
- strengthen agency capacity to use evidence (Burwell et al., 2013).

Responding to these mandates will be challenging for DHS. The agency does not have a history of experience with benefit–cost analysis and program evaluation generally. The research in this volume describes how the department can begin to address this directive.

SOME EXAMPLES OF DHS BENEFIT–COST ANALYSES

RIAs prepared by DHS provide the best examples of the problems encountered trying to quantify and value the benefit analysis for homeland security rules. We will examine two examples: the Western Hemisphere Travel Initiative (WHTI) and the proposed Air/Sea Biometric Exit Project (Exit). Both of these analyses were conducted in 2008 (see Industrial Economics Inc., 2008; US DHS, 2008). The WHTI states that, as of June 2009, US citizens and non-immigrant aliens from Canada, Bermuda, and Mexico entering the US at land and sea ports of entry from Western Hemisphere countries must present a valid passport, passport card, or other acceptable document in circumstances in which travel was previously permitted without such a document. The proposed Exit system would verify in a reliable and timely manner whether those people who entered the US legally had departed, and it was expected to significantly improve on the information available from the paper-based Form I-94 process.[5]

Using the Exit RIA as an example, the RIA summarizes the benefits and describes whether the benefits were monetized, quantified but not monetized or qualitatively assessed in a tabular form. It also maps the goals of DHS with the potential benefits of the proposed Air/Sea Biometric Exit Benefits rule. We reproduce both these tables in Tables 1.1 and 1.2, respectively. The RIAs for both the WHTI and Exit rules identified 'increased national security' as one benefit, and outlined three sets of information that would be needed to quantify and monetize the improvements:[6]

1. Estimates for the baseline probability that a successful terrorist attack will occur.
2. Estimates of incremental reductions in the baseline probability of a successful terrorist attack that would result from the implementation of the regulation and the consequences of the avoided event (collectively, the risk associated with a potential terrorist attack). Combining (1) and (2) would provide a measure of the risk reduction attributed to the rule.
3. Estimates of the average per individual (or household) willingness to pay (WTP) for the reduction in this type of risk. Using the incremental risk reduction together with estimates for the willingness to pay for a unit reduction in risk, the analyst has an assessment of the *ex ante* trade-off that an individual (or a household) would make to obtain the policy that is assumed to be responsible for the risk reduction.

The next step in the description in the RIA specifies that this average trade-off should be multiplied by the number of individuals experiencing the risk reduction.[7]

The RIAs identify the important data questions that arise in each of these steps. First, data on terrorist attacks and their consequences during the last decade are limited. Therefore, the task of assessing baseline risk is exceptionally difficult.[8] Moreover, the mechanism linking the policy to the risk reduction is problematic. The RIA outlines several reasons why DHS felt that historical data might not be appropriate. For example, it was difficult to determine whether documented attacks can be attributed to how entry procedures treat people who lack a passport. The RIA argued that

Table 1.1 Benefits categories with rationales for benefits

Exit Benefit	Rationale for Benefit from Exit	Monetized	Quantitative but not Monetized	Qualitative
Increased national security	● US-VISIT, which Exit is a fundamental part, improves the capabilities to manage and screen aliens against watch list records, which includes wanted persons and immigration violators.			X
Improved detection of visa overstays	● Accurate reporting of departure of alien travelers, coupled with information collected at entry into the US, may better indicate who has left the US beyond their allotted visa time period and by how much.	X		
	● Detection of visa overstays allows for better decision-making and management of the immigration and visa issuance systems and produces timely information and efficiencies for law enforcement.			X
	● Cost savings to the government from preventing an individual who has overstayed their visa and who has left the US from re-entering the US. Costs that would be avoided with successful Exit implementation include detection and possible detention, prosecution, incarceration, and removal for egregious cases.	X		
Improved Exit processing over I-94 System	● Automated processing of biometric data allows for more efficient matching with Entry data.	X		
	● Increased accuracy of matching arrival and departure records creates time savings for data analyst.	X		

Improved ICE efficiency attempting apprehension	● Accurate departure reporting of alien travelers allows ICE investigators to determine whether fugitive or targeted individuals can be apprehended within the US (value associated with the reduction of time spent seeking wanted persons).	X		
	● Accurate and timely departure reporting of alien travelers allows ICE investigators to identify more effectively and efficiently those individuals who have overstayed their visas and are still in the US.		X	
Improved DIG efficiency processing exit/entry data	● The timely collection and validation of biometric information will improve processing and analytical efficiencies within the Data Integrity Group (DIG).	X		
	● Expected decrease in the non-matched (entry to exit) population will reduce the total workload handled by the DIG.			X
	● Biometric matching of entry to exit will improve the certainty of a no-match designation.			X
Improved compliance with NSEERS requirements due to the improvement in ease of compliance	● Replacing the departure requirements under the National Entry-Exit Registration System (NSEERS) with the requirements under Exit will improve the compliance rates of NSEERS, because all out-bound alien travelers must be processed through Exit in order to depart the US from air and sea ports. The time savings of biometric information collection under Exit compared to the person-to-person processing under NSEERS will also result in more individuals willing to comply with NSEERS.		X	

Table 1.1 (continued)

Exit Benefit	Rationale for Benefit from Exit	Monetized	Quantitative but not Monetized	Qualitative
Increase in economic activity created through the expansion in the number of Visa Waiver Program (VWP) eligible countries	• Better data collection and analysis on a particular country's travelers' facilitates the process that determines if a country should become a member of the VWP. The economic impact of an expanded VWP is measured by increased economic activity in the US from more accessible tourism and business travel.			X
	• Implementation of a Biometric Exit Program is required before any new countries may be admitted to the VWP. However, another rule would have to be implemented to cause the specific admittance of any new VWP country. As such, this RIA considers the value of an expanded VWP, which is predicated on a Biometric exit system, but does not include those benefits in the aggregated present value of total benefits.			X

Source: United States Department of Homeland Security (2008). United States Visitor and Immigrant Status Indicator Technology Program. *AIR/SEA BIOMETRIC EXIT PROJECT Regulatory Impact Analysis* (April, 2008) DHS-2008–0039–0002. Table 5–1.

Table 1.2 Mapping of DHS goals with Air/Sea Biometric Exit benefits

DHS strategic goal/ objective supported	US VISIT goals/ objectives	Exit objectives	Exit benefit	Measure
Strategic Goal 2 – Prevention				
Strategic Objective 2.1 Secure borders against terrorists, means of terrorism, illegal drugs, other illegal activity	Security Enhance the security of United States (US) citizens and travelers	Biometrically verify aliens' identity	Increased national security	Qualitative in terms of cost of terrorism and reduction of costs due to border security as well as unquantified security benefits
Strategic Objective 2.6 Improve the security and integrity of our immigration system	Integrity Ensure the integrity of the US immigration system	Provide mechanism to identify visa overstays	Improved detection of visa overstays	Percentage of visa overstays (number of visa overstays detected as percentage of total alien travelers) Cost savings from preventing a prior visa overstayer from entering US (subsequent detection and prosecution cost avoided)
		Accurate matching of arrival and departure records	Improved exit processing over existing biographic systems	Dollar value of accurately matching records Percentage of exit records matched to entry records (Number of exit transactions matched to entry transactions as percentage of total exit transactions)

Table 1.2 (continued)

DHS strategic goal/ objective supported	US VISIT goals/ objectives	Exit objectives	Exit benefit	Measure
		Improvement in effectiveness of government resources	Improved ICE efficiency attempting apprehension	Value associated with the reduction of time spent seeking wanted persons no longer in the country
				Qualitative improvement in efficiency in geographic targeting of visa violators
			Improved DIG efficiency processing exit/entry data	Value of improved processing efficiency
			Improved compliance with NSEERS requirements due to the improvement in ease of compliance	Quantitative, not monetized: increase in expected NSEERS compliance rates
		Facilitate travel	Increase in economic activity created through the expansion in the number of Visa Waiver Program eligible countries	Value of additional domestic economic activity created by the increased number of travelers arriving from countries with relaxed visa requirements Measured but not included in the aggregate present value of benefits

Source: United States Department of Homeland Security (2008). United States Visitor and Immigrant Status Indicator Technology Program. *AIR/SEA BIOMETRIC EXIT PROJECT Regulatory Impact Analysis* (April, 2008) DHS-2008–0039–0002. Table 5–2.

using existing data to project the future probability of attack requires an understanding of the socio-economic and political conditions motivating and facilitating attacks, and foresight about how these factors may change in the future. Faced with these limitations, the RIA did not attempt to construct quantitative estimates for either the baseline probability of terrorist attacks or the incremental reductions from this baseline.

Estimating willingness to pay (WTP) for the reduction in risk also posed challenges. The value of lost property and the opportunity costs associated with supply-chain effects can be determined from market data. However, it is difficult to estimate the WTP for a reduction in personal risks of loosely specified events that *may* pose threats to an individual's health. Indeed, as we noted earlier, this task may be better characterized as an effort to reduce the ambiguity in risk. That is, people may feel that without the policy they are less secure. This interpretation assumes that their anxiety arises from observing terrorist events outside the areas where they live. These events serve as reminders that 'it could happen here'. People may feel that their day-to-day activities are also insecure. There is evidence that such concerns do affect people's attitudes and behaviors. For example, Slovic's (1987) early and influential research found that the public is less willing to tolerate risks related to incidents they dread,[9] such as nuclear accidents or terrorist attacks, than incidents that are not dreaded but that pose similar or higher risks, such as riding a motorcycle. The RIAs note that while some of these effects may be qualitatively described, the literature lacks quantitative estimates that account for factors like dread. The literature does contain estimates of the value of changes in fatal and nonfatal risks; however, the RIAs discuss how the value of a risk reduction may depend on risk perceptions.

These examples support our suggestion that the evaluation of security policies is especially challenging. We need to distinguish policies that reduce prospective threats from those that provide mechanisms to respond to events (whether terrorist-related or due to natural disasters) after the fact. While there are parallels at the conceptual level between the needs for these assessments and other applications of benefit–cost analysis, the information needs for security-related policy are especially pronounced.

The first step in building a framework for the economic impact analyses envisioned in the evaluation of either new rules (or for large modifications to existing regulations) requires policymakers to decide what simplifications can be tolerated for the sake of getting started. In some respects, the RIAs we selected as examples reflect an effort to jump into benefit–cost analysis without answering this question. The analysis structure for RIAs associated with the DHS rules is not necessarily a simple modification of practices used in different contexts. We argue in the next chapter that the process of building a framework for security policy assessment should start with a conceptual analysis of the types of outcomes influenced by policy, and their effects on people. It is possible to decide which analysis compromises can be tolerated and which cannot. Once an initial strategy for conducting analyses of DHS proposed rules is developed, it is then possible to learn from the process of doing assessments. The research presented in the chapters that follow was developed with this idea in mind. It outlines the elements that need to be addressed in order to structure an initial 'analysis platform'. In the next chapter, we use the analysis platform concept to describe the architecture of policy analysis and evaluation.

WHAT IS NEXT

The Exit RIA contains a table (reproduced in Table 1.2) that maps the DHA strategic goals to the benefits of the rules. The benefits listed in the table are high-level benefits. The next step would be to describe exactly how the rules affect specific classes of households and businesses (including the public sector), in order to make clear the pathways through which the rules will have an impact on society's welfare. Chapter 2 in this volume discusses the importance of developing such a framework to link regulations to consequences for people, firms, and other institutions. After describing some of the important steps in a benefit–cost analysis, the chapter provides a short summary of revealed and stated preference methods. We use the stated-preference surveys we conducted that were designed to map into security-related policy questions for our examples. The chapter suggests a candidate for an architecture or framework for assessing benefits and costs of homeland security policies, and describes how an existing RIA could be used to help build this type of framework. An important distinction highlighted in this chapter is the *ex ante* versus *ex post* perspective on policy evaluation. The former naturally fits policies designed to protect against security threats.

After these two introductory chapters, the volume is organized into three further parts. Part II is composed of four chapters. It considers several perspectives on security policy when such policy is characterized as an effort to reduce risk. We selected the Environmental Protection Agency (EPA) policy architecture as an example relevant to DHS, because EPA has developed protocols for a wide array of risk assessments. Chapter 3 discusses the potential parallels between EPA's generic risk-assessment methodology and DHS risk assessment. Chapter 4 provides an overview of the theoretical and empirical issues that help analysts parse the diverse estimates of the trade-offs people would make to reduce the risks of premature death. Chapter 5 provides a UK perspective on how these trade-off measures have been used in an array of policy contexts. Its author, Michael Jones-Lee, has been at the center of many of these assessments, and he provides both conceptual and practical insights into their role in policy analyses. Chapter 6 discusses the parallels between security risks and the risks posed by natural hazards, considering both *ex ante* and *ex post* issues.

Turning to the first contribution in Part II, Chapter 3 provides the insider's view of the risk assessment process in EPA, emphasizing the interaction between the design of risk assessment methods and the flexibility of consistently linking the outcome measures and the risks to the economic measures of the trade-offs people would make to reduce risk. EPA's process has four distinct steps:

1. hazard identification;
2. dose response assessment;
3. exposure assessment; and
4. risk characterization.

Coordination in the definition of important health endpoints and risk measures is a key theme. An effort, such as that envisioned in developing these definitions requires collaboration and genuine interdisciplinary research. It demands an understanding of the fact that endpoints need to be defined from two potentially different perspectives that can be conflicting in their implications. First, they must allow for meaningful health science research that characterizes the role exposures to the regulated pollutants play in influencing the risks of these outcomes. At the same time, the second requirement is that the outcomes be meaningful and understandable to the people who would experience health effects and potentially be willing (*ex ante*) to give up resources to reduce the risks. The two perspectives do not necessarily lead to the same set of definitions.

Both the temporal dimensions of outcomes and the physical responses that result from exposure to pollutants can be different. For example, we might be able to accurately characterize how exposures to ozone over short intervals affect lung function measured in terms of forced expiratory function of lungs. What does this outcome mean to the person experiencing it? How does it relate to their longer-term health and life expectancy? The authors, Dockins and Wheeler, use thyroid condition versus thyroid cancer to make the same point. Disparities that cannot be reconciled may imply different strategies for evaluating rules such as cost effectiveness or breakeven analyses. The chapter highlights these and other alternatives. The authors implicitly suggest that it may be possible to design these analyses so they serve to complement benefit–cost analyses in situations were measurement is currently impossible. That is even in cases where some of the outcomes of a policy can not be defined in terms that would reconcile the outcome measures from the risk assessment perspective with the needs for examining economic trade-offs, there is value in being consistent with the overall logic of a benefit–cost analysis. The consistency in describing the process has direct value to those attempting to use quantitative and qualitative information to make decisions.

Chapter 4 by Viscusi describes the definition and properties of *ex ante* trade-off measures for reductions in mortality risks. Labeled as the value of statistical lives (VSL), these estimates are among the most important elements in EPA's benefit–cost analyses. Viscusi's work has been a major influence on these analyses for the past two decades. His chapter explains the reasons for heterogeneity in these estimates as a result of differences in people's circumstances: age, health conditions, income, and other factors. As he acknowledges, there are many important economic reasons why we should expect trade-offs to be different. Of course, the differences do not mean the estimates used in policy evaluations should incorporate heterogeneity. He notes that:

> Policies that affect the population broadly and do not have targeted effects might well rely on overall VSL estimates without recognizing the potential variation in these values across the population . . . when the VSL estimates are derived from segmented labor markets in which different labor market groups force quite different opportunities, it may be quite inappropriate to incorporate such differences in the analysis.

After a brief summary of the history of using VSL estimates for policy he comments on recent controversies such as:

- the so-called 'senior discount' associated with adjusting VSL estimates down for older groups;
- the income elasticity of the VSL and the importance of adjusting for income changes;
- the adjustment of the VSL for the size of the risk change;
- the treatment of VSL with risk having different latency and transition to death.

In each case the chapter provides a balanced summary of the context and issues in evaluating the relevance of each question for policy uses of VSL estimates.

The chapter closes with a discussion reinforcing an important motivation for the workshop and subsequent research leading to this volume.

Most people view the risks posed by terrorism differently from the context used for most VSL estimates. There are also important differences with the risks of natural disasters. As a result, there is a clear need for research to understand how the elements of security-related threats influence the trade-offs people would make. However, this need does not imply that reductions in security-related risks are so important that they trump all other risk reduction programs.

Chapter 5 builds on Viscusi's insights using the experience with incorporating benefit measures for policy-related risk changes in the UK. Jones-Lee's assessment of the implications of heterogeneity parallels that of Viscusi, concluding that for policy purposes, where the events at risk and the structure creating the mortality risk are comparable, a common value for all groups affected is likely the most feasible.

He describes experience in using VSL-type measures for policy related to workplace safety, transport, railways, environmental risks, and access to natural health treatments. As a rule, policies tended to adopt a common estimate for VSLs or for the value of a statistical life year. He concludes that there has been no policy consensus on attaching a differential premium for risks of multiple fatalities over what would be implied by ruling the expected fatalities by the consensus VSL.

Of course, he notes that benefit–cost comparisons should not be the exclusive criterion for decision-making. An important example is the case of the UK's decision to offer a new health treatment to participants in the public health insurance system without cost. One strategy for evaluating which treatments qualify would be based on a comparison of the cost of the treatment per remaining life year compared to the affected population, relative to estimates of the value of a statistical life year. Those treatments with costs per remaining year of life expectancy lower than this estimated trade-off would pass one criterion. Others are also included in the discussions. Moreover, as he notes, there has been increased consideration given to multiple objective scaling techniques for these assessments.

Chapter 5 concludes with a qualified recommendation. The UK evidence on policies to reduce the risks for multiple fatality railway accidents suggest people do not assign higher trade-offs per fatality than would be implied with risks associated with single-fatality events. Based on this result, security-related risks to people's lives might be able to use VSL estimates as a starting point. In interpreting this suggestion it is important to emphasize his 'starting point' qualification.

Chapter 6 by Farrow helps readers to understand the complexities that arise in attempts to transfer risk trade-off measures from one context to another in quite different situations. He considers how the interpretation of these trade-off measures changes with three separate variations on the models used to represent individual behavior: state-dependent preferences, non-expected utility models, and endogenous risk. We return to these distinctions in discussing research needs in our closing chapter.

Part III of the volume considers some of the effects that security policy is likely to have. Chapter 7 discusses how much we can expect the spatial distribution of economic activity (and people) to adapt in response to security threats. Using analogies to natural disasters Kahn argues that the productivity enhancing effects of central cities more than offsets suburbanization in response to security threats that differentially affect what might be labeled 'signature cities'. More generally, his argument identifies a set of important private responses to security threats. Economic activity adjusts, reducing the harm from terrorist threats based on the 'old' organization of economic activity. As a result, policy must consider both the endogeneity of risk due to the response of the agents creating threat responses to new security policy and the private, longer term responses by societies that face persistent threats.

How do we put these considerations together? We need a structural representation of behaviors that integrate all the margins for adjustment to the sources of threats, the entities providing security, and the agents responding to external threats to their well-being and assets. No doubt this is a tall order. It implies a very different type of general equilibrium model to characterize a wider array of market and non-market interactions.

Chapter 8 by Rose describes how general equilibrium effects can matter, and how the elements in computable general equilibrium models (CGE) can be modified to incorporate resilience and to account for behavioral responses to the 'fear' associated with threats to security.

The chapter provides examples of six types of threats including quantitative assessments of the impacts for specific examples from past research. Rose extracts common elements that can be used to characterize these threats, including: the lethality of the source of risk; the concentration of people affected and their ability to mitigate the risk; the level of protection of the target of a security attack; the duration of the event associated with the risk; the fear of repeated attacks; the ability to respond in the future; and the resilience of the social and economic systems to the attack. Using the template of a CGE model, the chapter discusses the elements that must be combined to structure a CGE model. The process highlights the information that can be consistently derived from these frameworks as well as the margins where future research is needed to reflect, more completely, the diverse elements in the security-related examples he presents. The result is a window into 'generalizing general equilibrium analysis' to address security policy.

Part IV, the last part of the book, addresses some of the issues associated with implementing policy evaluations. Chapter 9 discusses one of the most visible effects of security policy: people must spend more of their time in security-related lines for air travel and at some entry points into the US. Waiting in lines to clear security, process baggage, or obtain new documentation to undertake various types of travel and business all increase the costs of undertaking market and non-market activities. Often these costs are not routinely recorded as a market transaction would be. They are important costs nonetheless.

As a result, we begin our discussion of implementation issues in Part IV by asking what we know about measuring the opportunity cost of time. This chapter reviews the strategies that have been used to estimate the shadow value of time, recognizing that the task is not as simple as suggesting that it should be the wage rate for people who are working. Even for those working, the shadow value will depend on commitments, the timing and amounts of time required, and ability to multi-task. Fortunately, access to new data resources, for example the American Time Use Survey, is advancing our understanding of how people and new technologies are rapidly adapting to constraints imposed by protecting security.

The second chapter in Part IV, Chapter 10 by Boyle et al., addresses the practical reality that most policy evaluations must be undertaken with whatever information is available on the research shelf. While most policy analysts have been aware of this limitation for a long time, it has been underappreciated by academic economists. There is rarely time to conduct primary research to estimate the trade-offs people would make for security-related risk reductions, time savings, or whatever is identified as an outcome of new policies. Instead, analysts must adopt estimates for comparable situations in the literature to match the needs of policy.

This approach is labeled 'benefit transfer'. Of course, it can apply equally well to cost estimation, such as the estimates used to measure the opportunity cost of time. These become especially important when we are identifying implicit costs that might be associated with increased time commitments at airports due to a new screening requirement. Often other costs of a new policy are derived from informal engineering models. To date they have received less scrutiny.

Boyle et al. provide a readers' guide to the methods used in the literature, including a careful discussion of their limitations. Given that we never know the true value of these trade-offs, even when we have time for primary research to measure them, how should we use these adapted estimates developed from these benefit transfers applied to research that was designed for another purpose? We know in advance that they are flawed. Boyle et al. remind readers of the importance of being able to bound gains or losses due to a decision. Not only does this narrow the range for debate and therefore limit the possibility of significant errors, it also allows simple plausibility checks.[10] Every policy does not constitute a means to avoid another 9/11. Bounds also focus attention on the strategies used for implementing policies to identify ways to reduce the costs of meeting the policy's objective.

Our summary of each chapter here is deliberately brief. It is intended to pique your interest and explain why these chapters are here. We return to the themes they develop in the book's final chapter, Chapter 11, which discusses the design of a DHS platform for analysis and the new research needed to support it. An important lesson that emerges from all the chapters is that we can get started with analyses now. A council of perfection is a license to avoid hard decisions associated with the judgments that good policy analyses require. This book is intended to offer readers ideas to get started, and to advance the research that underlies these important judgments.

NOTES

1 Some authors have referred to this as another form of Frank Knight's (1921) classic discussion of risk versus uncertainty.
2. Department of Homeland Security (2011, p. 38).
3. Department of Homeland Security (2011, p. 50).
4. Department of Homeland Security (2011, p. 51).
5. We do not attempt to comment on the current status of either of these programs. Instead, we focus on the methods used to evaluate them from the perspective of the period before implementation began.
6. This is not an exact quote, but an edited paraphrasing of the statements in the RIA.
7. If the assessment of the average trade-off was per household, the approximate number to multiply would be the number of households. More generally, the issue of the 'policy extent of the market' is an important one, which we will return to in Chapter 11.
8. We return to this issue in our concluding chapter, Chapter 11, where we suggest strategies for using expert judgments that are implicit in past rules and explicit through the types of expert elicitation and risk encoding methods used by EPA and other agencies.
9. Dread associated with risk is defined as a 'perceived lack of control . . . catastrophic potential, fatal consequences, and the inequitable distribution of risks and benefits' (Slovic, 1987, p. 283).
10. This strategy allows one to ask a rhetorical question as part of the policy evaluation. This question concerns how large the error in the transfer would need to be to change the decision. A variety of indirect indicators can then be used to offer information relevant to this question. In the absence of the results of the transfer it is not possible to narrow the scope for debate over the net benefits of a proposed new rule.

REFERENCES

Burwell, S.M., C. Muñoz, J. Holdren, and A. Krueger (2013). 'Memorandum to the Heads of Departments and Agencies, subject: next steps in the evidence and innovation agenda', July 26, Executive Office of the President, Office of Management and Budget.

Hobijn, B. (2002). 'What will homeland security cost?' *Federal Reserve Bank of New York Economic Policy Review*, November, 21–33.

Hobijn, B. and E. Sager (2007). 'What has homeland security cost? An assessment 2002–2005', *Federal Reserve Bank of New York Current Issues in Economics and Finance*, **13** (February), 1–7.

Homeland Security Act (2002), 6 U.S.C. §111 (2002).

Industrial Economics, Inc. (2008). 'Regulatory assessment for the final rule documents required for travel within the Western Hemisphere: the Western Hemisphere Travel Initiative implemented in the land environment', prepared for US Customs and Border Protection, United States Department of Homeland Security, March.

Knight, F.H. (1921). *Risk, Uncertainty and Profit*, New York: Harper & Row.

Navarro, P. and A. Spencer (2001). 'September 11, 2001: assessing the costs of terrorism', *Milken Institute Review*, Fourth Quarter, 16–31.

United States Office of Management and Budget (OMB) (2010). *Report to Congress on the Benefits and Costs of Federal Regulations and Unfunded Mandates on State, Local and Tribal Entities*, Office of the President of the United States of America.

Samuelson, P.A. (1976). *Economics*, 10th edn, New York: McGraw Hill.

Slovic, P. (1987). 'Perception of risk', *Science*, **236** (April 17), 280–285.

United States Department of Homeland Security (DHS) (2008). 'Air/Sea Biometric Exit Project regulatory impact analysis DHS-2008–0039–0002', United States Visitor and Immigrant Status Indicator Technology Program, April.

United States Department of Homeland Security (DHS) (2011). *Final Plan for the Retrospective Review of Existing Regulations*, August 22.

United States Visitor and Immigrant Status Indicator Technology Program (2008). 'Air/Sea Biometric Exit Project regulatory impact analysis DHS-2008–0039–0002', April 17.

2. The design of benefit–cost architecture for homeland security policy analysis

V. Kerry Smith and Carol Mansfield

INTRODUCTION

Cass Sunstein (2010), the former Administrator of the US Office of Management and Budget's (OMB's) Office of Information and Regulatory Affairs during President Obama's first term, noted that the evaluation of new regulatory policies was especially important in times of acute economic distress. He concluded his remarks to the Administrative Law Review Conference at American University's Washington College of Law, noting that:

> Regulations must be designed in a way that promotes, and does not undermine, the continuing recovery. A transparent accounting of consequences – of costs and benefits – is indispensable. If we look before we leap, with a commitment to openness, we are going to be finding unprecedented opportunities for improving and even extending people's lives. (pp. 23–24)

Meeting these goals requires that those involved in rulemaking develop an architecture for policy analysis.[1] That is, a framework is needed to link the regulations they develop to the consequences for people, firms, and other institutions in ways that allow the benefits and costs of each change to be clearly articulated and assessed. Because resources will always be limited, this consistent structure for conducting policy analysis must be general enough to accommodate a wide array of rules. Developing an accepted logic for organizing these analyses, what we label as the 'architecture', also facilitates transparency in government decision-making. As Greenstone (2009) suggests, transparency is necessary but not sufficient for maintaining public confidence in the regulatory process. Just as important, significant past regulations should be evaluated after they are promulgated to see if they accomplish what was expected and to be sure they did not have important unintended negative effects. Retrospective analysis highlights the impacts of policies as implemented, and it can also inform judgments about the ability of *ex ante* analyses to anticipate and predict the major impacts of a policy.

Many might agree that developing an architecture for policy analysis within each regulatory agency seems reasonable, but how does one get started? We argue in this chapter that three sets of activities help meet this goal. The first selects a set of studies from past analyses of rules from the existing set of regulatory impact analyses (RIAs) or other economic analyses associated with homeland security conducted by US agencies. These examples are then evaluated using a simple template that aligns the elements of the RIA or other analysis with the components of a benefit–cost analysis, such as what we describe in the section on 'One Possible Template'. The second activity is to identify common analysis needs across rules. This common set of needs, together with the shared economic logic, can be combined to create a structure that outlines an agency's approach to analysis and identifies the type of analysts, data, and methods needed to implement it. We discuss and illustrate the types of economic methods used for benefit analysis later in this chapter. Finally, the last step is to develop a culture that ensures *ex post* evaluation will be part of a feedback loop used in considering the performance of past regulations and in assessing the quality of the methods used in prospective analyses of the new rules. The next sections of the chapter develop these ideas in more detail.

BACKGROUND

When the public sector (at any level) decides to invest in something or to regulate private actions in some way, analysis that follows the logic of benefit–cost can be used to gauge whether the aggregate benefits derived from the investment or the rule outweigh the costs. Benefits are measured by the resources people would give up (measured in monetary terms when possible) to obtain what the investment or policy provides. The costs should measure the full costs (private and social) of the investment or the restriction on private activity, again in monetary terms, when possible.

A great deal of research, much of it quite technical, has been devoted to theoretical issues associated with how to: (1) formally define each concept, especially the trade-off measures used for benefits (see Freeman, 2003); (2) deal with decisions that have effects over time (see Gollier, 2001; Just et al., 2004; Boardman et al., 2006); (3) adjust for uncertainty in outcomes recognizing differences in individuals' versus society's risk aversion (Freeman, 2003; Gollier, 2001); (4) account for pre-existing distortions that affect people's behavior in responding to a new public action (Just et al., 2004;

Goulder et al., 1999; Goulder and Williams, 2003); and (5) incorporate the effects of the size of the action in relationship to the economy, as well as other 'systems' that might affect it and the other changes that might stem from the action being evaluated (Carbone and Smith, 2008; Smith and Carbone, 2008; Klaiber and Smith, 2011, 2012).

In this chapter, we focus on what we view as the most significant elements in a benefit–cost analysis: the analysts' choices about how to frame the problem and structure the components of the analysis strategy. When the analyst chooses a framework and the set of components used for the analysis, this choice dictates the type of information that will be available to decision-makers and the public. These choices will be our focus here, and our discussion will highlight how the choices relate to analysis of rules and other policies.

ONE POSSIBLE TEMPLATE

In this section, we lay out one possible template that could be used to organize the components of a policy analysis. The template highlights the decisions that need to be made by the analysts along the way. Figure 2.1 provides a basic flowchart of the template.

Rules to Outcomes

Two dimensions of regulatory policy are especially important to benefit–cost analysis. The first is the rulemaking process that translates legislative goals into specific actions in a proposed rule. The second is given in the title of this subsection: taking the list of actions in the proposed rule and creating a parallel list of the outcomes expected to result from these actions. We use as our example the RIA for the Secure Flight rule (Department of Homeland Security, 2008). The Secure Flight rule was defined in response to section 4021(a) of the Intelligence Reform and Terrorism Prevention Act. It requires the DHS and the Transportation Security Administration (TSA) to transfer, from aircraft operators to federal agencies, the tasks associated with conducting preflight comparisons of airline passenger information with the federal government's watch lists. The October 2008 RIA identified six actions to be taken by the government and the airline industry (pp. 20–31):

1. TSA will fully assume the domestic watch list matching function from aircraft operators after conducting operational testing with each aircraft operator during a first implementation phase. Following this

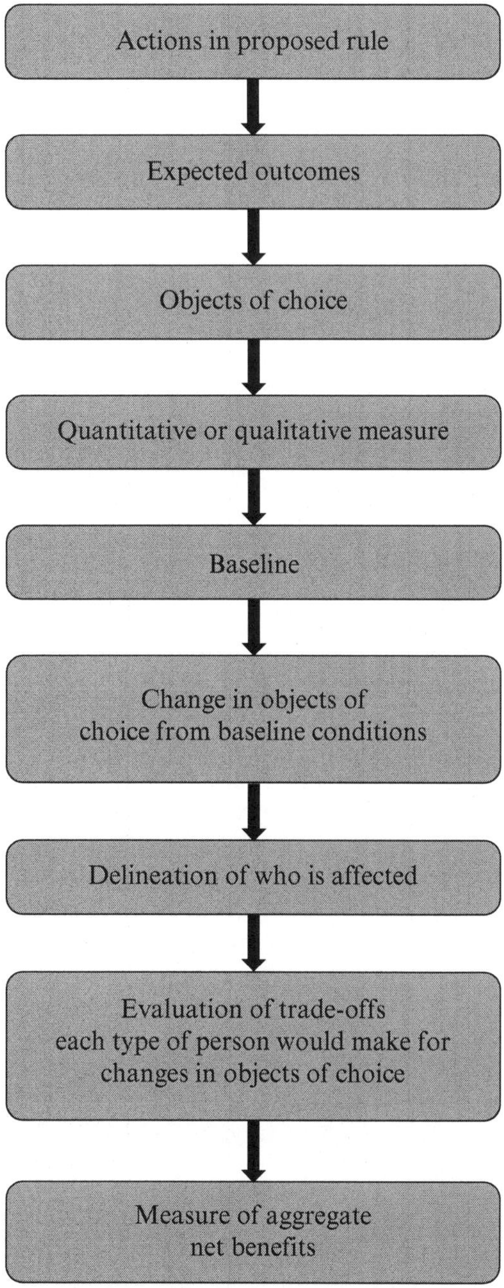

Figure 2.1 Basic flowchart of the template

initial domestic implementation phase, TSA will assume from the US Customs and Border Protection (CBP) the responsibility for comparing passenger information to government watch lists for certain domestic and foreign aircraft operators flying to, and from, and over the United States.

2. TSA requires covered aircraft operators to request and transmit to TSA each passenger's full name, date of birth, gender, and, if available, Redress Number, Known Traveler Number, and passport information. Covered aircraft operators will request and transmit to TSA an identical set of data elements from non-traveling individuals seeking authorization to enter an airport sterile area (such as to escort a minor or passenger with disabilities).
3. Covered aircraft operators must transmit to TSA certain non-personally identifiable information such as itinerary information and record locator numbers.
4. TSA will compare each passenger's and non-traveler's data to the federal government's consolidated watch lists and return a gate or boarding pass printing instruction to covered aircraft operators. If TSA is unable to differentiate an individual from a person on the Terrorist Screening Center's (TSC) Selectee or No Fly lists, covered aircraft operators must require the individual to present an unexpired government-issued photo identification document (ID) with the individual's full name and date of birth.
5. TSA will also provide instructions for placing separate bar codes on the boarding passes in the future in accordance with TSA instructions. The Secure Flight system will automatically generate a unique code for each watch list result returned to covered aircraft operators. Aircraft operators will be required to print this code separately from any other bar or optical code currently printed on a boarding or gate pass. Personnel at security checkpoints will use this code to verify the authenticity of the boarding pass.
6. Covered aircraft operators are required to take reasonable steps to make available a privacy notice to individuals on a website or self-service kiosk informing them why the information described above is being collected, how it will be used, and that provision of the requested information is voluntary.

This list is a mix of activities, including reassigning responsibilities across agencies, collecting and transferring information, and defining the monitoring systems. We can, as the RIA does, estimate the new costs and cost savings for each task.

To measure the benefits of these actions, the analyst must first define the expected outcomes associated with the list of actions. This is the first step in the analysis logic. The rule could be intended to maintain the outcomes associated with the current system for conducting preflight comparisons of passenger lists with watch lists, while reorganizing activities to reduce costs. If this is the goal of the rule, then the analysis (from a benefit–cost perspective) would compare the increased costs to some entities versus the reduced costs to others in order to determine if the net change leads to reductions in the overall costs (cost-effectiveness analysis). However, Secure Flight, like many rules, aims to improve conditions and reduce cost. In the RIA, the benefit categories (outcomes in our terminology) are enumerated as follows:

1. Improved security for travelers and non-traveling individuals, as well as additional access for the latter group.
2. Reduced false positives or misidentification of travelers as potential security threats.
3. Airlines relieved of watch list responsibilities.
4. More accurate matching of passengers and non-traveling personnel.
5. Increased watch list security.
6. Consolidated regulatory policy.
7. Boarding pass authentication.

Items (3) and (6) are the likely sources for cost savings. The other items are expected to be sources of benefits to different members of society. Explicitly linking the actions in the proposed rule to expected outcomes improves the analysis of the rule by forcing the analyst (and decision-makers who write the rules) to carefully consider what might happen when the actions in the rule are implemented.

Linking Defined Outcomes to Objects of Choice

The second decision (or set of decisions) describes the connections an analyst makes between the outcomes and a more specific characterization of things people want (the things people express preferences over). We use the term 'objects of choice' to describe the set of things people have preferences over, rather than the more common phrase 'goods and services'. This phrase is used in microeconomic theory to structure a general description for the relationship between consumers' choices and the patterns of demand we can observe.[2] We use the phrase 'objects of choice' to acknowledge that a person can have preferences for anything, including for example, less tangible goods like 'peace of mind when risks are reduced'. Describing these preferences in terms of commodities or services seems to imply that the logic is limited to a narrow set of decisions. It does not have to be, and recognizing the generality of the revealed preference logic has been important to designing economic methods for policy evaluation.

To make a decision, the consumer evaluates some set of alternatives, labeled the choice set. The choice set is a collection of the possible objects of choice the consumer considers in selecting their preferred option. In some cases, we can observe the consumer's choice. However, we do not always observe them making choices that allow an analyst to uncover how important people feel the outcomes are, especially for the less tangible objects of choice.

Rules and policies may affect the choice set available to the consumer. We can think of the objects of choice in the Secure Flight rule as the set of goods or services or other 'things' that the government is offering the people affected by the proposed rule. For the travelers, the objects of choice might include a reduced risk of injury or death from air travel, and a reduced risk that the passenger will be incorrectly identified as someone on the watch list and be barred from entering the gate area. Sometimes endogeneity makes it difficult to identify all the objects of choice and affected individuals.[3] As people change their behavior in response to a new rule, new impacts may arise and the number of people affected by the rule may change. Instead of consumers choosing, the regulatory analysis lays out how each bundle affects the public's welfare and a process specifies how society's preferred bundle is selected. The results of a benefit–cost analysis become one of the considerations in making these types of decisions.

When objects of choice are specified, this process requires identifying the different sets of individuals who will be impacted in different ways. A reduced risk of injury or death from air travel will be important to travelers and non-travelers, but for different reasons, and the value they place on the change in risk will probably be different too. Current travelers may directly experience reduced risk and greater peace of mind when traveling. Non-travelers may consider this risk important because friends or relatives are traveling.[4] People who do not currently fly because of concerns about terrorist risks may fly more. Terrorist attacks on airlines can also have a big impact on the airline industry and the economy as a whole. For the general public, the reduced risk of a successful terrorist attack on the airline industry reduces the risk of economic disruption.

Measuring the Objects of Choice

For a quantitative benefit–cost analysis, a measure for each element of the choice set must be created. The process of developing definitions for the objects of choice in any policy analysis balances the measure intended by the rule with the available data and methods, to produce a measurable index that the analyst can relate to the people who would be affected by the rule. For example, in the context of environmental regulations, assume that the objective of a rule is to protect human health. The specific consequences of a new rule in this context are usually measured by ambient concentrations of air pollutants. The actual measures used in setting the standard are based on how measures from monitored records of pollution concentrations affect the health outcomes that can be observed, such as mortality rates or hospital admissions in particular areas. The ideal measures for the objects of choice would broadly capture a physical measure of health, an activity-related index of mobility, or a perception-based assessment that could be linked to the ambient concentration of the pollutant. What we often settle for is a measure such as hospital admissions that can be related to monitored air pollution levels.

Specifying the Level and Policy-Induced Changes to the Baseline

Once measures for the objects of choice are defined, baseline conditions usually need to be defined. In the case of Secure Flight, before the policy non-travelers had access to the gate area under a very limited set of conditions. After the policy, they would have access under a more general set of conditions. The analyst needs to specify what changes as a result.

Sometimes it is not necessary to define a baseline condition if there is a means to estimate the change.[5] Suppose a rule saves time in security lines and the opportunity cost of this time is approximately constant. In this case, the aggregate cost savings can be measured without knowing what the amount of time spent waiting was under baseline conditions. In many situations this will not be possible because the trade-offs people make to obtain the change or the value they place on the change depends on the baseline level.

Defining the Extent of the Market for a Public Policy

The extent of the market for a public policy defines the set of affected individuals whose values are included in the analysis. Textbook discussions of the value of a public good usually consider the case of a pure public good and measure the aggregated willingness to pay ($AWTP$) for a change in the amount of this good as the sum of all individuals' willingness to pay (WTP_i) for a change in some commodity Δq as in equation (2.1).

$$AWTP(\Delta q) = \sum_{i=1}^{N} WTP_i(\Delta q) \tag{2.1}$$

The individuals are numbered from 1 to N, and N is the counterpart to the extent of the market.

In many areas of benefit–cost analysis, considerable effort is devoted to distinguishing different types of individuals, each with a distinct estimate for WTP_i. Usually these distinctions are due to differences in the activities that these different individuals undertake as part of using a common set of facilities. In our example the distinction between passengers and non-travelers who wish to access the gates would both experience a somewhat different 'commodity' (or Δq) because they are doing different things when they access the gates. In this case equation (2.1) would be rewritten as (2.2), with Δq the change experienced by passengers and $\Delta \tilde{q}$ by non-travelers. The commodities q and $\tilde{q}$ are different objects of choice associated with different outcomes of the rule.

$$AWTP = N_1\overline{WTP_1}(\Delta q) + N_2\overline{WTP_2}(\Delta \tilde{q}) \tag{2.2}$$

where $\overline{WTP_1}$ is the average value for passengers and $\overline{WTP_2}$ is the average value for non-travelers. For each group, the extent of the market is different, so we have different values for N_1 and N_2. In many situations the decisions made about the extent of the market are the most important factors influencing the aggregate benefit estimate for rules.[6]

Measuring Individual Trade-offs

To connect outcomes to observable choices, the analyst must identify situations where people can be observed making choices over something that matches some dimensions of one or more of the outcomes of the policy. Establishing this match is one part of the policy analyst's tasks in developing measures of the trade-offs people would make to obtain the outcomes of new rules. When it is possible to establish a close match between what people have done and what a rule would do, then the trade-off measures from these past decisions are more likely to be relevant to the changes anticipated with the rule. A variety of strategies can be used. One entails studying the choices people have made and trying to connect the things they pick to the objects of choice. This strategy involves revealed preference methods. A second involves offering hypothetical choices under well-defined conditions. This second set of methods falls under the stated preference logic.

Revealed preference theory is about what can be learned from people's choices. To answer this implicit question (that is: what do we learn from a person's choice?) we need to carefully define the object of choice: what is it and how it changes when an individual does something, as well as what happens when a person does not do anything. Notice that this means a baseline condition is implicitly specified. Equally importantly, we need to delineate completely the circumstance that might influence those choices. What does a person give up to obtain the object of choice? What are circumstances such as knowledge, background conditions about the person's economic commitments, and the other aspects of the context that might influence what this individual would do when the choice was made? An expensive umbrella may seem like a good choice when it is raining but would not be selected when it is a clear day. People react differently to health shocks experienced by a family member, altering the labor market choices for care giving, when they have made previous financial commitments such as a home mortgage compared with when they do not.[7] A more detailed description of the objects of choice along the dimensions described above allows the analyst to identify appropriate measures of WTP (or value) depending on the details.

There are a number of comprehensive discussions of the theory and methods used in measuring economic trade-offs as part of developing a benefit–cost analysis. We will not attempt here to summarize the methods and issues that arise in implementing them.[8] Instead our objective is to explain the process of developing trade-off measures with revealed and stated preference methods.

Revealed preference methods combine information about past observed choices, and assumptions about how individual preferences and constraints must have motivated these choices. That is, the composite of assumptions rationalizes the observed choices. This logic is important to the process of recovering measures of economic trade-offs implied by the choices. Purchasing a water filter to reduce contaminants in drinking water implies that the individual making this expenditure implicitly feels that the services provided by the device are worth at least the price paid. This logic requires that we identify what those services are – removing contaminants, improving taste, and so forth – the time period over which they are available with the device, and also that we define what the conditions would be without it.

A stated choice survey proposes a hypothetical situation and explains it as a change that could take place in relationship to a baseline (or default) situation. The features of what has changed and how the change would take place need to be aligned with the framing of the elements describing the baseline. The person asked about the change is told how an overall decision would be made and is also told there are specific amounts of resources, time, or both that would need to be given up for the proposed change to actually take place. Responses are then analyzed as if each respondent's decision is equivalent to an actual choice, with the financial consequences that are specified as part of the description of the object of choice and the circumstances associated with the choice. With a discrete choice framing of the offer the stated cost is interpreted as a lower bound for a person's WTP if they select the condition, and an upper bound if they do not.

Stated preference methods have been discussed for nearly as long as revealed preference. For our purpose, we will not discuss the debates in economics about the reliability of stated preference methods for measuring economic trade-offs. Our focus is on a separate issue. Beginning with a contingent valuation (CV) study conducted for a natural resource damage assessment associated with the *Exxon Valdez* oil spill (see Carson et al., 2003), and ultimately concluding with an expert panel (usually called the National Oceanic and Atmospheric Administration, NOAA, panel) that sought to evaluate contingent valuation (see Arrow et al., 1993),[9] stated preference studies in the CV format have favored the use of specific plans describing activities that are proposed to change a resource, a risk, or some other good or service that the person answering the question is unable to obtain in another way. The object of choice in this set-up includes the plan, not just the proposed change in the good. Including the plan in the questionnaire's presentation of the stated choice was important to the NOAA expert panel's assessment of the method (see Arrow et al., 1993).

Examples of Revealed Preference Approaches

The most common revealed preference methods used in benefit analysis combine parametric assumptions with data on observed choices to measure the trade-off.[10] We selected two examples to illustrate how this would work: a risk trade-off (the value of a statistical life), and measures for the opportunity cost of time.

The value of a statistical life (VSL) is one of the key trade-off measures that links the US Environmental Protection Agency's (EPA's) risk management strategy to benefit measurement. It is a transformation of the marginal WTP for a reduction in a fatality risk. The transformation involves implicitly defining the extent of the market for the reduction in fatality risk. This is done by assuming that a sufficient number of individuals are willing to pay for a one-unit change in risk to reduce the expected number of fatalities by one. Thus if the mortality measures used in the model we explain below are in ten thousands (that is, fatalities per 10000 individuals), then 1/10000 would be a unit change in risk. The logic asks the rhetorical question: suppose 10000 individuals were each willing to pay the estimate for the marginal WTP to reduce risk by one unit or 1/10000. Adding this up, or 10000 times the mean of what they would pay, is the aggregate value for this risk change experienced by these people. The aggregate is labeled the VSL. It is an estimate of what those individuals would trade-off for that risk reduction, assuming they all experience the change.

As a rule, labor market decisions and hedonic wage functions have been used for these estimates. To highlight some of the implicit assumptions, consider a slightly more general form of the model developed in Evans and Smith (2006).[11] Assume an individual's survival probability, π, is given in equation (2.3). π is a function of on-the-job fatality risk, p, and probabilities of death from J other causes, r_j, where $j = 1, \ldots, J$.

$$\pi = \pi(p, r_1, \ldots, r_J) \tag{2.3}$$

The survival probability is assumed to be decreasing in its arguments. Each of which is a mortality risk from a different source.

Let $U_s(W)$, $s = A, D$ represent the state-dependent utilities associated with income W (derived from work) in states *alive* (A) and *death* (D), respectively.[12] In addition assume that $U_A(W) > U_D(W)$, $U_s'(W) > 0$, for $s = A, D$, and $U_A'(W) > U_D'(W)$, with $U_s' = (dU_s'/dw)$. Expected utility is then defined in equation (2.4).

$$EU = (1 - \pi(p, r_1, \ldots, r_J))U_D(W) + \pi(p, r_1, \ldots, r_J)U_A(W) \tag{2.4}$$

Combining first-order conditions yields an expression for the VSL:

$$VSL = \frac{dW}{dp} = -\frac{(\partial\pi/\partial p)\,[U_A(W) - U_D(W)]}{\pi U_A'(W) + (1 - \pi)\,U_D'(W)} > 0 \tag{2.5}$$

The middle term in equation (2.5), (dW/dp), is estimated using a hedonic wage model (see Rosen, 1974) that is assumed to describe the equilibrium locus of wage or job attributes (including job-related risks).[13] The first argument in the numerator of the final term, $(\partial\pi/\partial p)$, represents the effect of a change in occupational mortality risk, p, on the survival probability, π. In the simplest case $\frac{\partial\pi}{\partial p} = -1$ and the VSL is measured as the difference in utility in the state *alive* versus a bequest adjusted by the expected marginal utility of income.

Our presentation of the logic highlights one issue. Are all sources of mortality risk interpreted equivalently? In this simple presentation, this question is about the survival function and the ability to consider all survival threats as making the same contribution to well-being.[14]

From the perspective of the policy analysis, the use of trade-offs in terms of mortality risk implies that a prior decision has been made about the link between the outcome relevant to policy and the object of choice used to measure the economic trade-off. More specifically the analysis is assuming that the rule being evaluated is delivering a risk change, among other things. The second example of revealed preference models used in measuring trade-offs concerns estimates of the opportunity cost of time. Here most efforts have also focused on the labor market.[15] In this case it is the labor–leisure choice. In situations where time at work can be adjusted and the wage rate is constant over the range of values for time working, then the wage provides a measure for the opportunity cost of time. Using it for all situations implies a comparable perfect substitution assumption to what was involved in the VSL example. If an analysis uses one VSL, the assumption is that the value of reducing any risk to survival is equivalent. In the case of time, we are assuming that all uses of time have an equivalent value to people.

A number of authors on labor and environmental economics have investigated this issue. People usually cannot adjust as economic models imply, and all uses of time are not equivalent. Finally, some activities may require blocks of time to be assembled (for example a concert must be attended when it is scheduled for a specific amount of time).[16] The opportunity cost of time varies depending on when the time is needed. We observe responses consistent with this conclusion by considering all the devices that allow some activities to be shifted in time (for example recording devices for television programs, movies). However these distinctions are difficult to measure.

For many policy applications, especially those associated with security, waiting time is a factor. Secure Flight involves changes in time requirements for reservation agents. The RIA estimates this time requirement as 25 seconds to collect the required information and uses the 'fully loaded' Bureau of Labor Statistics Estimates of the labor costs. What about the time of the passengers? Domestic passengers are assumed to have an opportunity cost of $28.60 per hour for the added time associated with trips for personal use, based on a Department of Transportation memorandum.[17] International travelers are assumed to have the same hourly opportunity cost.

One might ask about whether delay and waiting time are comparable to work time. It is possible to consider this issue in the context of a stated preference survey where the waiting time defined in the stated preference scenario was for security purposes. We discuss the specifics of this research effort in more detail in the section on 'Examples of Stated Preference Studies'. Our focus here is on the implied opportunity cost of time estimated from the research and summarized in Table 2.1. Two different payment vehicles (an income tax and a tax on gasoline) were used to describe the cost of the security programs. Regardless of the

Table 2.1 Stated preference estimates of opportunity cost of waiting time for enhanced airline security

Payment vehicle	Mean income of subsample	DOT-implied wage rate	Opportunity cost (2006)	Opportunity cost (2005)
Income tax	$51 665	$25.83	$44.07	$42.69
Gasoline tax	$53 992	$27.00	$168.48	$163.21

Note: The survey underlying these results was undertaken in March 2006 and income relates to the previous year.

payment vehicle used for the survey, compared with the Department of Transportation (DOT) estimates the choices implied larger opportunity costs of time for waiting time by nearly 50 percent for the lower of our two estimates. The issue is not that these estimates are superior but rather that consideration of the opportunity costs in this context could be important to cost estimates. The object of choice is not just time, but time spent waiting in an airport security line.

These two examples illustrate the logic associated with revealed preference measures of trade-offs. They offer estimates for a trade-off for a specifically defined object of choice. With the case of the VSL it is a change in mortality risk. For the opportunity cost of time it is the amount of time a person would be expected to lose in a particular situation. Using a single value for the VSL or the opportunity cost of time to assess benefits (or costs) implies that the outcomes of the rule can be converted into the units corresponding to the units used in the trade-off measures.

Examples of Stated Preference Studies

Following the logic we have presented, the tasks described in the language of the rule define the process used to achieve the outcomes. As the analyst moves from the tasks to defining the outcomes, to defining the objects of choice, the process for achieving the outcomes must be included. Usually, people are not indifferent about how an outcome is achieved; they care about the means, not just the ends. We illustrate this point in this section by reviewing a series of CV studies associated with homeland security plans.

Several years ago we initiated a modest program of research to design and implement three stated preference surveys. The surveys were exploratory. It was not clear whether we could explain the threats in ways that allowed survey respondents to make choices among policy options. The analysis for two of the three surveys is complete. For the third, the results

Table 2.2 Decomposing choice alternatives in stated preference examples

Object of study/choice alternatives	Attributes varied	Payment vehicle	Links for transfer
1. Threat: shoulder-mounted missile Missile defense technology Training pilots Patrol airports	Waiting time in security, price	Two-income tax, gasoline tax	Risk not quantified, only opportunity cost of time
2. Threat: food security Hire food inspectors to reduce risk Purchase home test kit for self-protection Purchase medicine to reduce severity of food-borne illness	Risk of food-borne illness, severity of incident of illness, time to use test kit	Income tax increase; price of kit, price of medicine	Risk of illness, severity of illness, opportunity cost of time
3. Threat: radiological dispersion device, dirty bomb Facilities to shelter in place Monitors and cameras to detect radioactive materials Public evacuation planning and practice	40 maps of metropolitan areas, paid-leave days given up	Income tax	Opportunity cost of time, geographic variation in responses (metropolitan areas)

reported here are preliminary. Each survey offers respondents a set of plans to reduce the risk or the consequences of a threat to homeland security.

Table 2.2 summarizes the highlights of the features of the three surveys concerning different threats to security. Here we report a brief summary of each to illustrate how the 'plan approach' to stated choice surveys describes the choices respondents are asked to make, and what those choices imply for the trade-offs that are estimated from such studies.

Protection against threats to commercial aircraft

The first survey considered policies to address a common threat: a terrorist attack on a commercial airline flight using shoulder-mounted missiles. The survey described the threat associated with terrorists' use of shoulder-mounted missiles and outlined three plans that were described as efforts to reduce the threat in some way. This is the connection between features of the baseline conditions and the activities associated with each plan. Each respondent answered questions in a 'choice experiment' context. That is, they were asked to select one of three options. Two were plans to address the threat, and the last was the default or 'do nothing' choice. A small number of attributes of the plans varied across respondents. The specific variants in each choice panel were selected to enhance the prospects of estimating a choice model from the responses.

Our objective was to describe the threat as one that affects the viability of the commercial airline sector, rather than increasing the risk to a passenger on any specific flight. To reinforce this logic the proposed plans were described as being paid for through either an increase in the income tax or an increase in the federal tax on gasoline. In the case of the gas tax, the design allowed the amount of the program's cost that was described to each respondent to adjust, based on the amount the person indicated was spent on gasoline during a year. This question about gasoline expenditures was asked at the outset of the survey, before respondents knew that this second question referring to adjusting fuel costs would be asked.

This survey and the next two we discuss were Internet-based surveys with the Knowledge Networks web panel. Box 2.1 provides the information used to describe the threat. Table 2.3 is an abbreviated form of the summary of three plans: (1) a system installed in planes to detect and divert heat-seeking missiles; (2) pilot training and fire suppression equipment on planes' fuel tanks; or (3) increased patrols on perimeters around the 20 largest airports.

The survey was administered to 2250 Knowledge Network panelists in March 2006. The response rate, considered in terms of the panelists invited to take the survey, was 74 percent. The choice panels describing the plans to respond to the threat varied across respondents. Two plans were offered in each panel. The information included a summary of the highlights of each plan as well as the cost of the plan expressed in weekly and annual terms, and the additional time required for security screening as another aspect of the plan. As we noted, half of the sample had the cost explained as an added income tax, and half used an increase in the federal gasoline tax. Each respondent saw two independent choice panels, each with two plans and a default status quo option.

Table 2.4 reports the estimated WTP for each plan using each of the two payment vehicles, based on a random utility model. Two models are reported for each subsample: one that assumes constant marginal utility of income, and another that allows it to vary across four income classes for household income.

The ranking of the plans is consistent based on WTP regardless of the payment vehicle, holding marginal utility of income constant. When the marginal utility is allowed to vary, the ranking of estimated WTP across plans is not maintained with income tax as the payment vehicle. However,

BOX 2.1 BACKGROUND GIVEN TO SURVEY RESPONDENTS

Airline Security

The terrorist hijacking of commercial airplanes and attacks on the World Trade Center and the Pentagon on September 11, 2001, led to major changes in airport security screening. Despite the increase in airport security, there are a number of continuing threats to air travel safety.

The Department of Homeland Security has identified ground-to-air missiles as an important threat to the security of the air transportation system in addition to the on-going threats posed by hijacking.

Ground Attacks with Missiles: Commercial aircraft can be attacked from the ground with small surface-to-air missiles (SAMs). These missiles can be carried by a single person and are fired from an area close to the airport.

The three main kinds of surface-to-air missiles are:

- Heat-seeking: target heat sources on an aircraft;
- Laser-guided: follow a laser path aimed at the aircraft and require extensive training and skill;
- Command line-of-sight missiles: directed using radio controls and require a very high level of skill;

It is estimated that there are at least 4 000 to 5 000 missiles that may be accessible to anti-Western terrorists. The majority of these missiles are heat seeking.

The chance that you would actually be on a plane experiencing a missile attack or a hijacking is very, very small, even if you fly a great deal.

In US airports, over 750 000 commercial airplanes depart on an average day, ranging from over 100 departures to over 1 100 departures a day at the 50 largest US airports.

An important reason for government concern is the security and reliability of the commercial air transportation system.

One successful attack would affect everyone in the US.

When people are killed in an attack it increases feelings of insecurity and reduces people's willingness to travel by air. The airline industry still suffers from the drop in air travel after 9/11. A 10% decline in airline travel reduces economic activity by about $40 billion a year. Another successful hijacking or missile attack would have serious impacts on our transportation system and on the whole US economy.

Source: Smith et al. (2009).

for the plan involving increased patrols the estimate is not precisely estimated. The difference in the WTP estimates for the fuel tank protection and training plan versus the patrol is not significant.

One of the most surprising aspects of the results is associated with the large difference in WTP estimates across the surveys using different payment vehicles. We conjectured in the full paper describing these results

Table 2.3 Abbreviated description of the plans (description of missile defense systems)

Detect and divert	Preventing fires and landing safely	Patrolling around airports
• All US airplanes install system to detect and divert heat-seeking missiles • Very effective as soon as it is installed • Only works for heat-seeking missiles • Heat-seeking missiles most common	• All US airplanes install fuel tank fire suppression systems • Additional pilot training to safely land missile-damaged plane • Moderately effective with sufficient time to develop systems and training • Works for all types of missiles	• Guards would patrol the area around 20 largest airports • Moderately effective • Works for all types of missiles as well as other threats to airports

Table 2.4 Estimated willingness to pay for security of commercial airlines to terror-related threats

Plan	Model				
	(1)	(2)			
		INC1	INC2	INC3	INC4
A. Gas tax					
Jamming device for infrared missiles (man pad)	220.8	149.0	210.1	266	394.8
	(4.90)	(3.72)	(3.80)	(3.54)	(1.55)
Fuel tank protection and pilot training	133.4	91.9	129.6	164.1	243.5
	(2.93)	(2.73)	(2.70)	(2.67)	(1.45)
Increased patrols	22.2	21.9	30.9	39.1	58.1
	(0.41)	(0.64)	(0.64)	(0.65)	(0.61)
B. Income tax					
Jamming device for infrared missiles (man pad)	99.6	82.3	84.5	181.9	119.4
	(7.66)	(6.02)	(6.09)	(3.32)	(2.17)
Fuel tank protection and pilot training	64.0	52.9	54.3	117.0	76.8
	(4.81)	(4.28)	(4.37)	(2.96)	(2.03)
Increased patrols	66.9	55.2	56.7	122.1	80.1
	(4.89)	(4.20)	(4.24)	(3.26)	(2.07)

Note: The numbers in parentheses are the asymptotic Z statistics for a test of zero marginal WTP.

(Smith et al., 2009) that these differences could be due to the linearity of the choice function and the difference in the range of costs implied with the two payment vehicles.

Nonetheless, we concluded our analysis of this survey with what seems to be clear evidence that respondents were able to deal with these types of choices. Comparing the plans, the jamming device and patrols were most closely associated with reducing the risk of a successful strike on a plane. The training and reinforcement to fuel tanks focused on consequences, given a successful hit by a missile. So prevention was favored over response to an attack in this context. Aside from the measure for the opportunity cost of time, these models do not lend themselves to extract a general trade-off measure for changes in a specific risk, or in other specific consequences associated with a different type of threat.

Food security

Our analysis of plans to reduce the risk or the consequences of food-borne illness was structured in a general format because of the difficulty (in focus groups) of explaining security-related threats to food security. Our analysis might offer a basis for wider transfers of the estimates. Participants in these focus group sessions acknowledged a wide range of threats to security due to terrorist activities. However they were skeptical of targeted activities to address specific threats. As a result, we posed a well-recognized threat to the quality and security of the food supply: food-borne illness. After presenting plans to address this threat in different ways, the survey then asked if a respondent's answers would be different if the threat were related to terrorist activities.

Two of the plans propose strategies that influence the probability of illnesses and represent *ex ante* responses to the risks posed by pathogens causing food-borne illnesses. They vary depending on whether the individual undertakes the averting activity himself or the protection arises as a risk reduction to everyone (through greater resources for FDA food inspectors). The third plan focuses on a medicine to reduce the severity of a case of food-borne-related illness. Figure 2.2 provides the text used to describe each of the plans:

- an *ex ante* private plan: a home test kit for food-borne contaminants;
- an *ex ante* plan to reduce risk by hiring more food inspectors; and
- an *ex post* option offering a medicine that influences the severity of the illness once it is contracted.

As we noted, all plans suggested that there would be an additional cost added to each person's federal income taxes for developing and implementing the plan that was selected. For the private options (that is, the test kit and the medicine), a further cost was associated with purchasing the test kit or the medicine. These added costs were described in monthly and annual terms (assuming each respondent would purchase them as prescribed). In addition, the test kit was described as involving some added time in food preparation each time the kit was used. This added time was not needed if a person selected a plan that did not involve the test kit. Knowledge Networks panelists completed the survey between August 24 and September 10, 2007. The sample included 1606 respondents. The focus of the results reported here is associated with using the choice questions illustrated in Figure 2.2 where a default 'no plan' option was included along with the choice of two other plans.

This design varied the plans presented and some of the attributes for each plan. However, the effects of variation in each plan's attributes (aside from the opportunity cost of time, and each plan's tax cost plus the annual expenditures required for the test kit and the medicine) could not be estimated separately from the alternative specific effect we attribute to the plan. These characteristics vary by plan in ways that had to be consistent with the context of each plan. As a result, the estimates of the effects of the plan's attributes could not be distinguished from the alternative specific effect we attributed to each plan.

Table 2.5 compares estimates of the WTP for each plan for the full sample along with subsamples identified by different subgroups. Marginal WTP for the private test kit and the increased inspections is not significantly different (using a Wald test with the robust covariance matrix for the McFadden, 1974 conditional logit model $\chi^2(1) = 0.95$, p-value $= 0.329$). A 'negative' marginal WTP for the plan to offer a medicine to reduce the severity of illness, which is not significantly different from zero, reflects respondents' strong dissatisfaction with the plan to address *ex post* outcomes.

The measures for opportunity cost of the additional time involved in food preparation, \$22.50 and \$37.70 per minute, are quite large and may be the result of the framing of the question. The survey presents the time requirements for using the test kit as time per use of the kit. The actual amount of time the respondents spend using the kit over a year will vary based on kit utilization, the number of meals eaten at home, and the type of meals prepared. The correct comparison with the value of time estimates in other contexts should scale the minutes per meal by the times the kit would be used. For example, adding a minute to each of 150 meals would imply a value of 0.15 per minute (using our estimate of \$22.50 per minute) or an opportunity cost of time of about \$9.00 per hour and \$15.00 per hour with the \$37.70 estimate. Increasing the number of meals tested reduces the opportunity cost further.

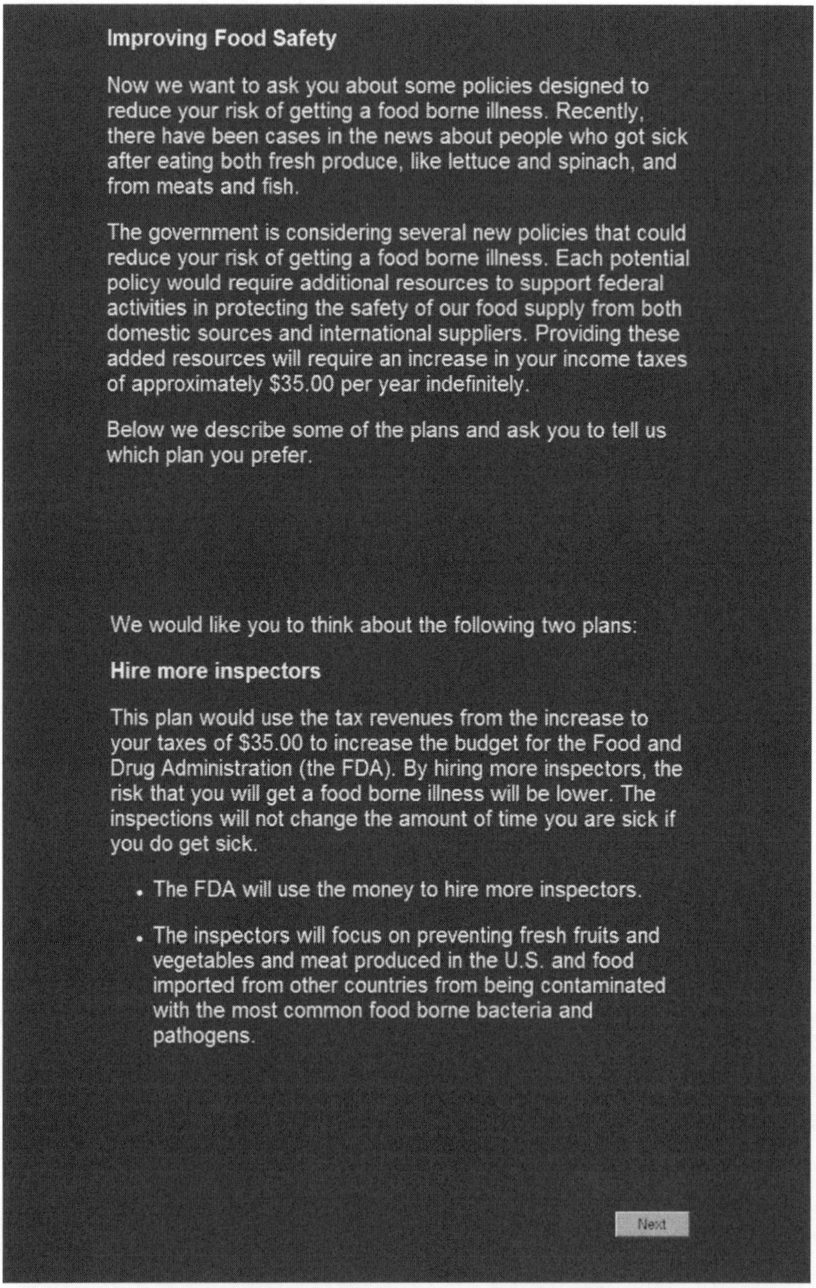

Improving Food Safety

Now we want to ask you about some policies designed to reduce your risk of getting a food borne illness. Recently, there have been cases in the news about people who got sick after eating both fresh produce, like lettuce and spinach, and from meats and fish.

The government is considering several new policies that could reduce your risk of getting a food borne illness. Each potential policy would require additional resources to support federal activities in protecting the safety of our food supply from both domestic sources and international suppliers. Providing these added resources will require an increase in your income taxes of approximately $35.00 per year indefinitely.

Below we describe some of the plans and ask you to tell us which plan you prefer.

We would like you to think about the following two plans:

Hire more inspectors

This plan would use the tax revenues from the increase to your taxes of $35.00 to increase the budget for the Food and Drug Administration (the FDA). By hiring more inspectors, the risk that you will get a food borne illness will be lower. The inspections will not change the amount of time you are sick if you do get sick.

- The FDA will use the money to hire more inspectors.
- The inspectors will focus on preventing fresh fruits and vegetables and meat produced in the U.S. and food imported from other countries from being contaminated with the most common food borne bacteria and pathogens.

Next

Figure 2.2 Description of the plans for food-borne illness

Purchase medicine

This plan would use the tax revenues from the increase of $35.00 to your taxes to subsidize the costs of a medicine that you can take if you get a food borne illness. Although the medicine does **not** change the risk that you would get a food borne illness, it will shorten the amount of time your are sick.

- The medicine is good for food borne illnesses caused by the most common food borne bacteria and pathogens in fresh fruits and vegetables and meat. The medicine causes very mild side effects, but no serious or lasting side effects.
- This medicine will be available without a prescription, but you have to order it ahead of time from the pharmacy and delivery takes several weeks. You need to have the medicine on hand -- you will not have time to order it once you got sick.
- After 1 year the medicine expires and will no longer work, so you need to buy more medicine each year.

Home test kit

This plan would use the tax revenues from the increase in your taxes of $35.00 to subsidize the costs of a home test kit that would allow you and your family to test all of your food. By testing your food, the possibility that you would become sick would be reduced (your risk of getting a food borne illness would be lower). Testing will not change the amount of time you are sick if you do get sick.

- **When you answer this question, please assume the results from tests with these kits would be very reliable**. You can test fresh fruits and vegetables and meat for the most common food borne bacteria and pathogens.
- Raw food is tested before cooking using the kit. This means that preparing a meal will take longer.
- If the test is positive and the food contains bacteria, the only way to completely protect yourself and your family would be to throw the food away without eating it.
- After 1 year, the test kit materials expire and the test no longer works. So each year, you will have to buy a new kit.

Figure 2.2 (continued)

Table 2.5 Marginal willingness to pay estimates for food safety plans: subsamples for different consumer groups

Plan Models	Adjusted full sample*	No children under 17 years of age	Experience food-borne illness	Primary food shopper	Consider the survey consequential
Test kit	195.2	99.5	241.1	256.6	253.2
	(2.11)	(4.42)	(1.06)	(1.05)	(1.33)
Food inspectors	156.6	83.5	259.1	211.6	256.4
	(2.35)	(5.94)	(1.09)	(1.12)	(1.39)
Medicine	−118.0	−15.5	−154.1	−227.7	−50.3
	(−1.15)	(−0.68)	(−0.66)	(−0.71)	(−0.51)
Opportunity cost of time	37.7	7.00	27.4	29.5	19.5
	(1.60)	(2.25)	(0.82)	(0.82)	(0.97)

Notes:
Numbers in parentheses are asymptotic Z statistics for null hypothesis of zero marginal WTP.
* The choice model includes fixed effects for the plans as choice alternatives, the total cost relevant to each plan and an adjustment for selection effects. It also deletes respondents who had difficulty understanding the risk of illness based on a simple test of risk perceptions.

Dirty bombs

The last example of a stated preference analysis of alternative homeland security policies involves plans to reduce the threat posed by conventional bombs that include low-level radioactive material. These devices are intended to spread the material widely around a targeted area, such as an important area in a city or a location with political or cultural significance. Once dispersed, these materials are difficult and costly to remove and may pose significant, long-term health risks if people are exposed to them for prolonged periods. As a result, a successful attack could imply closing off large areas of a city for use for a long time. These devices are referred to as 'radiological dispersion devices' (RDDs) or dirty bombs.

In 2009 we designed a survey to investigate people's WTP for plans to address this threat. After conducting several sets of focus groups and a pilot survey, we had respondents complete two separate Internet surveys. Between December 15, 2009 and December 31, 2009, a total of 2690 Knowledge Networks panelists aged 18 and older, who lived in one of 33 metropolitan areas, were invited to participate in the survey. A total of 1901 panelists completed the survey by 31 December for a 71 percent completion rate, measured based on complete responses to these invitations. The four metropolitan areas with the largest samples were Chicago (170),

Table 2.6 Descriptive statistics

Variable	December 2009	April 2010	
	Full sample	Four metro areas	Four metro areas
Age (fixed effects)			
18–24	0.020	0.028	0.025
25–34	0.086	0.092	0.091
35–44	0.143	0.146	0.172
45–54	0.241	0.256	0.267
55–64	0.270	0.256	0.243
65–74	0.176	0.163	0.149
Female	0.586	0.570	0.629
Young children	0.092	0.090	0.108
No. of children	0.472	0.482	0.531
White	0.772	0.717	0.703
No high school	0.020	0.026	0.014
College	0.518	0.548	0.612
Married	0.576	0.536	0.517
Income (US$)	82 174	93 659	97 037
Importance of being prepared for disasters			
Very important	0.51	0.53	0.54
Somewhat important	0.43	0.40	0.40
Not too important	0.05	0.06	0.05
Not at all important	0.01	0.01	0.01

Los Angeles (169), New York (130) and Washington, DC (182). Each of the respondents in these cities was randomly assigned one of several maps of the downtown area of each city, identifying different landmarks. For the remaining 29 metropolitan areas, each respondent received one map from the city where they lived.

The second survey was conducted for the four larger areas between April 1, 2010 and April 19, 2010 and involved 482 different panelists from those included in the December interviews. The survey structure and design were not changed. Table 2.6 summarizes the demographic attributes of the full sample, the four metropolitan areas as a subset of the December sample, and this subgroup sampled in April. As the table suggests, the demographic attributes of the respondents are comparable across the subsamples in the two periods.

The questionnaire used a choice experiment format, with two of the three potential plans along with a default ‘do nothing’ alternative. Each respondent saw two choice panels, each with three possible choices,

Table 2.7 Estimates of willingness to pay for plans to protect against dirty bombs

Plan	Sample					
	Full sample	Major metro cities	NY	LA	DC	Chicago
Develop facilities to shelter in place	100.56 (p = 0.00)	117.38 (p = 0.00)	173.48 (p = 0.00)	51.12 (p = 0.20)	154.97 (p = 0.00)	84.38 (p = 0.02)
Monitor for radioactive materials and security cameras	167.55 (p = 0.00)	231.04 (p = 0.00)	303.93 (p = 0.00)	182.24 (p = 0.00)	226.10 (p = 0.00)	226.90 (p = 0.00)
Plan and practice evacuations	−61.42 (p = 0.01)	−13.16 (p = 0.65)	−14.13 (p = 0.85)	−106.59 (p = 0.15)	6.91 (p = 0.88)	52.94 (p = 0.29)

Notes:
A dirty bomb is not an atomic bomb. It is an ordinary explosive device with radioactive material. The objective is to use the explosion to spread the contamination associated with the radioactive substances.
The numbers in parentheses are p-values testing the null hypothesis that the WTP was zero.

including the 'do nothing' alternative. They were asked to consider each choice panel as if it was an independent choice situation.

Three different plans were included in the design (Table 2.7). The first labeled 'shelter in place' proposed that the federal government would provide support to local governments in the 50 largest metropolitan areas (including the respondent's location), to be used to create space in office and retail buildings for sheltering people in the downtown area in the event of a successful attack with a dirty bomb. The resources would allow space and supplies so that people could wait until the risks of exposure to radioactive material were reduced in the aftermath of a dirty bomb attack. The second plan would introduce 'radioactive material monitors and security cameras' in the high-threat areas of the 50 largest metropolitan areas (including the respondent's location). Finally, the last plan would provide federal support for evacuation planning and practice. It would require one practice evacuation each year. The plan would again affect the 50 largest metropolitan areas including the respondent's area. The costs of the plans were described as requiring increased income taxes for the foreseeable future, and in the case of the evacuation plan would also require respondents to give up some paid leave time for the practice evacuation each year.

The shelter and evacuation plans target the severity of the impacts

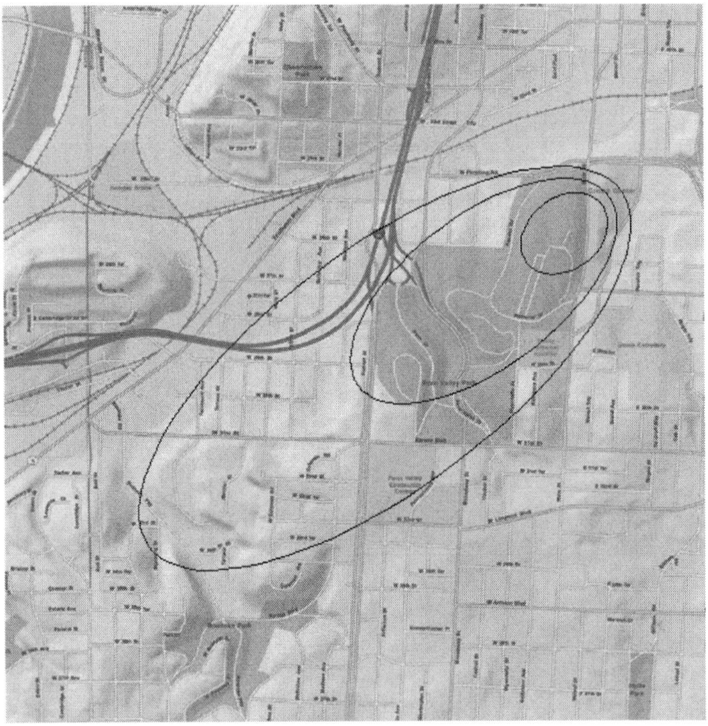

Note: The maps used in the original survey were higher resolution and in color.

Figure 2.3 Map used to describe the threat

should there be a successful attack. The monitoring device and security camera target both the risk of a successful attack and the identification of high-risk areas after such an event.

Figure 2.3 illustrates a map and Box 2.2 provides the text used to describe the threat. Table 2.8 presents our preliminary results using both surveys to estimate a simple random utility model. The full sample and a series of subsamples were estimated to illustrate how the survey could be used to estimate the WTP for a plan to address this source of threat.

The estimated choice model includes the increased tax, alternative specific constants for each plan, and in the case of an evacuation plan the amount of paid leave time that would be requested. In Table 2.8 we focus on the estimated WTP for each plan. It is clear that the plan with monitoring devices and security cameras is the approach with the highest estimates for WTP for the full sample and all subsamples. Developing facilities for

BOX 2.2 TEXT USED TO DESCRIBE THE THREAT

The table below describes the expected impacts on people living and working in the 3 rings shown on the map compared to the average risk of cancer. The risks from the contamination depend on what radioactive material was used and its spread throughout the area. For the purposes of the next set of questions please assume the information in the table provides the best estimate of the risks.

Ring	Expected deaths	Increase in cancer risk
Smallest ring in the middle	It is expected that about 1 in every 20 people in the smallest ring would be killed from the explosion.	Risk would be 100% higher than the average risk of dying from cancer – or about 38 out of every 10 000 people exposed to radiation from a dirty bomb in this area would die from cancer in the future.
Between the smallest ring and the middle ring	No one would be killed.	Risk would be 50% higher than the average risk of dying from cancer – or about 29 out of every 10 000 people exposed to radiation from a dirty bomb in this area would die from cancer in the future.
Between the middle ring and the outer ring	No one would be killed.	Risk would be 25% higher than the average risk of dying from cancer – or about 23 in every 10 000 people exposed to radiation from a dirty bomb in this area would die from cancer in the future.
Outside the outer ring in the rest of the city	No one would be killed.	Small increase in the risk of dying from cancer in the future.

Note: The online survey formatted the table in color to fit the design of the rest of the survey.

shelter would be second-highest. There appears to be a clear negative attitude toward planning and practicing evacuations.

Comparison of the results suggests areas that are more likely to be targets generally have a larger WTP than the average for all cities taken

Table 2.8 Definitions for major elements in preparedness

Term	Definition
Event	An incident that has a high enough level of severity, extends across state boundaries and involves resources that are managed or regulated at the federal level so as to call for federal action that falls within DHS's responsibility. Examples are terrorist attacks, natural disasters, industrial or transportation accidents, or releases of oil or hazardous substances in the environment.
Preparedness	'[T]o prevent, protect against, respond to, and recover from major events in order to minimize the impact on lives, property and economy' (National Preparedness Goal, December 2003).
Prevention	Actions taken to reduce the probability that an event defined under the above description will occur.
Protection	Actions, including direct and indirect resource allocations, information programs and other public and private activities that are taken prior to an event and are intended to reduce its consequences to people and property from the event. This could also include actions to protect the natural environment or cultural responses. For example, protection for unique natural wonders like the Grand Canyon or a historical monument would fall in this category.*
Response	Actions taken to address the short-term, direct effects of an event regardless of the cause. May et al. include in response a priority scheme with people designated as the first concern and property the second. Because they do not identify a distinction between private, natural and cultural assets, these are not prioritized. We would argue that this is part of the policy making process.
Recovery	Actions taken to restore functions and care for affected people over the longer term. The distinction between short and long term (for example, response versus recovery) may be vague. In practice it is context-specific.

Note: * May et al. (2006) note that protection was not explicitly defined in DHS documents. They also did not include natural environments and cultural responses in their specification, but we believe these should have been included.

Source: May et al. (2006, p. 4).

together. We did not explore the effects of the different maps at this stage in our analysis. Our intention was a preliminary assessment of respondents' ability to deal with these types of questions.

Comparing the results based on samples confined to the individual cities implies significantly different WTP measures for some plans in some of the cities. For example, comparing the overall sample's estimates for the two plans that had the largest WTP measures (monitoring devices with security cameras and areas for sheltering) to the trade-offs implied by the New York subsample indicates that New York respondents would pay more for both plans. By contrast a similar comparison of the overall mean with estimates from the Los Angeles sample implied much smaller values.

DESIGNING THE ARCHITECTURE FOR DEPARTMENT OF HOMELAND SECURITY (DHS) POLICY ANALYSIS CAPACITY

The development of an organization's analysis capacity takes place within a context that defines how the analysis contributes to the group's goals. The most direct way to illustrate what we have in mind is to describe how the analysis capacity of the US EPA's Office of Air Quality Planning and Standards (OAQPS) developed. Under the initial Clean Air Act, the agency was charged with the responsibility to protect human health with an adequate margin of safety. Over the decades since that initial legislative mandate was established, the analysis capacity within the agency was organized around the logic of risk assessment. In effect, protecting human health with an adequate margin of safety has been interpreted as risk management.

When benefit–cost analysis for environmental rules was first introduced, the connection between the policy goals of the rules (for example, compliance with an air quality standard) and outcomes from the activities listed in the rule was often somewhat tenuous.[18] The federal requirement to conduct benefit–cost analysis for rules, usually attributed to Executive Order 12291, changed the nature of EPA's activities. The logic governing the design of regulations did not change, but the structure of the interactions between those analysts defining the rules and those who are charged with developing the RIAs for them did. As a result, the information developed from the rulemaking process evolved to define EPA's architecture for benefit–cost analysis.

Although many of EPA's activities associated with rulemaking and evaluation can be organized under the risk management logic, some do not fit within this framework. Benefit–cost assessments of rules related to recreation under water quality regulations, air pollution rules related to visibility, or section 316(b) dam relicensing evaluations, are examples where the risk orientation does not adequately describe the activities. In these cases the tasks associated with these rules and management choices follow a somewhat different logic. Our point is generic. With a single logic for organizing an analysis it is possible to develop the information and experience to define a set of protocols that provide a systematic template for evaluating each new rule. This is what we labeled the 'analysis capacity'. This structure builds research experience with specialized literature. The strategies must be periodically evaluated to be sure they are consistent with best practice. Nonetheless, as long as they remain consistent, analysis protocols (such as the EPA Guidelines for Economic Analysis) and models such as EPA's Environmental Benefits Mapping and Analysis Program (BenMAP) can be developed and used for analyzing a variety of policies.

Risk management is an important function for DHS, but another organizing structure could be preparedness. As an example, we use a framework developed by May et al. (2006). They define the major elements of preparedness for homeland security as prevention, protection, response, and recovery. These authors provide a careful definition for each element and explain their interconnections. Table 2.8 paraphrases and extends (in some cases) the definition for each element in their framework. Figure 2.4 extracts from their report the logic that connects the elements. It expands the issues identified as cross-cutting themes to include incentives for private action and endogenous risk. Complementary private action (citizens taking actions on their own to prepare) will always play a big role in preparedness; the government does not have the capacity to take all the responsibility. Citizens can be encouraged to take action with incentives and information programs. In addition, the level of risk reduction achieved by a policy may be endogenous to the design of the policy. That is, when protective policies are undertaken, the nature of the risk changes in response to the policy. For example, laws requiring seat belt use lead to increased driving speeds. The final level of risk reduction will depend on how individuals respond to the policy as it is implemented.

Finally, an issue that is implicitly considered in the May et al. discussion is the indirect effects of policy. Security policy can create either ancillary benefits or costs. A potentially important component of these costs arises when a new security policy has indirect effects that reduce the effectiveness of other policies. An example of an alternative complementary situation where we could realize ancillary benefits as an indirect effect of a new security policy would be a situation where efforts to prepare to respond to and recover from a successful terrorist attack may also be

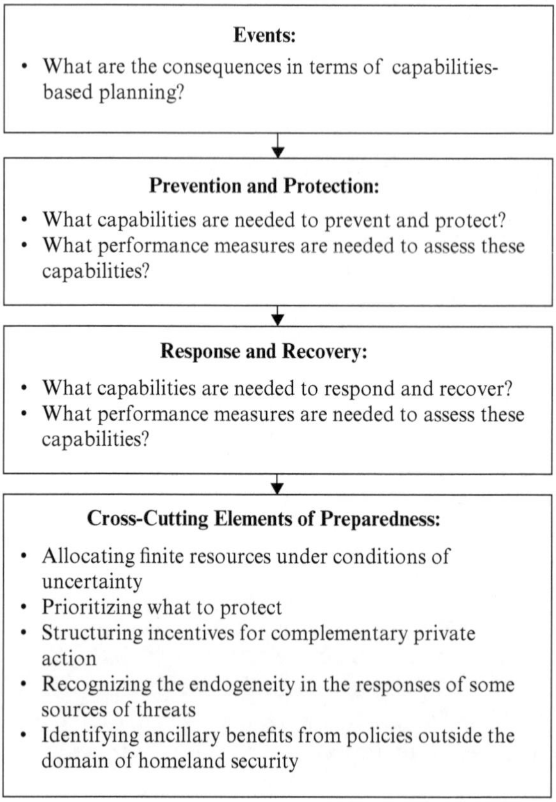

Note: We have edited some elements from their original presentation, deleting some elements and substituting others. The changes were made to the cross-cutting elements. See pp. 3–5 of the May et al. report for original.

Figure 2.4 May et al. (2006) logical structure

helpful in reducing impacts of natural disasters such as earthquakes or hurricanes.

On the cost side, reducing population density to reduce the exposed population to targeted threat areas might also increase sprawl. Similarly, decentralizing storage of financial processing systems may yield increased security for these records, but it could also reduce agglomeration economies from more centralized positioning.

Table 2.9, also taken from May et al. (2006), illustrates the generic point that some actions can have spillover effects across hazards. In the case of this table, the ability to serve multiple threats is highlighted.

Table 2.9 Potential complementarities in protection activity

	Terrorist attack	Natural disaster	Industrial disaster
1. Prevention to stop attacks	X		
2. Prevention to deter attacks	X		
3. Prevention to eliminate natural or industrial disasters		X	X
4. Protection to reduce damage	X	X	X
5. Protection by physical separation	X	X	X

Source: May et al. (2006).

To our knowledge DHS is in the early stages of the reductionist process associated with developing themes that would be used for one or more analysis strategies. This process depends on the ability to identify a set of outputs, services, or types of risk reductions that can be used to describe the outcomes of several different classes of policies. It is what we have labeled structuring the 'architecture' of the agency's policy analysis capacity.

Benefit–cost analysis will never be the exclusive basis for judging specific rules or resource management plans. It does provide an important disciplinary logic that ensures policymakers will have a systematic evaluation of what policies that restrict private activities, invest public resources, or manage resources held in public trust are expected to accomplish.

NOTES

1. In this context, policy analysis represents a systematic assessment of the economic impacts of some intervention whether a regulation, management change or public investment. For example, in the case of regulation it would be part of an RIA.
2. See Kreps (1990, pp. 18–19).
3. An example in the case of recreation would be a rule that required lifeguards at public beaches. This requirement could lead to greater use and increased congestion at beaches, and the net effect might not be clear. See Timmins and Murdoch (2007) for an example of a model of recreation site selection that treats congestion as endogenous.
4. In this context these individuals would be comparable to non-users in the literature of environmental economics. They would be willing to give up resources for the risk reduction even though they are not flying. See McConnell (1998) for a discussion of the distinction between altruism and non-use value.
5. If we can assume that the trade-offs people would make to obtain the change do not depend on this level.
6. See Kopp and Smith (1989) for examples of how these assumptions contributed to differences in the measures for natural resource damages.

7. See Chetty and Szeidl (2007) and Evans and Smith (2008).
8. See Freeman (2003) for an overview of theory and methods. Champ et al. (2003) is an introductory primer. More advanced discussion of theory can be found in Bockstael and McConnell (2007).
9. The report for the state of Alaska's natural resource damage assessment associated with the *Exxon Valdez* oil spill was completed in 1991. The Carson et al. (2003) citation is for a published paper describing the study. The original report was available to the NOAA expert panel who evaluated CV at the time they undertook their assessment.
10. Recent research in applied economics, including environmental economics, has focused attention on the source of identifying information that is associated with estimating an effect. In the context of measuring economic trade-offs, this has meant assumptions about the functional form used to describe an equilibrium relationship such as a hedonic wage function or to specify a preference or production function. The most recent literature (see Angrist and Pishke, 2010) has called for greater attention to the source of identification and effort to use data-based information as opposed to parametric information in these processes. These issues are very important and would require considerable space to develop. They do not alter the general points we are making. The focus of the analysis remains a factor that is assumed to be outside an individual's direct control that serves to bound the trade-offs they would make.
11. The discussion below is taken from their development.
12. We can think of the utility in the state *death* as associated with a desire to leave bequests.
13. The W is the annual earnings. Comparable issues to what have been raised with hedonic property value models concerning omitted variables and endogeneity could be raised for these applications (see Deleire et al., 2013 for an alternative model). However, these are beyond the scope of our objectives here.
14. There are many other issues. For example, are the individuals who we observe making risk–earnings trade-offs representative of typical individuals who might experience the risk associated with a policy being evaluated?
15. The VSL work considers choices across jobs and as a rule does not consider how many hours a person works.
16. See Palmquist et al. (2010).
17. The 1997 memorandum that was available to us distinguishes several types of transportation. All are based on percentages of earnings. Air travel for personal was 70 percent with a plausible range from 60 to 90 percent. A weighted average of incomes for passengers taking domestic business and other trips in 1998 was used. It was adjusted by 8.4 percent from 1998 to 2000.
18. See Fisher and Smith (1982) for a discussion of some of these early assessments. Today one need only consider the compliance documents of state and county officials responding to a notice that they were not in compliance with a standard for a criteria air pollutant. The State Implementation Plan describing how they will achieve compliance is often a litany of activities with little connection to how the actions collectively contribute to reducing ambient concentrations of the pollutant and meeting the standard.

REFERENCES

Angrist, J.D. and J.-S. Pischke (2010). 'The credibility revolution in empirical economics: how better research design is taking the con out of econometrics', *Journal of Economic Perspectives*, **24** (2), 3–30.

Arrow, K., R. Solow, P.R. Portney, E.E. Leamer, R. Radner, and H. Schuman

(1993). 'Report of NOAA Panel on Contingent Valuation', *Federal Register*, **58**, 4601–4616.
Boardman, Anthony E., David H. Greenberg, Aidan R. Vining, and David L. Weimer (2006). *Cost–Benefit Analysis: Concepts and Practice*, 3rd edn, Upper Saddle River, NJ: Prentice Hall.
Bockstael, N.E. and K.E. McConnell (2007). *Environmental and Resource Valuation with Revealed Preferences: A Theoretical Guide to Empirical Models*, Dordrecht: Springer.
Carbone, J.C. and V.K. Smith (2008). 'Evaluating policy interventions with general equilibrium externalities', *Journal of Public Economics*, **92**, 1254–1274.
Carson, R.T., R.C. Mitchell, W.M. Hanemann, R.J. Kopp, S. Presser, and P.A. Ruud (2003). 'Contingent valuation and lost passive use: damages from the Exxon Valdez oil spill', *Environmental and Resource Economics*, **25**, 257–286.
Champ, P.A., K.J. Boyle, and T.C. Brown (eds) (2003). *A Primer on Nonmarket Valuation*, Dordrecht: Kluwer Academic Publishers.
Chetty, R. and A. Szeidl (2007). 'Consumption commitments and risk preferences', *Quarterly Journal of Economics*, **122** (2), 831–877.
Deleire, T., S. Khan, and C. Timmins (2013). 'Roy model sorting and the value of a statistical life' (with Thomas Deleire and Shakeeb Khan). *International Economic Review*, **54** (1), 279–306.
Department of Homeland Security (2008). *Regulatory Evaluation Final Rule Secure Flight (49 CFR 1560)*, October 17.
Evans, M.F. and V.K. Smith (2006). 'Do we really understand the age–VSL relationship?' *Resource and Energy Economics*, **28**, 242–261.
Evans, M.F. and V.K. Smith (2008). 'Complementarity and the measurement of individual risk tradeoffs: accounting for quality and quality of life effects', *Environment and Resource Economics*, **41**, 381–400.
Fisher, A.C and V.K. Smith (1982). 'Economic evaluation of energy's environmental costs, with special reference to air pollution', *Annual Review of Energy*, **7**, 1–35.
Freeman, A. Myrick III (2003). *The Measurement of Environmental and Resource Values: Theory and Methods*, 2nd edn, Washington, DC: Resources for the Future.
Gollier, C. (2001). *The Economics of Risk and Time*, Cambridge, MA, USA and London, UK: MIT Press.
Goulder, L.H., I.W.H. Parry, R.C. Williams III, and D. Burtraw (1999). 'The cost-effectiveness of alternative instruments for environmental protection in a second-best setting', *Journal of Public Economics*, **72**, 329–360.
Goulder, L.H. and R.C. Williams III (2003). 'The substantial bias from ignoring general equilibrium effects in estimating excess burden, and a practical solution', *Journal of Public Economy*, **111** (4), 898–927.
Greenstone, M. (2009). 'Toward a culture of persistent regulatory experimentation and evaluation', in David Moss and John Cisternino (eds), *New Perspectives on Regulation*, Cambridge, MA: Tobin Project, pp. 111–126.
Just, R.E., D.L. Hueth, and A. Schmitz (2004). *The Welfare Economics of Public Policy: A Practical Approach to Project and Policy Evaluation*, Cheltenham, UK and Northampton, MA, USA: Edward Elgar.
Klaiber, H.A. and V.K. Smith (2011). 'Preference heterogeneity and non-market benefits: the roles of structural hedonic and sorting models', in Jeff Bennett

(ed.), *The International Handbook on Non-Market Valuation*, Cheltenham, UK and Northampton, MA, USA: Edward Elgar, pp. 222–253.
Klaiber, H.A. and V.K. Smith (2012). 'Developing general equilibrium benefit analysis for social programs: an introduction and example', *Journal of Benefit–Cost Analysis*, **3** (2), 1–52.
Kopp, R.J. and V.K. Smith (1989). 'Benefit estimation goes to court: the case of natural resource damage assessments', *Journal of Policy Analysis and Management*, **8** (4), 593–612.
Kreps, D.M. (1990). *A Course in Microeconomic Theory*, Princeton, NJ: Princeton University Press.
May, M., L. Eden, P. Roberts and J.N. Shapiro (2006). *An Analytic Approach to Preparedness for Homeland Security*, Stanford, CA: Center for International Security and Cooperation and Freeman Spogli Institute for International Studies.
McConnell, K.E. (1998). 'Does altrusim undermine existence value?', *Journal of Environmental Economics and Management*, **32** (1), 22–37.
McFadden, D. (1974). 'Conditional logit analysis of qualitative choice behavior', in P. Zarembka (ed.), *Frontiers in Econometrics*, New York: Academic Press, pp. 105–142.
Palmquist, R.B., D. Phanuef, and V.K. Smith (2010). 'Short run constraints and the increasing marginal value of time in recreation', *Environmental and Resource Economics*, **46**, 19–41.
Rosen, S. (1974). 'Hedonic prices and implicit markets: product differentiation in pure competition', *Journal of Political Economy*, **82** (1), 34–55.
Smith, V.K. and J.C. Carbone (2008). 'Environmental economics and the "curse" of the circular flow', in JunJie Wu, Paul W. Barkley and Bruce A. Weber (eds), *Frontiers in Resource and Rural Economics; Human–Nature, Rural–Urban Interdependencies*, Washington, DC: Resources for the Future, pp. 43–62.
Smith, V.K., C. Mansfield and L. Clayton (2009). 'Valuing a homeland security policy: countermeasures for the threats from shoulder mounted missiles', *Journal of Risk and Uncertainty*, **38**, 215–243.
Sunstein, C.R. (2010). 'Humanizing cost benefit analysis', remarks prepared for the Administrative Law Review Conference, American University, Washington College of Law, Washington, DC.
Timmins, C. and J. Murdock (2007). 'A revealed preference approach to the measurement of congestion in travel cost models', *Journal of Environmental Economics and Management*, **53** (2), 141–290.

PART II

Security policies and reducing risks

3. Lessons from risk assessment, economics, and risk management at EPA

Chris Dockins and William Wheeler[1]

INTRODUCTION

Economic analysis is a key component of risk management; it has been required for 'economically significant' federal regulations as part of regulatory review requirements under Executive Orders 12291 (issued in 1981) and 12866 (issued in 1993) and their successors. Even without the requirements of 12866, economic analysis, and particularly benefit–cost analysis, of proposed regulations is an important undertaking in its own right. Benefit–cost analysis can identify where investments of scarce resources provide positive net returns, and can be a valuable input into prioritizing policy actions. Those actions that cannot demonstrate positive net benefits should be considered carefully because they are not a step toward economic efficiency, although they may well be justified on other important grounds. Even when all benefits and costs cannot be quantitatively included in an analysis, careful enumeration of the types of benefits and costs expected, and qualitative information on their importance, can inform policy makers and the general public.

Fundamental to any of these analyses is quantitative assessment of risk reductions (or countervailing increases) that are expected as a result of the regulation. Over the course of decades, the United States Environmental Protection Agency (EPA) has built an infrastructure for risk assessment, as well as for economic analysis, although these have not always been fully compatible. The steps EPA has taken to develop risk assessment and economics, both separately and together, may prove useful to similar efforts at the United States Department of Homeland Security (DHS). DHS engages in a broad array of risk activities in a variety of contexts: terrorism, biological threats, natural hazards, cyber security, and others. When it was created, DHS combined 22 different agencies.

Risk analysis at DHS was recently reviewed by the National Research

Council (NRC, 2010), focusing primarily on risk analysis for terrorism threats, where DHS has focused its own efforts. Based on an examination of illustrative risk analysis models and processes, the report describes the general risk analysis framework used by DHS and identifies deficiencies. The primary deficiencies were in assessment of individual components of risk and their integration, and in assessment and communication of the underlying assumptions and surrounding uncertainties in risk analysis. The report views these as major deficiencies, concluding that, 'Until these deficiencies are improved, only low confidence should be placed in most of the risk analysis conducted by DHS' (NRC, 2010, p. 11). The NRC report made several specific recommendations for improving risk analysis at DHS, including a call for the department to develop scientific guidelines for risk analyses.

EPA's mandate, which focuses on protecting human health and the environment, is broad relative to many other regulatory agencies, but narrower than that of DHS. But it still encompasses an array of chemicals, microbial pollutants, and even radiation, under a variety of different statutes (each with its own requirements for what guides regulatory decisions). From a risk assessment perspective, its mandate requires EPA to assess risks to human health and to ecosystems and the environment. EPA has divided these into distinct 'human health risk assessments' and 'ecological risk assessments'. These assessments often rely on different expertise and are conducted separately, but they are both guided by a common approach detailed in various guidance and other documents developed by EPA since 1983.

Although EPA's risk assessment methods are well established and have been in use for over 30 years, they are not without criticism. In fact, one of the earliest criticisms was that risk assessments did not fully and clearly communicate the underlying assumptions in various components of the risk assessment process and their policy ramifications.[2] More recently, the NRC undertook an expansive review of the state of risk assessment at the EPA and offered several recommendations for improving how risk assessment is conducted, communicated, and used.

Two NRC recommendations are notable in the context of risk assessment and economic analysis. First, while risk assessments for cancer and non-cancer effects have typically taken very different approaches (something we describe more completely below), the NRC recommended that EPA harmonize these assessments. An important step is for non-cancer risk assessments to estimate probabilities rather than establish safe thresholds. This has major implications for economic analysis.

Another key recommendation was that risk assessment be performed within a framework that seeks to maximize the usefulness and relevance of risk assessment for making decisions.[3] The NRC provided such a framework, with an emphasis on defining clear goals, involving multiple disciplines, and communicating effectively throughout the assessment process. Importantly, the NRC recommendations did not replace EPA's existing paradigm for risk assessment. Instead, they suggested that the essential four-step EPA approach be embedded within a larger framework for decision-making, representing an expansion of EPA's current practice rather than a substitute.

A BRIEF HISTORY OF EPA RISK ASSESSMENT AND ECONOMIC DOCUMENTS

The history of risk assessment at EPA is well documented and summarized elsewhere (NRC, 2010, Appendix B; US EPA, 2012), but an overview is useful for the current discussion. EPA performed quantitative risk assessments in the mid-1970s and early 1980s, and even published interim procedures and guidelines on risk assessments for carcinogens in 1976.

In 1983, in response to concern about the wide variety of approaches to risk assessment taken by federal agencies, the NRC produced *Risk Assessment in the Federal Government: Managing the Process*, a report more widely known as the 'Red Book'. The Red Book defined a structure for risk assessment and risk management that underlies EPA's approach to those tasks. Essentially, risk assessment consists of four distinct steps:

- Hazard identification: what health problems are caused by the pollutant?
- Dose-response assessment: what are the health problems at different exposures?
- Exposure assessment: how much of the pollutant are people exposed to? (Includes frequency, timing, and number of people.)
- Risk characterization: what is the risk of health problems for the exposed population?

The last step integrates information from the first three and conveys the assessor's judgment about the nature and presence of risk, and about how the assessment was conducted. This may, but often may not, include estimated probabilities of adverse health outcomes, or the number of expected illnesses, cancers, or deaths associated with exposure to one or more environmental contaminants.

EPA adopted this structure as a foundation for risk assessment in 1984, and has since produced multiple guidance documents on the conduct of risk assessment for cancer risks, non-cancer risks, and ecological risks.[4] Some of these documents recommend specific practices or methods for risk assessment including guidance on assessing risks from carcinogens, microbials, and evaluating exposures. Others provide agency-wide principles and frameworks for developing risk assessment in a particular context (e.g., US EPA, 2007). These guidance documents were supported and informed by the reports of EPA's Science Advisory Board (SAB), which reviews agency analyses and science products. SAB reports often influence and inform guidance documents and, therefore, the EPA approach to risk assessment.

In the early 1980s, EPA was also beginning to establish its general framework for regulatory economic analysis, including assessment of benefits and costs. The need to establish a benefit–cost framework was driven in part by the new requirements for benefit–cost analysis under Reagan's 1981 executive order on regulatory review (Executive Order 12291). In 1983, EPA published its first economic guidelines for performing benefit–cost analyses. The guidelines contained recommendations for risk assessment of carcinogens and non-carcinogens, and predated any overarching risk assessment guidance for the Agency. EPA substantially revised its *Guidelines for Preparing Economic Analyses* in 2000 and in 2010, but no longer included significant recommendations for risk assessment.

To a large extent, practices in risk analysis and economic analysis at EPA were developed simultaneously. However, there were very few guidance or policy documents that addressed both disciplines and how they relate to one another.[5] The recommendations in *Science and Decisions* (NRC, 2009) on improving the utility of risk assessments by making them more informative for economic analysis may have arisen, in part, from the separation found in EPA documents.

ROLES OF RISK ASSESSMENT

The Red Book made a clear conceptual distinction between risk assessment (analysis) and risk management (decisions), and generally recommended that these be operationally separate. While there are advantages to separation – for example, it helps preserve the integrity of the scientific process – analyses may become insular and not as informative to the decision-maker as they could be. Still, separation does not imply isolation, and a risk assessment should be responsive to the needs of the risk manager.

Risk assessment itself, like any applied analysis, is not free from policy decisions. Judgments must be made about the default assumptions, standard models, and data suitability. But these 'science policy' decisions, which are inherent in the assessment process, are distinct from those that guide the choice of which regulatory option to adopt. Many of EPA's risk assessment guidance documents essentially codify specific risk assessment policy decisions based on scientific data, judgment, consensus, and expert consultation.

Risk assessment practices are also driven by the decision rules enumerated in EPA's enabling statutes. For example, Title I of the Clean Air Act (40 CFR part 50.2) requires primary national ambient air quality standards to be set to protect human health with an adequate margin of safety. A risk assessment designed to respond to such a standard would need to incorporate, to the extent possible, that adequate safety margin. Such an assessment might not need to predict risks in either the baseline or the policy contexts. In fact, it might not need to provide probability estimates at all because it might be sufficient to provide the level of exposure that ensures or predicts an absence of effects, that is, the level that is 'protective'.

But this approach is problematic for benefits analysis, something recognized by economists since at least the mid-1980s (Nichols and Zeckhauser, 1988). Economic analysis requires not only probabilities of outcomes, but also estimates of these probabilities that that are broadly applicable to affected populations. That is, economic analysis requires risk assessment to be predictive rather than protective, or benefits estimates will be biased or infeasible.

Figure 3.1 illustrates this. Many decisions can be directly informed by risk assessment that is protective, and this orientation has been the core consideration for risk assessment practice. Tools and methods have been developed to ensure that risk assessment provides information on exposure levels that are protective of public health, and these are sufficient for many policy decisions. Risk assessment directly informs those decisions.

But risk assessment may also indirectly inform policy or provide information to the public as an input into economic analysis.[6] In that case, the economic analysis uses risk data on changes in the probabilities of adverse health effects, or on the changes in incidence, to calculate net benefits, cost-effectiveness, and other economic impacts. This is often referred to as a 'damage function' approach to benefits analysis, where risk and exposure analyses are performed first and the results are provided to the economist, who will typically value the changes with benefit-transfer methods.

EPA's economic *Guidelines* (US EPA, 2010) describe this as an 'effect-by-effect approach' to estimating benefits consisting of: (1) identifying benefit categories; (2) quantifying significant endpoints; and (3) estimating values of the effects. EPA details considerations for each step, including

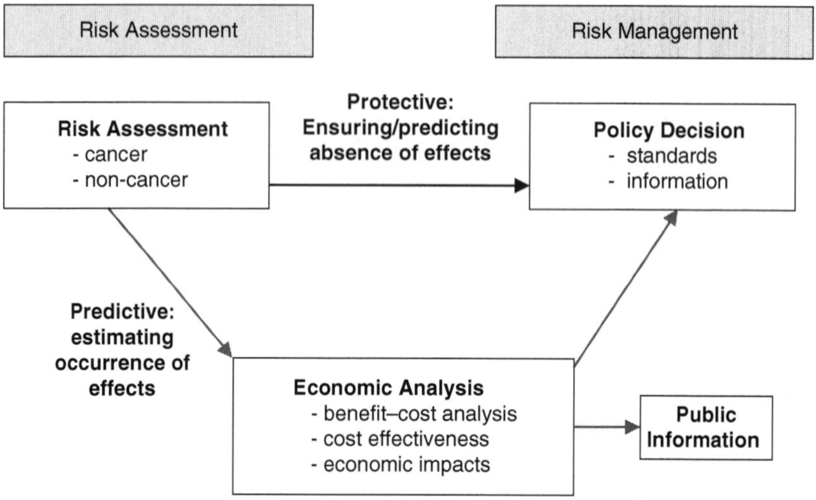

Figure 3.1 Roles of risk assessment

consultation with other disciplines involved in risk assessment, but the process is essentially linear, with a 'handoff' from risk assessment to economics somewhere in the sequence.

The EPA approach can be generally mapped into the vertical framework described in Chapter 2, where the steps can be roughly divided into two sets of typical tasks (see Figure 3.2). After the actions in a proposed rule are specified, the next six tasks generally fall under the purview of risk assessment (including exposure assessment). The final two tasks, evaluating trade-offs and measuring net benefits, are typically done by economists, often well after the first stages are completed. While there is generally some consultation among the health scientists and statisticians working on the risk assessment and the economists responsible for benefits analysis, the consultation procedures are often informal.

Choices made in the risk assessment portion of the analysis will constrain and define the boundaries of the economic analysis. This limits the information that can be provided to the decision-maker and to the public about the economic consequences of the rule. Three aspects of the risk assessment deserve particular attention because the risk approaches chosen have significant implications for the economic analysis.

Objects of choice are the health or ecological endpoints that will be modeled in the risk assessment. There are at least three key considerations when deciding on endpoints for use in economic analysis. Firstly, some endpoints may be useful for a 'protective' risk management decision but

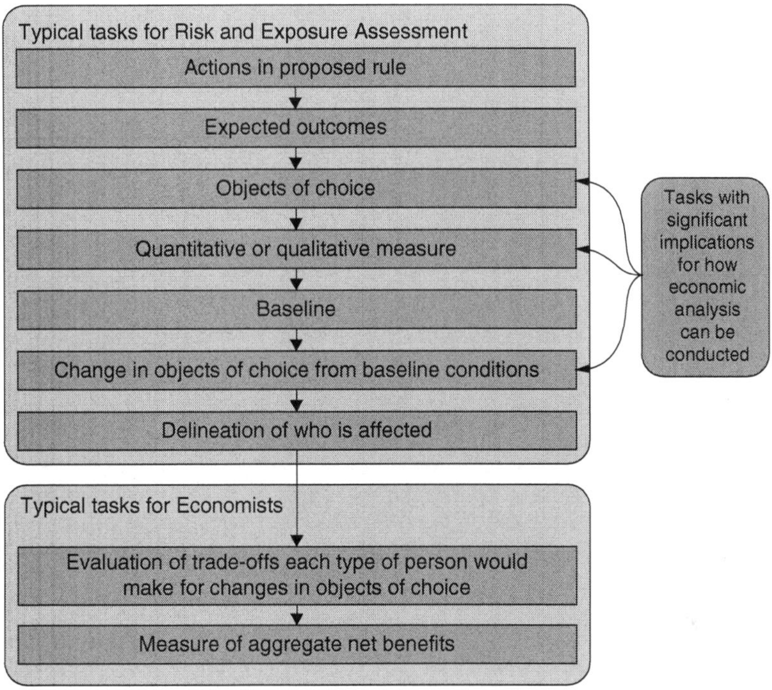

Figure 3.2 EPA approach mapped onto vertical process

cannot be linked to economic welfare. For example, the health outcome observable in human health studies may be only a precursor or an indicator of a welfare effect.[7] Secondly, economic analyses need an assessment of all meaningful effects, not just the most sensitive. The latter might be sufficient for making a risk management decision because it ensures that other effects do not occur. But the benefits analysis will be incomplete and biased downward unless all effects are included, because the most sensitive effects might not be the most valuable. Finally, economic valuation depends on dimensions such as severity, frequency, duration, and timing that may not be described in the risk assessment.

The quantitative or qualitative measure to be used includes whether to focus on probabilities of given health outcomes and whether those probabilities will be for specific individuals or for the population as a whole. In the case of individuals, the estimate may be for a 'reasonable maximum exposure', or 'most exposed individual', measures that are useful for characterizing the upper tail of the risk distribution and for evaluating whether policies protect the most vulnerable. However, these risk measures cannot be applied to the population and are not useful for the economist tasked (later) with producing aggregate benefits measures. In fact, this problem has been an obstacle for estimating the benefits from the Superfund program. The only risk assessments were considered too conservative to use (US EPA, 2006), although some attempted to partially adjust the risk assessments for use in benefit–cost analysis (Hamilton and Viscusi, 1999).

For many non-cancer health effects, the measure will not be risk at all, but will instead be defined relative to a reference dose (RfD), which is a level of exposure that is 'likely to be without appreciable risk' over a lifetime.[8] The ratio of potential exposures to the RfD is defined as a hazard quotient. A hazard quotient greater than one indicates that adverse health effects are possible, but the probability of adverse health effects is not necessarily proportional to the hazard quotient. This threshold-based approach might be sufficient for a management decision – exposures are below the 'safe' level – but economics has no general method for estimating benefits of risk described this way. Instead, the economic analysis requires probabilities of health outcomes or predicted changes in continuous measures of health or functioning (for example, intelligence quotient, IQ, changes from lead exposure).

Changes in objects of choice from baseline conditions must be characterized in terms of changes in absolute probabilities. Changes in a hazard quotient indicate some change in the objects of choice – the health outcomes – but without a specific change in probabilities they cannot be fully included in the economic analysis. Even an assumption that the reference dose is a safe level allows only for a step-function approach to benefits analysis, where all benefits are received upon exposures being reduced to the RfD. The marginal benefits of reductions prior to the RfD level are zero, as are those after the RfD level is attained. Unless there are other benefits from the action, there is no justification for regulating below the RfD level (and no way to determine whether there is an optimal level above this level).

Changes in other dimensions of our objects of choice factor into the economic analysis, as well. For example, changes related to asthma may not be in incidence but in frequency, severity, or duration of asthma attacks. These changes each have economic value, and the ability of an economic analysis to capture this value depends upon the risk assessment's ability to characterize the changes. The timing of health effects is another factor that requires attention, because reductions realized sooner will be more valuable than those realized later. In principle, even if a regulation only delays an outcome instead of reducing the probability that it will occur, there are economic benefits: the change in the object of choice in this case is a change in the timing of the risk and not a reduction in the risk.

INTEGRATING ECONOMIC CAPABILITY INTO RISK ANALYSIS AND RISK MANAGEMENT PRACTICES

The role of economic analysis at EPA has grown over time, as evidenced by the founding and growth of the National Center for Environmental Economics, and the expanding role of executive orders for economic analysis.[9] The demands on risk assessment from economists have grown commensurately. Our experience is that the best results are achieved in an integrated process involving economists, risk assessors, and other scientists and analysts.

Better integration of economics and risk analysis with risk management has been an EPA priority for the last several years, and the agency has just released its own description of a human health framework for decision-making. If economists and risk assessors collaborate early in the process, it is often possible to produce risk analyses that support economic analysis. In some cases, of course, the data may not be available to fully characterize risks, but economists can provide other assessment tools to help inform policy. Two examples below illustrate such cases.

Example: Risk Assessment for Benefits Analysis

To address some of the challenges of integrating risk assessment and economic analysis, EPA undertook a cross-office case study to explore how benefits could be quantified for the case of a toxic chemical. The case study was designed to integrate animal toxicology data, dose-response modeling, data on human disease incidence and medical treatment, and economic analysis, to develop illustrative benefits analysis for both cancer and non-cancer endpoints. Axelrad et al. (2005) provided the framework for the analysis.

The first essential step of the project, known as Risk Assessment for Benefits Analysis (RABA), was to establish a cross-disciplinary team. Importantly, this team included not only toxicologists, epidemiologists, and statisticians, but also economists who could be involved from the beginning to help define health endpoints and risk measures that were economically meaningful and could be valued using known techniques.

The interdisciplinary nature of the exercise was fundamental to its success, and many critical early decisions were made only after considering perspectives from multiple disciplines.[10] Key among these was the decision of how health endpoints, all thyroid-related, were to be defined. The original targets for risk modeling were health effects found in the animal data, such as increased liver weight and then increased thyroid hormone levels. These endpoints might have been sufficient for setting a protective standard based on the premise that preventing the upstream effect also prevents the health effects that occur as their result. However, the endpoints could not be meaningfully included in an economic analysis, and they had to be transformed into the probability of developing hypothyroidism. This case contrasts with the more typical kind of case, where a risk assessment is provided to economists who must then attempt to find endpoints that can be valued.

A benefit of the process used in RABA is that available valuation data can be factored into the decision about which health endpoints to spend time and resources modeling. If an analysis must be produced before original valuation work can be done, and resources require that we not pursue all possible risk assessment endpoints, then there is utility in knowing which endpoints can be carried through to the final quantitative benefits analysis. Additionally, economic value can be used to prioritize potential endpoints for modeling where highly valued risk reductions would be more important to include in the benefits analysis, all else being equal.

The risk estimates from the RABA case study consisted of probabilities for hypothyroidism and thyroid cancer, using a non-linear dose-response function. Because the team was integrated, the final probabilities also accounted for the likelihood of seeking treatment for a thyroid condition and thereby mitigating the risk of progression to thyroid cancer. There were other health endpoints that the analysis could not address in either the risk assessment or the economic analysis, but the case study laid the groundwork for performing a robust analysis when data are available.

Alternatives to Cost–Benefit Analysis

In cases where a risk assessment does not lend itself to economic analysis, there are still tools that can be used to get a sense of the likely cost–benefit ratio. These tools have been applied in the drinking water program. Several drinking water regulations protect the public from harmful organisms such as fecal coliform, *E. coli*, and other pathogens. These are typically controlled using disinfectants such as chlorine or chlorine dioxide, although residual amounts of disinfectants can remain in drinking water. These residuals can interact with other substances in the water to produce disinfection byproducts. Disinfection byproducts were first identified in 1974; since then, toxicological studies have found them to be carcinogenic and to cause adverse reproductive and developmental effects in laboratory animals. Epidemiological studies have suggested a small association among bladder, rectal, and colon cancer and exposure to chlorinated surface water; some epidemiological studies have also suggested adverse reproductive or developmental effects in laboratory animals. In 1998, based on mounting health evidence and because an estimated over

200 million people in the United States were thought to be exposed to disinfectants and disinfection byproducts in drinking water, EPA regulated these substances in the Stage 1 Disinfectants and Disinfection Byproducts Rule (DBPR; US EPA, 1998).

The risk assessment for the Stage 1 rule was hampered by a lack of occurrence data on disinfectants and disinfection byproducts in drinking water. EPA estimated that the annual number of cancer cases caused by disinfectants and disinfection byproducts in drinking water was 0–100 cases based on toxicological data, and 0–10 000 cases based on epidemiological data, and that the rule would reduce the number of cases by 24 percent. With such a range of uncertainty, EPA did not present a calculation of net benefits with point estimates, but only compared ranges of estimates of costs and benefits. EPA also presented the results from two techniques meant to clarify decisions when uncertainty is present: a breakeven analysis and a minimizing regrets analysis.

Breakeven analysis is a technique that works backward by taking what is most accurately known, and then determining what the levels of what is unknown have to be to break even. In the case of the Stage 1 DBPR rule, EPA knew the costs and value of risk reduction fairly certainly, but the actual risk levels were highly uncertain, so the breakeven analysis first calculated the cost and value of risk reductions, and then identified the risk reduction necessary to break even. EPA included several competing assumptions to test the sensitivity of its results.

In the breakeven analysis, EPA used the estimated costs of the regulatory option at both 3 percent and 7 percent discount rates. EPA then assumed that 23 percent of all bladder cancer cases would be fatal and valued those using the value of a statistical life (VSL) ($5.6 million per life), while the remaining non-fatal cases were valued at $587 500 per case (using a willingness-to-pay estimate) and $121 000 (using a cost-of-illness estimate). Across all of these assumptions, the breakeven analysis estimated that the number of bladder cancer cases attributable to DBPs in drinking water would need to range from 1630 to 2390 annual cases in order to break even. This range is well within the estimated range of 0–10 000 cases of cancer caused each year by disinfectants and disinfection byproducts.

A minimizing regrets (also known as minimizing social losses) analysis is used in situations where there is a lot of uncertainty about the level of risk. The analysis compares regulatory options across a variety of risk levels and identifies the option that minimizes losses at each risk level. Losses are calculated as the costs of the option plus the cost of the cancer cases not prevented by the regulatory option; these cases are valued using the VSL. The option that minimizes regrets is the one that has the lowest social losses.

Table 3.1 Social losses for Stage 1 DBPR minimizing regrets analysis (billion $, 1998)

	Number of cancer cases avoided						
	<1	100	1000	2500	5000	7500	10 000
Alternative							
No action							
Social costs	$0	$0.176	$1.755	$4.388	$8.776	$13.164	$17.552
Social losses	**$0**	**$0**	**$0**	$0.352	$1.405	$2.458	$4.129
Final rule							
Social costs	$0.701	$0.832	$2.036	$4.036	$7.371	$10.706	$14.041
Social losses	$0.701	$0.656	$0.281	**$0**	**$0**	**$0**	$0.617
Strong option							
Social costs	$2.892	$2.998	$3.945	$5.525	$8.158	$10.791	$13.423
Social losses	$2.892	$2.823	$2.190	$1.489	$0.787	$0.085	**$0**

Note: The option that minimizes social losses is indicated in **bold**.

Social losses are calculated as the social costs of an option minus the social costs of the option that has the lowest social costs at a given risk level. For the Stage 1 DPBR rule, EPA compared a no-action alternative, the regulatory option, and a strong option from the proposed rule[11] over risk levels of <1, 100, 1000, 2500, 5000, 7500, and 10 000 cancer cases. The results are shown in Table 3.1. From <1 to 1000 cancer cases, the social losses are lower for the no-action alternative than the other options; from 2500 cases to 7500 cases, social losses are lower for the regulatory option; and at 10 000 cancer cases, social losses are lower for the strong option. Regrets are minimized by identifying the greatest social loss for each option and picking the option with the lowest such loss. The greatest social loss for the no-action alternative is $4.129 billion, the greatest social loss for the regulatory option is $701 million, and the greatest social loss for the strong option is $2.892 billion, so regrets are minimized with the regulatory option, which has the least-bad option for any risk level. Although not dispositive, both the breakeven and regrets analysis supported the regulation.

CONCLUSIONS

What should one conclude from the EPA risk assessment and economic analysis paradigm? We believe there are four key points relevant for development of risk analysis and economics at DHS.

Economic analysis is valuable for informing decision-makers and the public of the relative merits of alternative policy choices. Rigorous and clear benefit–cost analysis can demonstrate which regulations are efficient and cost-effective, something that depends crucially on risk assessment inputs to the benefits analysis process. Programs that lack the capacity for robust economic analysis will struggle to justify specific decisions, even if those decisions are likely to be welfare-enhancing.

It is important to establish a clear framework for analysis, and robust guidelines to implement that framework, as well as to have ongoing consultation with external experts. Guidelines, even if they are limited, improve transparency and facilitate peer review and formal peer input into the best available analytic practices. Regular and frequent public consultation with EPA's SAB, as well as with the National Academies, has proven to be extremely valuable for the rigor and credibility of EPA's economic and science products. Taken together, transparency and scientific review will lead to improvements over time.

One problem, and one that EPA has experienced, is that established guidelines have momentum, particularly if they are specific to some disciplines and exclude others. Heavy reliance on risk paradigms developed for narrow purposes may squeeze out other approaches, including economic analysis. Inertia, ingrained culture, and incremental budgeting can also be problematic. For example, the Office of Research and Development at EPA organized itself – and made budgetary decisions – around the risk assessment framework in its 1996 Strategic Plan (US EPA, 1996). The office now has no economic research or other social science component, although the SAB has repeatedly encouraged it to build one.

To the extent that guidance can be integrated across disciplines or operate under a unifying framework, these problems can be reduced. EPA continues to work toward integrating economic analysis and risk assessment; it released a draft framework for human health risk assessment for external peer review in July 2012 and finalized the framework in 2014. The framework, which builds on the model provided by the NRC, emphasizes the importance of economics and the role of risk assessment as an input into other analyses. Ideally, such a framework would be established prior to development of specific guidance and general practice; DHS now has a valuable opportunity to do just that.

NOTES

1. The views expressed in this chapter are those of the authors and do not necessarily represent those of the US Environmental Protection Agency. No official agency endorsement should be inferred.
2. The 1983 'Red Book' (NRC, 1983) recommended a Board on Risk Assessment Methods to address this and other issues.
3. NRC (2008) devotes a full chapter to improving the utility of risk assessment.
4. These documents and many related references are available at EPA's Risk Assessment Portal (www.epa.gov/riskassessment).
5. One notable exception is the *Framework for the Economic Assessment of Ecological Benefits* (US EPA, 2002).
6. Risk assessment here can be thought of as both an intermediate and final good in the regulatory production process, in the same sense that an ecosystem service can be both an intermediate and final good in an ecological production process (Boyd and Banzhaf, 2007; Boyd and Krupnick, 2013).
7. Consider the case of forced expiratory volume (FEV) that relates ground-level ozone to maximum amount of air capacity in lungs. While this is a useful measure of lung functioning, its relation to something that can be valued in an economic analysis is not clear.
8. Strictly speaking, the RfD is for ingestion or dermal exposure to contaminants. For inhalation risks, the analogous measure is a reference concentration (RfC).
9. Even Executive Order 12866 and its successors will require more analyses over time to be subjected to benefit–cost analysis because the $100 million threshold for 'economically significant' rules remains unadjusted for inflation since 1981.
10. The approach taken in RABA is similar to recommendations received by EPA to 'develop a strong social science capability and incorporate it fully in risk analyses and risk management practices' (NRC, 2010, p. 100).
11. This strong option was presented for comparison purposes only.

REFERENCES

Axelrad, D.A., K. Baetcke, C. Dockins, C.W. Griffiths, R.N. Hill, P.A. Murphy, and L.K. Teuschler (2005). 'Risk assessment for benefits analysis: framework for analysis of a thyroid-disrupting chemical', *Journal of Toxicology and Environmental Health*, **68**, 837–855.

Boyd, J. and S. Banzhaf (2007). 'What are ecosystem services? The need for standardized environmental accounting units', *Ecological Economics*, **63** (2–3), 616–626.

Boyd, J. and A. Krupnick (2013). 'Using ecological production function theory to define and select environmental commodities for nonmarket valuation', *Agricultural and Resource Economics Review*, **42** (1), 1–32.

Hamilton, J.T. and W.K. Viscusi (1999). *Calculating Risks: The Spatial and Political Dimensions of Hazardous Waste Policy*, Cambridge, MA: MIT Press.

National Research Council (NRC) (1983). *Risk Assessment in the Federal Government: Managing the Process*, Washington, DC: National Academies Press.

National Research Council (NRC) (2009). *Science and Decisions: Advancing Risk Assessment*, Washington, DC: National Academies Press.

National Research Council (NRC) (2010). *Review of Department of Homeland*

Security's Approach to Risk Analysis, Washington, DC: National Academies Press.
Nichols, A.L. and R.J. Zeckhauser (1988). 'The perils of prudence: how conservative risk assessments distort regulation', *Regulatory Toxicology and Pharmacology*, **8** (1), 61–75.
United States Environmental Protection Agency (EPA) (1983). *Guidelines for Performing Regulatory Impact Analysis*, EPA-230–01–84–003.
United States Environmental Protection Agency (EPA) (1996). *Strategic Plan for the Office of Research and Development*, EPA/600/R-96/059.
United States Environmental Protection Agency (EPA) (1998). *Regulatory Impact Analysis for the Stage 1 Disinfectants/Disinfection Byproducts Rule*, EPA 815-B-98–002.
United States Environmental Protection Agency (EPA) (2000). *Guidelines for Preparing Economic Analyses*, EPA 240-R-00–003, http://yosemite.epa.gov/ee/epa/eed.nsf/pages/guidelines.
United States Environmental Protection Agency (EPA) (2002). *A Framework for the Economic Assessment of Ecological Benefits*, http://www.epa.gov/spc/pdfs/feaeb3.pdf.
United States Environmental Protection Agency (EPA) (2006). *Advisory on EPA's Superfund Benefits Analysis*, EPA-SAB-ADV-006–002.
United States Environmental Protection Agency (EPA) (2007). *Framework for Metals Risk Assessment*, EPA 120/R-07/001, http://www.epa.gov/raf/metals-framework/pdfs/metals-risk-assessment-final.pdf.
United States Environmental Protection Agency (EPA) (2010). *Guidelines for Preparing Economic Analyses.*
United States Environmental Protection Agency (EPA) (2012). *Framework for Human Health Risk Assessment to Inform Decision Making* (External Review Draft). 601-D12–001, http://epa.gov/raf/frameworkhhra.htm.

4. The heterogeneity of the value of statistical life: evidence and policy implications[1,2]

W. Kip Viscusi

INTRODUCTION

The value of a statistical life (VSL) is a measure of individuals' money–risk trade-off and is the most widely used economic measure for valuing changes in risk. The academic literature includes dozens of labor market studies of VSL. There have also been studies of VSL based on price–risk trade-off for the product market as well as risk-taking decisions ranging from choice of highway speed to use of seat belts.

This chapter focuses on the variation in the VSL both across different studies in the academic literature and in different policy contexts. There are important differences in the VSL with respect to individual risk-taking behaviors as well as personal characteristics, including age, income, race, gender and immigrant status. What are these differences and what are the policy implications for benefit assessment? To assess such issues, I explore both the VSL estimates themselves and their implications for the structure of labor markets. In particular, I examine the role of segmented labor markets in which people face different labor market opportunities, giving rise to differences across the population in their estimated VSL.

This review of VSL findings is not intended to provide a detailed survey of the literature, as in Viscusi and Aldy (2003). Rather, after briefly summarizing the VSL concept and reviewing the thrust of the empirical evidence, I address different aspects of the heterogeneity of VSL. The examples that are selected address some of the most important determinants of the level of VSL. These examples also provide illustrations of the ways in which heterogeneity might enter. For the most part, this discussion concentrates on the implications of labor market studies. The particular aspects of heterogeneity considered are those for which we have the most knowledge based on current research. As a result, there is substantial evidence of differences based on age, income, race, and immigrant status. These differences pertain to different population groups, but there is also heterogeneity in the valuations based on the nature of the mortality risk and the associated morbidity effects. Because this volume is intended to inform decision-making on US homeland security policies, considerable attention is devoted to valuing terrorism risks, which often involve concerns pertaining to national security as well as risk of death.

It should be emphasized that inclusion of discussion of sources of heterogeneity does not imply that policy makers should incorporate these differences in their analyses. Policies that affect the population broadly and do not have targeted effects might well rely on overall VSL estimates without recognizing the potential variation in these values across the population. I also show that in some instances, such as when the VSL estimates are derived from segmented labor markets in which different labor market groups face quite different opportunities, it may be quite inappropriate to incorporate such differences in the analysis. Recognition of other sources of heterogeneity also may not be feasible due to political sensitivities. However, these controversies may become more muted over time as the estimates of VSL across the population become more refined and as more agencies recognize the heterogeneity of VSL.

The use of VSL for benefit assessment of government regulations has continued for almost three decades. After reviewing the academic literature, I then examine the policy arena's use of the VSL methodology beginning with the discussion of the adoption of the VSL methodology almost three decades ago and continuing through the recent controversies involving variations in VSL levels with age and income. Other aspects of risk heterogeneity that also are potentially prominent policy concerns include the size of the risk being reduced and the context in which the risk arises. For example, is the risk a voluntary risk and is it being incurred in a market context in which those subject to the risk receive monetary compensation for bearing the risk?

The main practical alternative to using the VSL approach is the use of economic loss measures in a tort damages context. Tort damages alone will undervalue life compared with VSL estimates. There have been recent suggestions that court-awarded compensation for wrongful death include both the VSL and the value of economic loss. Such a measure, if appropriate for compensatory damages purposes, surely would also be appropriate for regulatory analyses. Whether this expansion of the use of the VSL concept in conjunction with economic loss amounts is appropriate is explored later in this chapter.

VSL AND THE POLICY EVALUATION ARCHITECTURE

A useful starting point for addressing the potential role of VSL is to consider the policy analysis architecture. As Chapter 2 in this volume by Smith and Mansfield demonstrates, the policy decisions ultimately must be linked to outcomes of interest. The most prominent outcome for the activities of most agencies that reduce various kinds of mortality risks is the expected number of lives that are saved by the regulation. From the standpoint of benefit assessment purposes, it is essential to have some mechanism for monetizing these effects so as to put them on comparable terms with other policy effects, such as the policy's costs. Estimates of VSL serve this function.

Interestingly, there has been an interdependent relationship between VSL and economic analysis of risk policies. The use of benefit–cost analysis as a routine policy evaluation tool has boosted the policy prominence of VSL. The causality has been in the other direction as well in that the availability of economic estimates of VSL has stimulated agencies to develop more rigorous frameworks that incorporate the kind of systematic policy analysis architecture discussed by Smith and Mansfield.

The US executive branch's utilization of benefit–cost tests for regulations, as exemplified by Executive Order (EO) 12291, has made comparisons of estimated benefits and costs a routine part of policy assessments. The widespread use of these evaluation techniques in turn has pushed VSL estimates to the forefront, as these values provide the basis for monetizing the risk reduction effects. To the extent that policies cannot be approved unless the benefits can be shown to exceed the costs, it is essential to have some mechanism for monetizing these policy outcomes. Because a chief component of policy benefits is often the reduced risk of mortality, the VSL estimates have assumed a pivotal role.

The role of VSL in stimulating a systematic policy analysis architecture is less well understood but is also important. Consider the experience at the US Environmental Protection Agency (EPA) in the 1980s. EPA officials, with advice from economists such as V. Kerry Smith and A. Myrick Freeman, III, had identified key concepts pertinent to EPA policy valuation, including VSL. But what EPA had not yet accomplished at that time was the development of the full risk assessment logic in which the agency must first determine the health effects of the policy, after which it would then be possible to apply the VSL estimates. This understanding of the components needed for a meaningful policy assessment led to the development of the risk analysis sequence for air pollution policies of identifying sensitive population groups, measuring the risk from a criteria pollutant to an average member of that group, determining the benefits of reducing the risk, and setting a standard to protect the exposed population. Without the impetus provided by VSL and the benefit–cost test requirements, EPA would not have developed its current risk analysis architecture.

Conceivably the development of estimates of the heterogeneity of VSL will likewise stimulate more refined policy assessments. To what extent does it matter that particular population subgroups benefit disproportionately from a policy? For example, government policies often have very targeted effects on particular population groups that are exposed to risks disproportionately. Passengers on airplanes will benefit most from improved air safety. If airline passengers' VSL levels are greater than for the average worker, should that source of heterogeneity be taken into account? Does it matter who pays for the safety improvement? If the safety regulation will, in effect, be borne by the passenger through higher ticket prices, should that affect the acceptability of recognizing the heterogeneity of VSL? These and other concerns are likely to be stimulated by the ongoing advances in refining VSL estimates for different population groups and for different kinds of risk.

CALCULATING THE VALUE OF A STATISTICAL LIFE

Because the VSL concept is so widely misunderstood, particularly by critics of the approach, it is worthwhile to begin with the definition of the concept. The VSL pertains to the trade-off between money and very small risks of death. Suppose that there is a risk of one chance in 10000 to 10000 people, so that this group will experience one expected death. If each person would be willing to pay \$800 to eliminate the risk, the VSL in this instance would be \$8 million, or 10000 people × \$800 per person. The VSL figure is not an accounting measure of the present value of one's lost earnings. It does not reflect the amount the person would be willing to pay to avoid certain death or the amount that the person would need to be compensated to accept certain death.

Although many studies have used survey methods to try to elicit peoples' risk–money trade-off, the dominant approach in the economics literature has been to analyze wage–risk trade-offs. Properly designed stated preference studies are a useful technique for valuing many health risks, such as those for which there is no market evidence. But examining how workers in the labor market value risks offers the advantage of imputing values from actual risk-taking decisions.

The underlying theory of compensating wage differentials can be traced

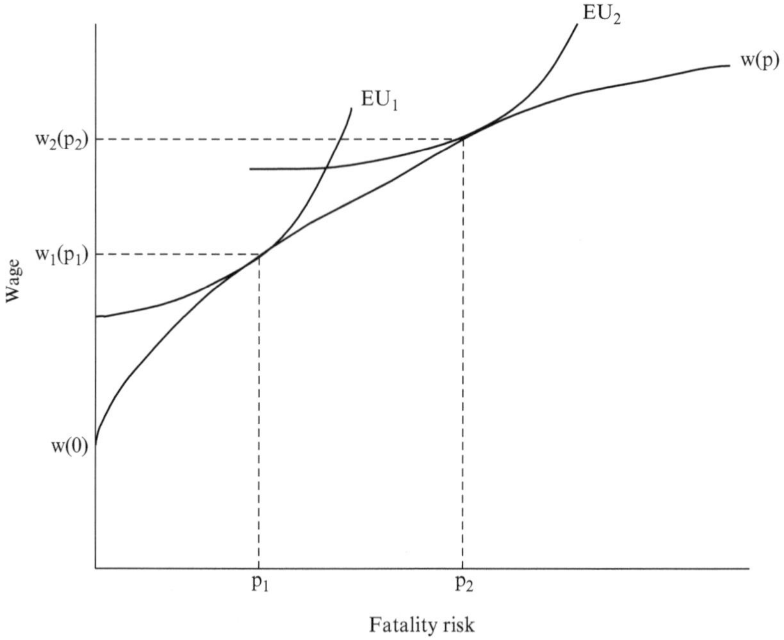

Figure 4.1 The standard hedonic labor market model

back to Adam Smith, who theorized that workers would need to be paid more for jobs that are risky or otherwise unpleasant. Thus, the empirical task is to control for the various aspects of the worker and the job and to determine how much pay workers receive for extra risk. This approach, which is known as hedonic wage models, involves workers picking an optimal risk–wage combination from the available set of opportunities in the labor market.

Figure 4.1 sketches the identical set of choices facing two different workers. The curve w(p) is the market opportunities locus. It is the outer envelope of all the individual firms' offer curves, which indicate the highest wage the firm will offer for any given risk. The envelope of such offer curves consequently represents the highest wage that is offered in the market for any given fatality risk. Workers consequently can choose any wage–risk combination that they would like from this offer curve based on their own preferences.

The figure shows two workers. Each worker will choose the wage–risk combination that offers the highest expected utility level given their own preferences. Worker 1 chooses fatality risk p_1 that offers a wage rate of

$w_1(p_1)$. Worker 2 is willing to face a higher risk of p_2 for a wage $w_2(p_2)$; in each instance the compensating differential the worker receives for risk is the difference between the wage they receive and the value w(0).

Conventional hedonic wage models fit a curve that passes through these various points of tangency, thus simultaneously reflecting both the wage–risk trade-off for workers and firms. The median estimate of the US VSL is $7 million ($2000) or $8.7 million ($2009) based on the meta-analysis in Viscusi and Aldy (2003). Thus, the worker receives an additional $870 to face an annual job fatality risk of 1/10 000.

Estimates from labor markets in countries other than the US have produced VSL levels in the expected range. For example, as one would expect, the labor market studies in countries such as India have found a lower VSL than in the United States where the income levels are much higher.

HETEROGENEITY OF VSL BASED ON THE RISK LEVEL

As indicated by Figure 4.1, the wage–risk trade-off for different workers depends on where they are settled along the market offer curve. Worker 1 is on a steeper part of the curve than Worker 2 and consequently will have a higher VSL. Workers who gravitate toward the higher risk jobs such as those with the fatality risk p_2 have a lower VSL reflected in their choices.

This heterogeneity in the level of VSL based on the risk level makes it possible to reconcile some of the early differences found in estimates in the literature. For the estimates of the VSL by Thaler and Rosen (1975), the average worker in the sample faced an annual job-related fatality risk of 1/1000. In contrast, the study by Viscusi (1978, 1979) analyzed a more representative group of workers who had fatality risks more in line with the national average at that time, which was 1/10 000. Thus, the Thaler–Rosen study focused on workers whose risk levels were about an order of magnitude greater than the US average. Thus, their sample of workers was concentrated on the right side of Figure 4.1. Not surprisingly, this focus on workers in very high-risk jobs led to a comparatively low value for VSL. The estimates in Viscusi (1978, 1979) were five times greater than those in the Thaler-Rosen analysis.[3]

What is interesting about these differences is that the disparate VSL estimates do not arise because of a failure by economists to find 'the value of life number'. Rather, there is substantial heterogeneity in VSL trade-offs throughout the labor market, and this heterogeneity is reflected in the different studies. What particular VSL number emerges from the analysis will depend in large part on the composition of the sample and their concentration along the w(p) curve in Figure 4.1.

These results have more general implications for what one would expect in terms of differences across the population. People who choose very high-risk jobs or very risky products or who live in very dangerous neighborhoods have revealed themselves to have lower VSL levels than the average person in society. They have money–risk trade-off rates such as those for workers located along the right side of the opportunities locus in Figure 4.1. Thus, an important role of selection occurs, and based on this selection one can often infer that fundamental differences exist in the risk–money trade-offs people are willing to make.

SEGMENTED LABOR MARKETS

The canonical hedonic labor market model assumes that workers face identical labor market offer curves such as w(p) shown in Figure 4.1. However, Viscusi and Hersch (2001) hypothesize that workers may in fact face different labor market offer curves and, as a result, settle into separate labor market equilibria. A definitive test that they propose for showing that labor market offer curves are different is that if workers who face greater risk levels receive less total wage compensation for risk than workers who face a smaller risk level, then they cannot be on the same market offer curve.

Figure 4.2 provides an illustration of the Viscusi–Hersch labor market model. The other labor market offer curve is indicated in the figure by v(p). As in Figure 4.1, Workers 1 and 2 settle into positions along w(p). Worker 3 does not have available the option of choosing off this higher labor market offer curve and consequently must pick the best of available choices from v(p). As indicated in the diagram, Worker 3 chooses a job risk p_2. However, that worker receives a lower total wage compensation for that risk than Worker 2 who chooses the same risk but from a more favorable labor market offer curve since w(p) is steeper at p_2 than v(p).

Labor market offer curves could, of course, shift upward or downward for a variety of reasons, such as differences in worker education level. What matters from the standpoint of VSL differences is not the vertical intercept but whether the rate of trade-off between money and risk also differs. Thus, is the slope of v(p) flatter than that of w(p), as indicated in the diagram?

In general we do not estimate all the different points along the curve and compare them; rather we obtain an average VSL number for a particular sample. Suppose that one group of workers facing an average risk

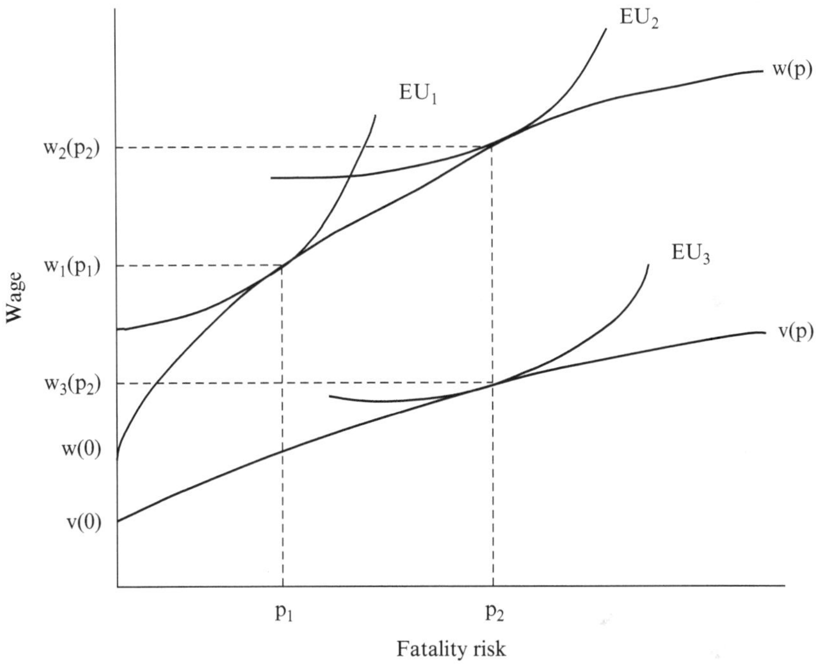

Figure 4.2 *The Viscusi–Hersch hedonic labor market model*

p_2 receives a wage rate of $w_2(p_2)$. Then that worker's compensating wage differential for risk p_2 is given by $w_2(p_2) - w(0)$ and is shown in Figure 4.2. In contrast, the workers who pick off the lower offer curve, on average, receive a wage $w_3(p_2)$ for risk p_2 and consequently earn an average compensating wage differential $w_3(p_2) - v(0)$. If workers face identical average risks but receive higher total compensating wage differentials for risk than another worker group, then we can conclude that they are on a different wage offer curve. A stronger version of this test is to compare workers at different risk levels. In particular, if one worker group faces a lower risk p_1, then their total compensating differential for risk should be lower than that for a worker group that faces a higher risk p_2. If this does not hold, then it clearly contradicts the assumption that the workers are on the same labor market offer curve.

To date three studies have analyzed whether labor markets are segmented from the standpoint of compensating wage differentials for risk. The first of these studies was Viscusi and Hersch (2001), which focused on the difference between smokers and non-smokers. Because smokers incur substantial personal risks as a consequence of their smoking behavior, one would expect them to be willing to accept job risk for a lower wage premium than non-smokers and to gravitate to the higher risk, low wage–risk trade-off jobs. Whether smokers will simply be located further to the right on the flatter portion of the market offer curve than non-smokers or whether they will be on different labor market offer curves is an empirical issue. What they found in their analysis of non-fatal injury risks is that smokers faced higher risks on the job than non-smokers, but they received a lower wage premium for risk, providing evidence of different labor market offer curves facing smokers and non-smokers.

This issue of labor market segmentation was also examined with respect to racial difference in compensation for risk. Viscusi (2003) analyzed the compensating differentials faced by black and white workers in the US economy. Although black workers faced greater risk than white workers, they received lower wage premiums for risk. Thus, the heterogeneity in the VSL levels observed across racial groups could be traced to different labor market opportunities that these groups faced.

An interesting policy-related example of this phenomenon is with respect to immigration. In particular, it is often suggested that recent immigrants perform the least attractive jobs in the economy that non-immigrant American workers are unwilling to do. Translated into economic terms, such statements imply that these immigrants have different rates of trade-off between risk and wages than native US workers. However, the welfare implications of these differences are quite varied if immigrant workers face different and less attractive wage offer curves than native US workers.

The potential importance of such heterogeneity is the focus of a recent article by Hersch and Viscusi (2010). Their analysis considered a wide variety of immigrant groups. Notably, immigrants in general often did not differ from native US workers in terms of the risk premiums they received. However, Mexican immigrants, particularly those who lacked English language skills, fared particularly poorly in the labor market.

Table 4.1 summarizes some of their results with respect to native US workers as compared with Mexican immigrants. The first set of results in Table 4.1 consists of estimates derived from the Current Population Survey (CPS). As indicated, Mexican immigrants face an average fatality risk on the job that is almost one and a half times that of native US workers, where these fatality rate estimates are conditional on the worker's industry, immigrant status and age. Native US workers receive wage compensation for risk that implies a VSL of $7.95 million. However, the fatality risk variable is not statistically significant in the log wage equation for Mexican immigrants, indicating that they do not receive statistically significant compensation for risk. Taken together, these results provide evidence of labor market segmentation as hypothesized in Figure 4.2.

Table 4.1 Value of statistical life and immigrant status

	Fatality risk*	VSL ($millions)
		Estimates based on the CPS
Native US	4.35	7.95
Mexican immigrants	5.97	Not statistically significant
		Estimates Based on the NIS
All immigrants	4.50	9.35
Mexican immigrants	5.70	Not statistically significant
Mexican immigrants who speak English	5.70	3.44

Note: * Fatality rate by industry–immigrant status–age. Risk is annual fatality rate per 100 000 workers.

Source: Figures are from Hersch and Viscusi (2010).

A somewhat different comparison is provided in the lower panel in Table 4.1 in which all immigrants are compared with Mexican immigrants using data from the New Immigrant Survey (NIS). Immigrants generally face a risk level similar to that of native US workers and, based on the results from this study, have an average VSL of $9.35 million. However, Mexican immigrants once again face a much higher risk level and do not receive statistically significant compensation for the risk.

What these results indicate is that in analyses that seek to identify different types of heterogeneity in the VSL trade-offs in the labor market it is essential to ascertain whether the groups do in fact face similar labor market offer curves. How one interprets the observed heterogeneity in estimated VSL levels is quite different if the estimated VSL is derived from selecting a different point on a particular wage offer curve, as opposed to the worker being relegated to a less attractive set of labor market opportunities with different available wage–risk trade-offs. If the differences in labor market opportunities arise from influences such as discrimination, then whether and how one would choose to use the estimated labor market estimates of VSL based on the estimates across different groups will be affected as well.

HETEROGENEITY BASED ON AGE

The VSL varies with individual age because the length of the remaining life varies, so the amount of life at risk varies with age. Expenditures to reduce the risk of death will extend life expectancy but will not lead to immortality. How the role of age influences the VSL depends on various life-cycle effects, as individual wealth over the life cycle affects one's willingness to pay (WTP) for risk reductions. In part, this difficulty arises from imperfect capital markets that prevent people from borrowing and lending money across time and from being unable to purchase perfect insurance at actuarially fair rates.

There have been numerous studies of age differences and the VSL using labor market data for over two decades. In the early studies in the literature, one typical approach was to include in the wage equation an interaction term of the fatality risk and the age variable. However, the fatality risk variable in these studies was not age-specific because such data were not available. As a result, the degree of refinement that was permitted by the data did not extend beyond estimating an average value per statistical life year, based on the assumption that all discounted years of life were equally valued. My series of studies with Michael Moore, such as Moore and Viscusi (1988), provide examples of this approach.

More recent studies of the influence of age have taken advantage of the additional refinement made possible by using the Census of Fatal Occupational Injuries (CFOI) data. Using these data, which provide a comprehensive inventory of each US job-related fatality, it is possible to construct age-specific risk measures by industry, occupation and other matters of interest. The result of wage equation estimates using these measures is that the age–VSL relationship reflects an inverted U-shaped pattern.[4] This finding is consistent with the implications of theoretical models in which the life-cycle pattern of VSL is estimated based on an assumption of imperfect capital markets, as in Shepard and Zeckhauser (1984).

Because of the role of imperfect capital markets, the life-cycle pattern of income is instrumental in influencing the value of VSL at different age groups. In particular, the estimated VSL is flatter if one controls for consumption over the life cycle or for cohort effects. The pivotal role of life-cycle effects is borne out as the VSL shape over workers' lifetimes tracks the lifetime income and lifetime consumption profiles quite closely, as demonstrated in Kniesner et al. (2006).

Figure 4.3 presents estimates of the VSL by age group from Aldy and Viscusi (2007). The bold curve indicates the cross-sectional estimates of VSL, whereas the dashed line adjusts the VSL estimates for the particular cohort that the individual is in. As indicated, the cohort-adjusted VSL is lower for younger age groups and higher for older age groups, reflecting the fact that those in older age groups are from an earlier labor market cohort. The peak estimate for the VSL is just under $8 million in the cohort-adjusted estimates and occurs around age 50.

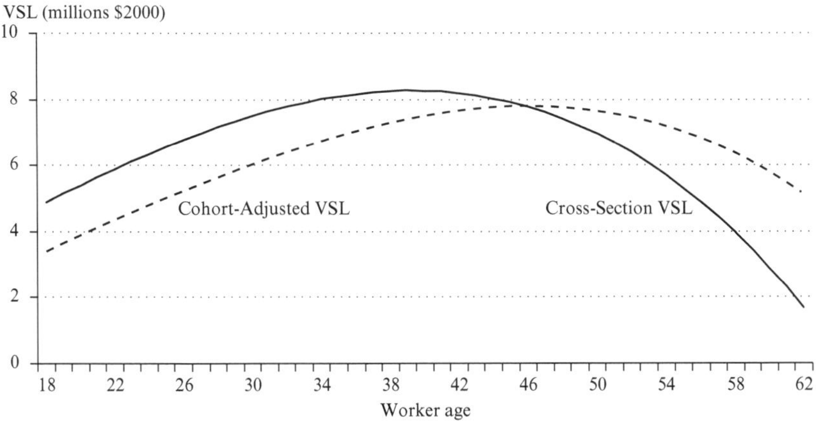

Source: Aldy and Viscusi (2008).

Figure 4.3 Cohort-adjusted and cross-section value of statistical life, 1993–2000

To summarize, what do we know about the age–VSL relationship based on the labor market evidence? First, the VSL does not peak at birth as would be the case if all that mattered is the total remaining life expectancy. Second, the VSL does not plummet as we age. Notably, the VSL for workers around age 60 in Figure 4.3 is higher than the VSL for workers at age 20. This result is not unique to this particular study but rather is the norm in recent analyses of VSL. In particular, because the VSL represents the individual's personal wage–risk trade-off, which in turn will be affected by one's resources in a particular stage of the life cycle, the total remaining life expectancy alone is not the sole factor influencing the VSL estimate.

VALUE OF A STATISTICAL LIFE YEAR

In many contexts, such as those involving regulations that affect people with very short remaining life expectancy, it is not appropriate to use the standard VSL measure. Rather, taking into account the difference in longevity often leads to using the value of a statistical life year (VSLY). The basic formula for this method developed in Moore and Viscusi (1988) divides the VSL estimate by the discounted expected remaining years of life to obtain the valuation per discounted expected life year.

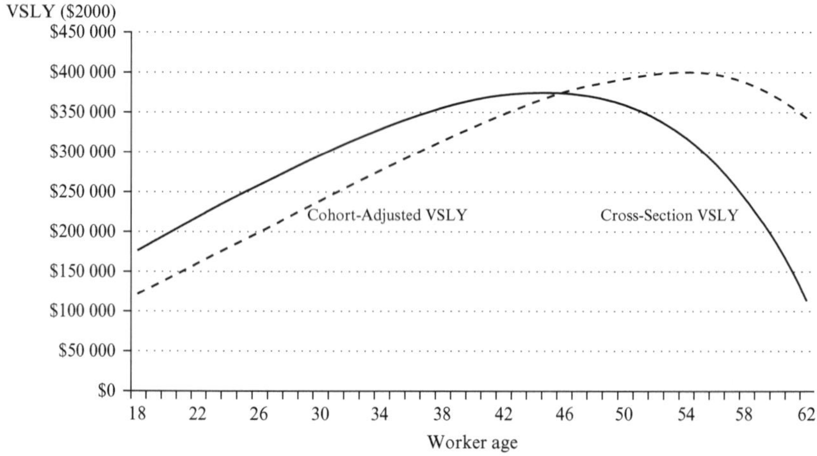

Source: Aldy and Viscusi (2008).

Figure 4.4 Value of a statistical life-year based on cohort-adjusted and cross-section value of statistical life, 1993–2000

Whereas that article assumed a constant valuation per year of life, the advent of more refined fatality risk data that make it possible to construct measures of the fatality rate for workers of different ages has greatly extended the kinds of analyses that can be undertaken. Viscusi and Aldy (2007) and Aldy and Viscusi (2008) use a job fatality rate measure that is specific to the worker's industry as well as the worker's age group. The estimates derived from this approach imply that VSLY is not a constant and is not steadily declining with age even though individual health may decline. Rather, the VSLY rises fairly steadily before eventually tapering off.

Figure 4.4 presents one such set of estimates using the CPS. Consider the cohort-adjusted VSLY estimates indicated by the dashed lines in the figure. The value per statistical life year rises from about $125 000 for those in their late teens, reaching a peak of about $400 000 around age 54. Thereafter, the VSLY tapers off but nevertheless remains quite substantial, at a level of $350 000 for workers age 62. These results, in conjunction with those in Figure 4.3 for VSL, indicate why the VSL does not plummet with age. Over the life cycle there is a substantial rise in the valuation that people place on each year of life.

INCOME EFFECTS

Compensatory damages for wrongful death include as a standard component compensation for the present value of the lost earnings that the family experiences because of the death. Although there may be adjustments for taxes and consumption, depending on the particular state law, the net result is that this component of compensatory damages is proportional to the value of the income that is lost. In much the same way, the WTP to decrease fatality risks also is likely to increase with one's income given that one's health is a normal good. The main empirical issue is how great the responsiveness is to the level of income.

Two principal estimation strategies have been used to assess the income elasticity of the VSL. In each instance, the estimates yield an average income elasticity across the population. The models are not structural approaches in which it is possible to ascertain the effect of changes in income levels on preferences of any particular individual. The first consists of meta-analyses across different VSL studies. The meta-analysis approach estimates the income elasticity based on how the VSL responds to differences in the wage level in the studies. The component VSL values are average estimates across each particular sample and consequently do not reflect the full range of heterogeneity within the sample.

The meta-analysis estimates by Viscusi and Aldy (2003) yield an elasticity estimate in the range of 0.51 to 0.61. Their study used a series of ten different specifications that spanned all the possibilities that have been considered in the previous VSL meta-analysis literature. The estimates were not greatly sensitive to the specification used.

An alternative approach to estimating the income elasticity of VSL is to use quantile regression estimates within a sample to analyze how the VSL for workers at different wage levels differs depending on the level of the fatality risk. A much more substantial estimate of the income elasticity is reported in Kniesner et al. (2010) who use quantile estimates using the Panel Studies of Income Dynamics data on worker wages in conjunction with CFOI fatality risk data. They estimate a mean income elasticity across the different quantiles of 1.44. Although the equation specification used in this study parallels that of a standard hedonic wage analysis, the resulting estimate of the income elasticity is quite different than that implied by meta-analyses. One possible explanation is that meta-analyses may suppress some income elasticity because of their focus on differences in the average VSL across studies, which does not fully account for the within-study heterogeneity that is evident in the quantile analysis. Notwithstanding these differences in the magnitude of the income elasticity, it is clear that the value of the income elasticity of VSL is positive.

VSL IN THE POLICY ARENA

Although policy makers were originally reluctant to adopt the VSL approach, this methodology has now become standard practice for agencies in performing their regulatory analyses of risk regulations. There have also been policy implications involving age adjustments and income adjustments to VSL, and it is useful to explore how these variations have been treated in policy assessments.

Before the advent of the use of the VSL methodology to value risks to life in regulatory impact analyses, the government nevertheless did attach a finite benefit value to these losses. Typically the approach parallels that used in personal injury cases based on the present value of lost earnings and medical costs. In its assessments of a proposed hazard communication regulation, the Occupational Safety and Health Administration (OSHA) suggested that this benefit measure, in fact, calculated the 'cost of death', which the agency regarded as less controversial than using the value of life methodology because life is too sacred to value. After reviewing OSHA's regulatory impact analysis of its proposed hazard communication regulation, the Office of Management and Budget (OMB) concluded that the benefits did not exceed the costs. As a result, OMB rejected the regulatory proposal.

OSHA then appealed the issues to then Vice-President Bush. I was asked to resolve the dispute between the two agencies by analyzing the merits of the proposal as well as the OMB critique of it. By using my estimates of the value of life, which has since been termed the VSL, I showed that the benefits exceeded the costs. In particular, using the VSL estimates increases the value of the benefits by a factor of ten.[5]

As a result of this analysis, the regulation became attractive on benefit–cost grounds. Calculated benefits now exceeded the value of costs, and the day after the White House received my report in support of the regulation, the regulation was issued. What is particularly noteworthy about this case study is that in this historical context using the VSL estimates approach was more supportive of risk regulation than making lives 'priceless'. Somewhat surprisingly, the VSL methodology is now under attack for pricing lives, even though at the time the VSL methodology was adopted, the main critique was not that the lives were being priced at too low an amount but rather that the number was so large and so far in excess of the present value of lost earnings that many questioned whether it was a reasonable basis for benefit assessment.

THE 'SENIOR DISCOUNT' CONTROVERSY

Although empirical evidence indicates that there are age variations in VSL, whether and how these age variations should be taken into account for purposes of benefit assessment is controversial. In its analysis of the Clear Skies Initiative in 2002, the US EPA used a senior discount of 37 percent in a benefits analysis sensitivity test. This senior discount estimate was based on survey studies in the UK with respect to valuation of deaths from railroad accidents. The use of a lower valuation figure for the lives saved for people over 65 led to a political firestorm. Protesters adopted slogans such as 'Seniors on Sale – 37% Off'. EPA subsequently backed off the approach. Although such demographic adjustments have evoked controversy with respect to regulatory analyses, such adjustments are the norm for calculating *ex post* compensation in personal injury and wrongful death cases.

The controversy did not abate, and Senator Barbara Boxer proposed legislation banning all demographic adjustments to VSL. It is important to note that this proposed prohibition against demographic adjustments for differences in the VSL only pertained to differences at a point in time rather than adjustments over time.

Although the resistance in the United States for any such age adjustments appears considerable, there are international precedents for such policies. In Canada government officials have used a VSL that is 25 percent lower for those over 65 compared with those under 65. Similarly, in 2001 the European Commission recommended that the VSL measure should have a declining value with individual age.

Although VSL estimates do not plummet with age, there are clearly age-related variations in VSL. Moreover, use of age-specific VSL measures in some instances may boost the values placed on those who are older because they have higher VSL amounts than workers at the other end of the age spectrum. Unfortunately, labor market evidence does not provide information on the VSL magnitudes for those outside the labor market at both extremes of the age spectrum.

If instead of using the efficiency-based measure of the VSL–age relationship one sought to value policies based on fairness, it is not clear whether appeals to fairness would resolve the controversy. One way of posing the fairness question would be to ask whether using the same VSL is equitable. That approach appears to have some symmetry across different age groups and is certainly the kind of fairness approach that the opponents of the senior discount incident would favor. Alternatively, one might pose the fairness question in terms of whether having the same VSLY is equitable. If equalizing the VSLY across people is the objective, use of a uniform VSL number irrespective of a person's life expectancy will create inequities by overvaluing the life years of those with very short remaining life expectancy.

Such appeals to fairness simply do not resolve the choice of the appropriate age adjustment to VSL. The main guidance should be derived by returning to basic economics principles. In particular, the guide for any age adjustment should be based on individuals' willingness to pay (WTP) for the risk reduction. This WTP value does, in fact, vary with age but is not a steadily decreasing function of age.

SHOULD INCOME LEVELS MATTER?

Although empirically VSL has a positive income elasticity, whether income-level differences should be taken into account for purposes of regulatory analyses is seldom confronted by regulatory agencies. Use of a uniform VSL irrespective of the income group being targeted by the policy will result in regulatory policies that the poor do not value, given their particular wage–risk trade-off. If the cost of the policy will, in fact, be shifted to this beneficiary group in some way, then from their vantage point they will be made worse off by using a VSL that exceeds their personal value.

A prominent example where the VSL–age relationship comes into play is with respect to airline safety. In particular, should we regulate airline safety more stringently than highway safety given that the passengers on airlines have a much higher income level than the average person killed in an automobile accident? In a study prepared for the Federal Aviation Administration (FAA) that was subsequently published as Viscusi (1993), I showed that based on the respective income levels of those being protected and available income elasticity estimates at the time, a higher VSL amount was more pertinent for airplane fatalities than for valuing the reduction in motor-vehicle accident deaths associated with the installation of guardrails.

The US Department of Transportation became the first government agency to formally adopt an income elasticity for VSL. Based on the Viscusi and Aldy (2003) income elasticity estimates, the agency selected a value of 0.55, which was the midpoint of their estimated range. If the Department of Transportation subsequently uses these higher numbers for valuing airline safety, then the rationale for doing so is more compelling than in most policy contexts because the beneficiaries of the safety regulation will be bearing the cost of the higher levels of safety mandated by more stringent regulations. The Department of Transportation's proposed adjustment of the VSL based on income levels is a very bold policy initiative to account for within-population differences.

In contrast, income changes over time have received much more widespread support. In the nearer term, income adjustments might occur to account for the fact that society is gradually becoming more affluent, and the VSL numbers should be updated to reflect changes in societal income levels. In the more distant future, such as analyses of policies pertaining to climate change or similarly remote environmental problems, the income changes involve future generations rather than those who are currently alive. Making adjustments for differences in income is efficient, but upward adjustments for future generations will redistribute income from the poorer current generation to a more affluent future generation.

In their conceptualization of the proper role of income adjustments, policy makers often fall prey to reference dependence effects. The current VSL level serves as the reference point, and upward adjustments are viewed much more favorably than decreases. In keeping with this reference dependence bias, proposed Senate legislation in 2008 required annual income adjustments for VSL based on changes in income. However, the proposed legislation also required that only increases in VSL will be permitted. Thus, even if there is a pertinent positive income elasticity of VSL and if income levels declined, perhaps because of severe economic downturns, then the higher VSL value from the more affluent period would be maintained. There is no economic efficiency rationale for such an asymmetry.

Such attempts to constrain the benefit values based on the political acceptability of different kinds of benefit adjustments are inconsistent with the fundamental principles underlying benefit–cost analysis. The proper benefits measure should be grounded in the willingness to pay of the beneficiaries of the policy. Whether these individual preferences indicate a positive income elasticity or other types of heterogeneity in preferences does not invalidate the importance of adhering to reliance on individuals' willingness to pay for guidance in setting benefit levels. To impose constraints on income adjustments or any other aspects of the benefit assessment process in effect overrides individual preferences and the pivotal economic role of consumer sovereignty.

THE DEVALUATION OF LIFE CONTROVERSY

This kind of asymmetry in treating changes in the VSL amount is also borne out in the devaluation of life controversy that emerged in 2008 with respect to the US EPA Office of Air Quality Planning and Standards (OAQPS) change in the VSL figure used in its regulatory analyses. This branch of EPA based its update of the VSL amount on the results of two meta-analyses: Viscusi and Aldy (2003) and Mrozek and Taylor (2002). Based on its assessment of the implications of these analyses, OAQPS lowered the VSL from $8 million to $7 million. From an external vantage point, this downward shift in the VSL presented an economic puzzle since income levels have risen over time. Moreover, the agency did not articulate why the studies differed or whether the results of one of the studies were more credible and consequently should serve as the basis for selecting the VSL. One of the principal differences between the studies is that the Viscusi and Aldy study used only the single best estimate of the VSL from each study, whereas Mrozek and Taylor used all reported estimates, which in some cases involved a very large number of different alternative econometric specifications based on the same underlying data. However, by including multiple estimates from each study the Mrozek and Taylor analysis included observations that were not independent of one another. It should be noted, however, that their econometric analysis did account for the effect of multiple observations using a clustering adjustment for the standard errors.

Irrespective of the studies' differences or whether the downward shift in the VSL is warranted, it is clear that, in general, agencies should have the freedom to reassess the scientific evidence pertaining to the VSL and make whatever adjustments they believe are appropriate, even if doing so involves a decrease in the VSL. The public reaction to the decrease in the VSL was less sympathetic. The substantial political and public disapproval resulted in many people suggesting that this devaluation of life was a conspiracy on the part of the Bush administration to undermine regulatory policies. There is, in fact, no evidence that this was the case because it was a decentralized decision within EPA. Moreover, other branches of EPA, such as the Office of Water, did not decrease the VSL that they used in their regulatory analyses.

This devaluation of life controversy largely stimulated the draft Senate legislation in fall 2008 that proposed that agencies must only raise the VSL over time. What is particularly remarkable about this incident is that it is the change in the VSL that generated the controversy, not the level. Even with the downward adjustment to the VSL figure, the OAQPS number for valuing risk to life was still relatively high compared with the value used by other federal regulatory agencies. For example, OAQPS was taken to task for decreasing the VSL to $7 million even though that figure exceeded the US Department of Transportation's VSL estimate at that time by more than $1 million.

ADJUSTMENTS FOR THE SIZE OF RISK

Government estimates of VSL are based on analyses of trade-offs involving very small risks. The chief source of evidence is labor market studies, and these analyses pertain to risks that workers actually face rather than very large hypothetical risks. Other hedonic studies, such as those of housing markets and product markets, likewise are restricted to risk levels that are observable. Stated preference studies have no such limitation, but these analyses have generally focused on small risks as well.

Suppose that we know the shape of w(p) in Figure 4.5 or the locus of observed risk–wage combinations that workers find attractive. Armed with this functional relationship, what can we say about workers' willingness to accept (WTA) jobs with much larger risks than the small risk levels considered in hedonic wage analyses? Consider Worker 1 who currently incurs a job risk p_1. If that risk level was increased to p_2, then applying the results from the hedonic wage function w(p) would imply that Worker 1 would be willing to accept risk p_2 if the wage were increased to $w_2(p_2)$. However, that wage level will not keep Worker 1 on the same constant expected utility locus. A higher wage rate $w_1(p_2)$ is required, where this wage is necessarily greater than that implied by the hedonic wage analysis due to the curvature of EU_1.

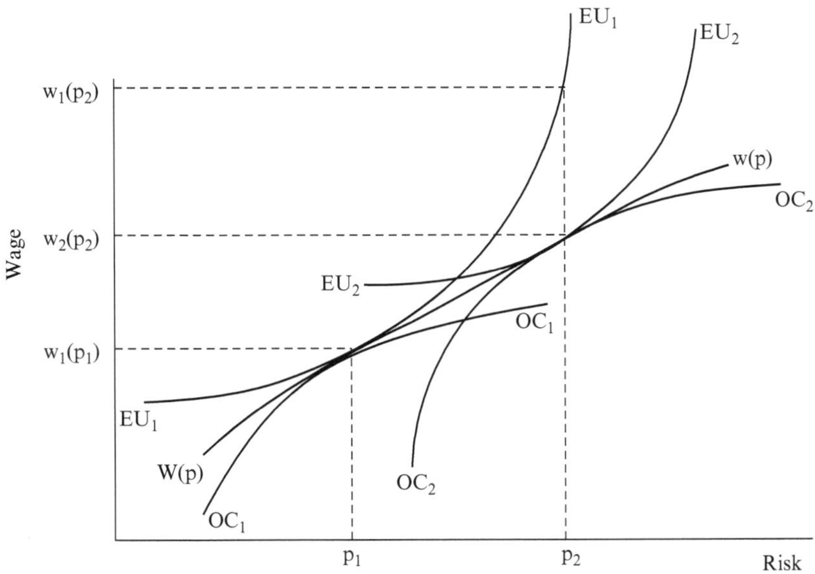

Figure 4.5 Hedonic market equilibrium for fatality risks

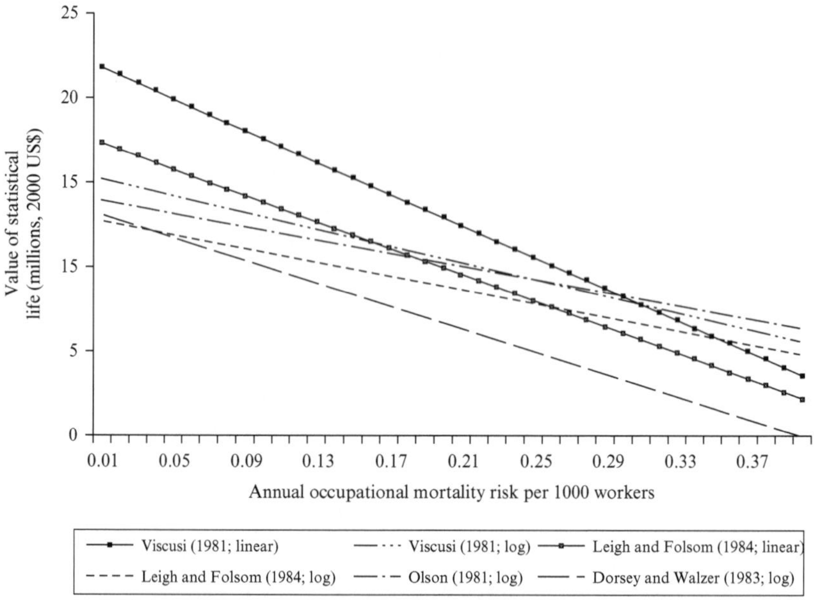

Figure 4.6 Relationship of value of statistical life to risk level in hedonic wage studies

By similar argument, one can analyze the worker's WTP for large risk reductions below p_1. As a first approximation, one might wish to assume that the curve w(p) approximates that value. However, as shown in Figure 4.5, EU_1 lies above w(p) for risk levels smaller than p_1 so that the WTP values (or the drop in wages that workers are willing to accept) for substantial decreases in fatality risk will be less than that implied by the hedonic wage function.

Hedonic labor market studies of fatality risks of different magnitude will capture two sets of influences. First, because such wage studies are focusing on WTA values for risk, as the risk levels become very large the wage–risk trade-offs should increase as well, for any given worker. Second, people will sort in the labor market based on their risk preferences, and the workers who are in the very high-risk jobs have different preferences than those in the more modest-risk jobs. Workers who self-select into high-risk positions will tend to have lower VSL values for any given risk level.

Figure 4.6 presents the Viscusi and Aldy (2003) results from six different hedonic wage studies that included a quadratic risk term to capture the curvature of the w(p) locus. Although the steepness of the decline in VSL with risk levels varies with the particular study, in every instance there is a downward-sloping relationship. The dominant influence is the sorting of lower VSL people into high-risk jobs. These w(p) curvature results consequently provide little insight into any particular individual's WTA large risk increases or WTP for large risk decreases because the main factor is the influence of individual sorting based on risk preferences, not changes in any particular individual's VSL trade-off along a constant expected utility locus. Put somewhat differently, government agencies looking for guidance in valuing major shifts in risk levels will have to rely on information beyond that conveyed by the hedonic wage estimates.

The risk levels analyzed in the hedonic wage studies have varied over time, in part because the workplace has become safer. The meaningful risk measures are those that attempt to isolate the risk associated with the worker's particular job.[6] The first such measures were those based on the early US Bureau of Labor Statistics fatality risk data by industry. These data are based on a sample of firms who reported fatality statistics voluntarily. These risk data imply an average risk level on the order of 1/10 000 for the time period beginning in the 1970s. The next wave of studies used data that were believed to be a more comprehensive tally of workplace fatalities. The National Institute of Occupational Safety and Health developed the National Traumatic Occupational Fatality (NTOF) data, which reduced the amount of measurement error in the fatality variable. Notwithstanding the name of the dataset, the information is available by industry and by state, and not by occupation. The average risk levels in studies using these data are from 1/10 000 to 4/10 000.

The current gold standard for fatality risk data is the US Bureau of Labor Statistics (BLS) Census of Fatal Occupational Injuries (CFOI). This database consists of a complete census of all occupational fatalities rather than a sample. Each fatality is verified with multiple source documents, with four being the average number used. The confidential micro data files can be used to construct risk measures by industry, occupation, industry–occupation combination, age, gender, race or other matters of interest. The average annual fatality risk level in the studies using these data is about 1/25 000.

Although there are exceptions, for the most part the hedonic wage literature has focused on WTA amounts for risk levels averaging from 1/25 000 to 1/2500. By most standards, these are comparatively small risks. For such small risk changes, the WTP amounts for EPA benefit assessments should be fairly similar to the WTA amounts. As indicated with respect to Figure 4.5, for larger non-incremental risk changes, the estimated VSL from labor market studies will overstate the implied VSL based on WTP amounts and understate the implied VSL based on WTA amounts for large risk changes.

A CALIBRATION EXAMPLE FOR NON-INCREMENTAL RISK CHANGES

If we have information on the shape of individual utility functions, it is possible to analyze how the WTP amounts and WTA amounts vary depending on the magnitude of the risk change. We begin with the general formulation for VSL and then consider specific functional forms. Let $u(y)$ be the utility function of income y when healthy, and let p be the probability of death. For simplicity, suppose that bequests have a value of zero. Then VSL is given by:

$$VSL = u(y)/[(1 - p)u'(y)]. \tag{4.1}$$

Suppose that the utility function takes a logarithmic form $u(y) = a + \ln(y)$. Such utility functions are specified up to a positive linear transformation, but the parameters must be set to be consistent with the estimated VSL. Assume that VSL = \$7 million and that the worker faces an annual fatality risk of 1/10 000. Also let the value of y = \$27 200, which is roughly the current average annual wage income of blue-collar workers in the CPS. This information is sufficient to pin down the shape of the utility function.

Consider an order of magnitude increase in the size of the risk from 1/10 000 to 1/1 000. The associated risk change is 9/10 000. Based on a VSL of \$7 million, the estimated WTA amount would be \$6300. But to keep the worker on the same constant expected utility locus, the required WTA is \$6966. Thus, the WTA is about 10 percent greater than would be predicted based on the local rate of trade-off.

Similarly, the implied VSL for the discontinuous change in the risk level is greater as well. The additional required wage compensation implies a VSL of \$7.7 million based on the WTA amount. Large risk increases consequently generate a WTA value greater than that implied by the estimated VSL from local trade-offs, but the changes in the valuations are not stark within this particular range.

Government policies generally involve WTP amounts for decreases in risk rather than WTA values for risk increases. Suppose the starting annual fatality risk is 1/1000, the starting income is \$27 200, and the VSL based on local wage–risk trade-offs is \$7 million. Suppose the risk is reduced to 1/10 000, which, based on an extrapolation from the estimated VSL, implies a WTP amount of \$6300. Based on the WTP amount that will put the worker on the same constant expected utility locus, the WTP value is \$5825, which is 8 percent less than would be predicted by the local trade-off rate derived from the hedonic wage relationship. The estimated VSL associated with this non-incremental risk change is \$6.5 million.

Large risk changes consequently have a different associated VSL than implied by local rates of trade-off. The implied VSL amounts for these shifts are greater than the locally estimated VSLs from a WTA perspective and less than locally estimated VSLs from a WTP perspective. For the risk change amounts of 9/10 000 considered here, the WTA values were 10 percent lower than predicted and the WTP amounts were 8 percent lower than predicted. That the discrepancy should be greater for the WTP amounts is expected given the curvature of the same constant expected utility locus. As Figure 4.5 indicates, the curvature of EU_1 ensures that the WTP magnitude of risk change relationship will be on a flatter portion of the EU_1 than the WTA risk change relationship. Thus, to the extent that agencies are largely concerned with WTP estimates more than WTA values, the change in the rate of money–risk trade-offs with large changes in risk is less than would be the case for WTA values.

An interesting application of these results is with respect to a VSL diagram that appeared in Appendix D of the 'Review of the revised analytical plan for EPA's second prospective analysis – benefits and costs of the Clean Air Act 1990–2020', 2004. Figure 4.7 is drawn from that report. The risk–WTP combinations r_1 through r_5 indicate the observed results of hedonic wage studies being pooled in a meta-analysis. The counterpart VSL amounts for each of these studies assuming a constant linear rate of trade-off is indicated by VSL-1 through VSL-5. The indicated WTP function in the diagram indicates the estimated WTP function based on a meta-analysis. Thus, the WTP value rises with the risk change based on the pooling of results across studies and leads to a flatter WTP function than that implied by any particular estimate.

What is potentially confusing about such discussions, which often refer to labor market estimates as 'empirical measures of WTP for risk reductions', is that for hedonic labor market studies they are not WTP measures but WTA measures. In the case of stated preference studies, the reference point usually is WTP values. From a theoretical standpoint, for large risk increases the WTA should be greater than the estimated value based on a linear extrapolation of VSL levels. To the extent that labor market meta-analyses are fitting curves such as that in Figure 4.7, the implied VSL should be steadily rising as the risk change increases. That the estimated VSL does not increase with the level of the fatality risk is a consequence of the self-selection of different workers into the high-risk jobs, as shown in Figure 4.6.

To avoid the complicating considerations of multiple studies across different groups, Figure 4.8 presents the results based on a single study. Linear extrapolation of the estimated VSL for large risk changes will overstate the WTP amounts for very large changes in risk because people

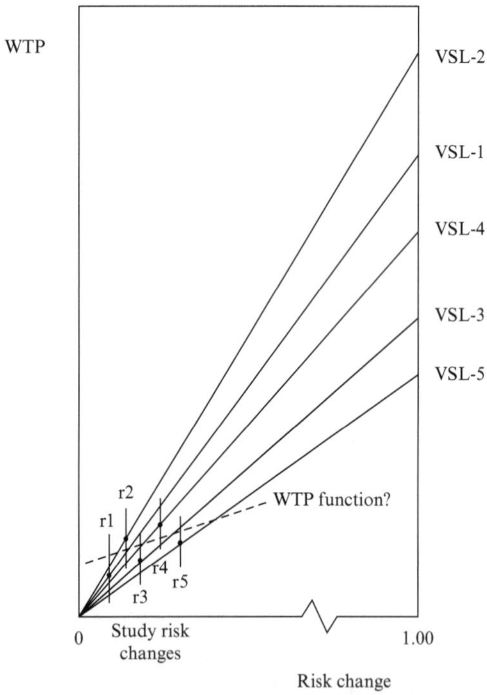

Source: 'Review of the revised analytical plan for EPA's second prospective analysis – benefits and costs of the Clean Air Act 1990–2020', Draft report, EPA-SABCOUNCIL-ACV-XXX-XX, March 5, 2004.

Figure 4.7 Illustrative analysis of meta-analyses

have a positive but diminishing WTP for risk reductions. Whether these effects of major shifts in the risk level are of practical consequence to EPA depends on the magnitude of the risks being considered.

Although some environmental risks are relatively large, whether they are large compared with the labor market risks that form the basis of most VSL studies is less obvious. For the labor market reference point, consider the risk levels in the recent BLS CFOI data. These annual fatality risks average 1/25 000, which is smaller than the risk levels in other hedonic wage studies. As a result, focusing on these data will provide an upper bound on the extent to which one should view environmental risks as comparatively large.

EPA benefits assessments typically focus on lifetime risks rather than annual risks. Assuming a 40-year work life, an annual occupational fatality risk of 1/25 000 corresponds to a lifetime job-related mortality risk of

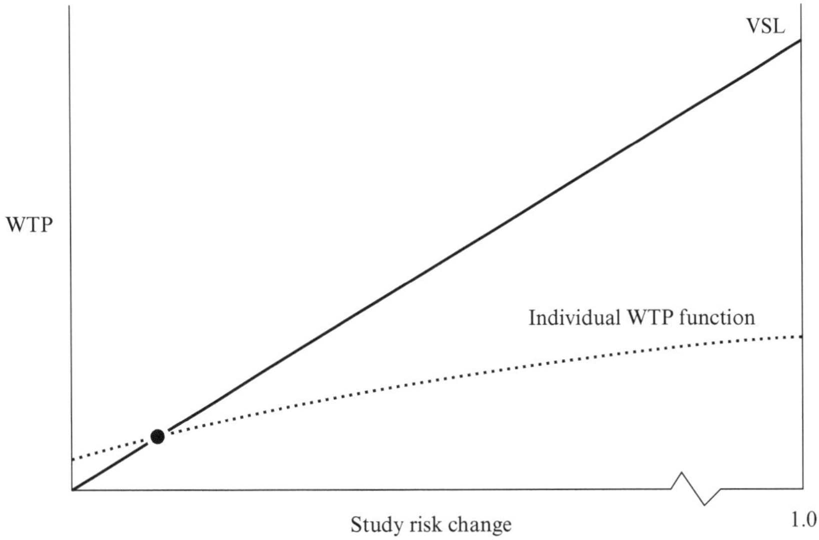

Figure 4.8 Individual willingness to pay as function of risk level

1.6/1000. For a VSL of $7 million, the annual required wage compensation is $280. The undiscounted lifetime wage premium is $11 200. For benefit assessment purposes, such values should be discounted using a reasonable discount rate such as 3 percent.

For an example of a large environmental risk subject to EPA regulation, I used the Draft Benzene Case Study (March 2008). This draft Clean Air Act regulation would reduce the lifetime risks of leukemia to the exposed population. The high-risk county affected by the regulation is Brazoria County for which EPA estimates that the lifetime leukemia risk would decrease from 2/10 000 to 3×10^{-6}. This risk change is two orders of magnitude. But whether the decrease is two orders of magnitude or even more is not the key issue because the post-regulation leukemia risk is about zero.

What is consequential is the absolute magnitude of the lifetime risk reduction of approximately 2/10 000. Even this lifetime risk level is not completely outside the range of the annual risk levels that have been considered in hedonic wage studies. How great the risk probability reduction is depends on the nature of the risk exposure. Suppose that the lifetime leukemia risk of 2/10 000 is based on a series of exposures over a ten-year period. Then the annual leukemia risk is about 2/100 000. The CFOI annual risk of 1/25 000 is 4/100 000, which is twice as great as this amount. Thus, even using the fatality risk data series posing the smallest risk level, the leukemia risk reduction is of fairly similar magnitude. If the lifetime risk exposure is the result of exposures of even more than ten years, then the annual risk is even smaller.

Whether the environmental risk reduction is large or small depends on how the benefits question is framed. Knowing that there is a lifetime risk reduction of a particular magnitude is not sufficient. Does the risk arise from a one-time exposure that results in leukemia at a particular future date? Or, more reasonably, does the risk arise from a series of exposures over time that produces a future distribution of risk across many future time periods? In all likelihood, focusing on the lifetime risk overstates the risk reduction achieved by the policy in any given year in much the same way as focusing on workers' lifetime risks would overstate their annual fatality risk level.

In the case of the labor market risks, the wage compensation for risks occurs in small annual amounts. Policies often do not involve annual payments but instead may involve substantial fixed costs leading to more costs being incurred upfront. How the payment mechanism is structured will matter for survey valuations. Most policies are not in fact funded through actual payments of this type, so it is usually the publicly financed benefit valuation thought experiment that is pertinent.

LATENCY AND CANCER BENEFIT ISSUES

Leukemia and other cancer risks involve a substantial latency period. From the standpoint of benefit assessment, the WTP for reducing these risks at some future date should be discounted by a usual government rate such as 3 percent. An alternative is to incorporate the latency period aspect into a stated preference survey and ascertain individuals' own rates of time preference with respect to cancer. As fascinating as this might be as an academic exercise, it is unlikely to provide meaningful guidance for policy. Decisions involving an intertemporal component are fraught with error. Among the problems identified in past studies is that of hyperbolic discounting whereby individuals display inordinately high rates of discount for the initial period, as shown in Viscusi et al. (2008). Thus, estimated implicit rates of time preference may largely reflect a form of individual irrationality. Decisions involving risk and uncertainty are also potentially fraught with error so that combining a latency period element with a risk valuation task may lead to an overly complex stated preference task.

Even putting aside both the issues of latency and the magnitude of the risk, more refinement of the benefit estimates for cancer risk reduction is needed. The valuations of cancer risk reduction will differ depending on the type of cancer, the associated morbidity effects, and the effect on premature mortality. Some stated preference studies of cancer simply denote the disease as 'cancer' with little description of the health consequences. Such studies will not yield meaningful valuations. Unless the respondent knows the characteristics of the health risk being valued and the consequences for personal welfare, the commodity being valued may bear little relationship to what is needed for benefit assessment.

Two studies that have obtained cancer risk valuations after providing a detailed description of the health consequences are Magat et al. (1996) and Van Houtven et al. (2008). Each of these studies used a risk–risk methodology whereby respondents determined the personal auto accident risk that would be equivalent to a given risk of cancer. The Magat et al. (1996) study presented respondents with detailed descriptions of the health effects of leukemia developed in conjunction with cancer specialists at Duke University Medical Center, USA. One would expect the studies to generate different values because of the different descriptions of the health consequences. However, the extent of the differences is quite large; Magat et al. (1996) found cancer risks occurring without any latency period as having a value equal to auto accident risks, whereas Van Houtven et al. (2008) found that even with a five-year latency period, cancer risks were valued three times as highly as auto accident risks. Other studies yield different results, so clearly there is a major research need to refine the estimates of cancer valuations.

SHOULD VSL BE ADDED TO THE PRESENT VALUE OF ECONOMIC DAMAGES?

There have been efforts to use the VSL measure to determine levels of compensation for wrongful death cases. This approach, known as hedonic damages, has been rejected by most courts but has been admitted in some jurisdictions. To the extent that compensatory damages serve an insurance function, setting compensation amounts at the level of VSL provides excessive insurance. In situations in which the injury arises in a market context, such as product-related injuries addressed by product liability, compensation based on the VSL levels will force people to buy excessive amounts of insurance because the liability costs will be incorporated in the product price. Use of VSL amounts in legal contexts is, however, appropriate for determining the appropriate cost–risk trade-off under a negligence standard or for setting the appropriate level of punitive damages when deterrence is a matter of concern.

Notwithstanding economists' reservations about using VSL as the standard approach for setting compensatory damages amounts, Posner and Sunstein (2005) advocate an even more generous compensatory damages formulation than using VSL for wrongful death cases. Here I briefly review their proposal and its limitations. Although the focus of their discussion is using VSL in the courtroom, since the optimal deterrence amount is never less than the optimal insurance amount for wrongful death, their proposal also has potential implications for valuing government regulations as well.

The Posner–Sunstein proposal is to provide two different components of compensatory damages. The first component is the standard compensation for economic loss consisting of the present value of lost earnings and medical costs. They propose, as the second component, augmenting this compensation with the VSL amount. They describe four different methods for calculating the VSL value. Irrespective of the method, their procedure ensures that the payment amount will provide both excessive deterrence and excessive insurance so that there is no sound economic rationale for damages at this level. In what appears to be an enormous understatement, they observe that their proposal would 'have a significant impact on tort awards, especially for the elderly in non-hedonic loss states'. The four different ways that they suggest for calculating the VSL are of potential interest from the standpoint of analyzing the heterogeneity of VSL for government policy.

The first approach that the courts might use is the government number for VSL. This is ultimately the approach that they suggest judges adopt. Unlike the present value of lost earnings and medical cost number, this VSL will not be specific to the individual and is a 'one size fits all' approach not unlike what government agencies generally do. As a result, it is inconsistent with common law practices for setting compensation for personal injury cases in which the compensation is linked to what the particular injured party has lost. At a more fundamental level, there is also the question of what is the 'government number', in that the VSL number differs not only across agencies but also within agencies; for example, air pollution and water pollution regulations are valued by EPA at different VSL levels.

The second approach is to determine the victim's VSL. Thus if R is the compensation the person received for risk q, the VSL amount that would be used is R/q. The difficulty is that rarely do we have individual-specific information on the level of R or the value of q. Using the CFOI data it is possible to estimate the value of q for the worker's industry–occupation cell or some other basis. Wage equation estimates could also be used at an aggregative level to determine the wage–risk trade-off associated with the person's job, assuming of course that the individual who died was employed.

Their third approach is to ask how much the victim would have paid to avoid the risk and then infer a VSL from that calculation. This procedure is a hypothetical calculation in hindsight on behalf of a person who is deceased. One could use evidence from other risk-taking activities, whether job risks or personal consumption activities such as smoking, to make some inferences about the valuation. However, for government policy this procedure appears much less reliable than obtaining *ex ante* valuations using stated preference surveys. The temporal reference point for government policies is also *ex ante*, unlike the role of the court system, which compensates people after injuries.

The fourth approach suggested by Posner and Sunstein is to ask the jury to set a 'value of life's pleasures lost by the victim'. This concept is entirely different from the VSL approach, although they suggest it is simply an alternative procedure for calculating VSL. The VSL reflects attitudes toward lotteries involving small probabilities of death. The value of life's pleasures is a quite different concept than that embodied in the VSL. The economic content of the value of life's pleasures concept is also not clear. Is this damages amount the amount of money that the person must be paid after death to be indifferent to life or death? Thus, is it the bequest amount that would have restored the deceased's welfare using the bequest function of the deceased? Or is the value of life's pleasures the WTP amount to avoid certain death? In either case, the amount that is being calculated is quite different conceptually from the VSL.

Although the Posner–Sunstein proposal is not a workable approach to setting damages for tort cases or for determining benefit values for regulatory analyses, their discussion highlights the importance of recognizing the role of heterogeneity. Damages in wrongful death and personal injury cases generally are linked to the amounts that are lost by the specific victims. In much the same way, government regulations should be assessed using the specific benefit values of those who are being protected by the regulation.

CONTEXTUAL SOURCES OF VARIATION IN VALUING LIFE: DEATHS FROM ATTACKS BY TERRORISTS

How people die matters. There may be morbidity effects associated with different kinds of death that will affect the valuation. In addition, the fatalities may be bundled with other types of consequences so that what is

Table 4.2 Subjective level of risk by type of fatality

Subjective level of risk	Auto fatality risk	Natural disaster fatality risk	Terrorism fatality risk
	(%)	(%)	(%)
Below-average fatality risk	43.9	58.6	50.6
Average fatality risk	47.6	34.9	41.4
Above-average fatality risk	8.5	6.5	8.0

valued is not the risk per se but also the risk in the particular context and the attendant losses associated with it.

A prominent example of distinctive risks of death pertains to victims of terrorism. What is at stake with respect to terrorism risks is not only the lives of the individuals affected but also the general idea that the United States is under foreign attack. Such deaths evoke more general concerns pertaining to national defense and security.

Because the valuations of reducing terrorism risks may be affected by one's perception of the risk, a useful starting point is to examine risk beliefs regarding deaths from attacks by terrorists. Table 4.2 provides the results from a national survey administered by Knowledge Networks and analyzed in Viscusi and Zeckhauser (2006). Respondents were given background information on the number of US deaths from auto fatalities, natural disasters and terrorist attacks. They were then asked to rate their relative risk compared with the average American's. Most people tend to rate their risk levels as being average or below average when compared to the general population. Doing so, in effect, enables them to not find fault with themselves, particularly when elements of personal choice are involved. Consistent with the framing effect of the question that generates an optimism bias response, few people rate their risk exposure as being below average. Terrorism fatality risk beliefs have a pattern not unlike the other causes of death; the percentage of the population with below-average risk beliefs is between that for auto fatalities and natural disasters. Interestingly, auto fatality risks have the lowest percentage with below-average risk beliefs, which is inconsistent with the usual claim that people underestimate those risks because of their apparent belief in control over the risk.

The variables that influence these risk beliefs are examined in Table 4.3, which presents the ordered probit regressions for the terrorism risk response. Variables that were not statistically significant, including a comprehensive set of locational and demographic variables, are not reported. The specter of the 9/11 attack apparently influences expectations, because

Table 4.3 Ordered probit regressions on subjective terrorism fatality risk

Independent variables	Coefficient (asymptotic std. error)
Age	−0.005*
	(0.003)
Black, non-Hispanic	0.389**
	(0.139)
Metropolitan residence	0.508**
	(0.118)
More than 6 plane trips per year	0.545+
	(0.296)

Note: + Significant at 10 percent level; * significant at 5 percent level; ** significant at 1 percent level; two-tailed test.

people who live in metropolitan areas or who fly more than six plane trips per year have higher risk beliefs. Older respondents have lower risk beliefs, while blacks have higher risk beliefs.

Should there be another terrorist attack, how willing are people to provide for government relief of the victims and their families? For the different risk–belief categories, support for such aid ranges from 72 percent to 85 percent of the population. As indicated by Table 4.4, among the more interesting factors linked to support of such victims are that current smokers, women, blacks, and those with average terrorism risk beliefs are supportive of such aid, while older respondents and Republicans are less supportive.

Although the 9/11 attack was a surprise to most Americans, a substantial number claim that they knew about the risk all along; a variant of hindsight bias that Viscusi and Zeckhauser (2005) term 'recollection bias'. For three samples in 2002, 2003, and 2004, respondents were asked the following question: 'Take yourself back to the World Trade Center disaster. Do you believe that the risk of a terrorist attack over the next year on an airplane is higher or lower than you thought it was before the September 11th disaster?' The results of these surveys are summarized in Table 4.5. A surprisingly low percentage views the risk as being higher despite the likelihood that expectation of a terrorist attack was probably not perceived as a significant risk before the 9/11 attack. This apparent bias in risk perceptions has ramifications for their support of anti-terrorism measures in a survey for which the trade-off was between civil liberties and risk. Respondents subject to September 11 recollection bias are less likely to favor targeting passengers for screening, presumably because they do not believe that an enhanced threat exists that must be addressed.

Table 4.4 Ordered probit regressions for government relief for terrorism victims

Independent variables	Relief for terrorism victims
Age	−0.011**
	(0.003)
Female	0.198+
	(0.106)
Black, non-Hispanic	0.570*
	(0.229)
Years of education	−0.041+
	(0.025)
Republican	−0.298**
	(0.110)
Current smoker	0.326*
	(0.136)
More than 6 plane trips per year	0.356
	(0.327)
Above-average terrorism fatality risk	−0.643**
	(0.211)
Below-average terrorism fatality risk	−0.408**
	(0.115)

Note: + Significant at 10 percent level; * significant at 5 percent level; ** significant at 1 percent level; two-tailed test.

Table 4.5 Percentage change in terrorist risk estimates after September 11

	2002 Sample (N = 94)	2003 Sample (N = 117)	2004 Sample (N = 122)
Risk is now higher	43	54	33
Risk is same as before September 11	17	24	34
Risk is now lower	40	22	33

Anti-terrorism policies also may entail trade-offs borne by the individual. Instead of targeting people for screening, there may be a choice of waiting longer in line for screening. In this instance the trade-off is between civil liberties and waiting time. For scenarios in which the screening was designed to only affect others, not the respondent, the willingness to favor risk profiling based on personal characteristics ('the person's age, race, gender, national origin, appearance and baggage') increased from

Table 4.6 Determinants of the probability of favoring targeting of passengers for airport screening

Independent variable	Coefficient (std. error)	
Waiting time (in min.)	0.0038**	0.0065***
	(0.0015)	(0.0022)
Respondents targeted for screening	0.0190	0.1870
	(0.0627)	(0.1140)
Non-white	−0.2653***	−0.2655***
	(0.0696)	(0.0697)
Waiting time × Respondent targeted for screening		−0.0052*
		(0.0030)

Notes:
* Indicates coefficient is significantly different from zero at 10 percent level, two-sided test.
** Indicates coefficient is significantly different from zero at 5 percent level, two-sided test.
*** Indicates coefficient is significantly different from zero at 1 percent level, two-sided test.

45 percent to 74 percent as the waiting time increased from ten minutes to 60 minutes. As the regression results in Table 4.6 indicate, each ten minutes of waiting time increases the overall percentage supporting targeting by 4 percent. Non-whites, who may have been previous victims of discrimination and who may believe that they will be targeted, are 27 percent less likely to support a targeting policy.

To analyze different societal preferences toward reducing risks, Viscusi (2009) analyzed results of a stated preference experiment using a nationally representative sample. The survey focused on two sets of risk–risk trade-offs. How much one would value the risks of death from terrorism as compared with comparable risks from natural disasters? How are terrorism risks valued compared with traffic-related deaths? And how are traffic-related deaths valued compared with natural disasters? Box 4.1 presents an example of such a question in which terrorism deaths are compared with traffic-related risks.

The results of the series of compared comparisons implied by the random utility model estimates are reported in Table 4.7. A principal result of the study is that although the number of deaths is the same in each case, preventing 0.56 terrorism deaths is equivalent to preventing a death from natural disasters for those with average risk beliefs. Thus, respondents value terrorism risks by a factor that is more than double the value attached to victims of natural disasters. Terrorism deaths are valued almost the same as traffic-related deaths for those with average risk beliefs. The different valuation amounts in Table 4.7 are quite responsive to individuals' risk beliefs, because the relative valuations are boosted by

BOX 4.1 EXAMPLES OF RISK TRADE-OFF QUESTIONS

Sample Terrorism Question:
Suppose you can vote for one of two different policies that cost the same amount but reduce different kinds of risks. Traffic safety policies reduce isolated deaths. The terrorism policy prevents deaths from a single major attack. Which of the two policies would you prefer?

	Traffic safety	Terrorism policy
Type of deaths prevented	Isolated accidents	Major terrorism attack
Average number of deaths prevented	150	50
Which policy would you prefer?	Policy 1	Policy 2

Table 4.7 Relative risk valuations after accounting for risk beliefs

Fatality risk trade-off categories	Implied relative valuations
Average disaster death risk/Average traffic death risk	1.7888
Above-average terrorism death risk/Average traffic death risk	0.6794
Average terrorism death risk/Average traffic death risk	0.9940
Below-average terrorism death risk/Average traffic death risk	1.3642
Above-average terrorism death risk/Average disaster death risk	0.3798
Average terrorism death risk/Average disaster death risk	0.5557
Below-average terrorism death risk/Average disaster death risk	0.7626

believing that one faces above-average risks and are reduced if the risks are believed to be below average.

The high valuation of terrorism deaths compared with natural disasters does not stem from a difference in risk perceptions whereby people thought they might be victims of a terrorist attack but not a natural disaster. The analysis controlled for differences in risk beliefs, personal characteristics and other factors likely to influence valuations. Political factors also came into play; those who were registered Republicans placed a higher valuation on the terrorism risks, even accounting for differences in income levels and other likely determinants of the valuation amounts.

Although studies such as this provide evidence on a risk–money trade-off, their perspective is different than a traditional VSL study. A hedonic labor market analysis of job market safety only captures the individual's valuation of personal risks. In contrast, these stated preference valuations are yielding society's general valuation of the hazard, where this will include the personal risk but also may include a substantial altruistic component irrespective of whether one is at risk personally.

The high valuation of terrorism risks as compared with traffic-related risks is striking in that people are much more likely to view themselves at a higher risk of personal death from motor vehicle accidents, thus leading to a strong personal risk valuation component as part of their valuation response. The low valuation of natural disaster risks also may stem from a belief that those exposed to the risk exhibit a form of moral hazard. The analysis of attitudes towards victims of natural disasters in Viscusi and Zeckhauser (2003) found that individuals who continued to expose themselves to natural disasters after previously experiencing catastrophic losses were not regarded as being highly deserving of continued public assistance.

This kind of result pertaining to personal responsibility for risk exposures very much parallels a finding in the UK by Covey et al. (2010). Their UK study focused on the public's valuation of reducing risks of people who exhibit irresponsible behavior. The risk context they considered was that of railway trespassers and suicides involving railroads. Their finding was that the public placed a lower value on reducing the risks of life to those who were willing to expose themselves to risk.

Both the US natural disasters results and the UK railroad results could reflect two sets of influences. First, people who have self-selected into choosing risky pursuits by either continuing to expose themselves to risks of natural disasters or taking high-risk actions with respect to railroad hazards have revealed through their actions that they place a lower value on risks to their life. As a consequence, a lower societal value for reducing their risks is simply a valuation that is consistent with the person's own revealed preferences and evidence of moral hazard. Second, it is also possible that respondents view such risks as hazards that will affect others and not necessarily themselves, to the extent that people believe they are responsible risk-takers even if others are not. However, even accounting for differences in individual experiences of natural disasters in Viscusi (2009), there remains a substantial gap in valuations of the risks of terrorism versus natural disasters.

CONCLUSION

The VSL has been an integral part of benefit assessment for a quarter-century. Much of the continued controversy over the approach is based on the misunderstanding of the 'economic' value of life. As a result, the opposition to the VSL approach is often misguided.

With improved fatality rate data and survey data, researchers have greatly expanded the questions that can be addressed. The estimates of heterogeneity and the sources of heterogeneity are becoming more refined. A challenge raised by this increased refinement in estimates of VSL heterogeneity is that new policy challenges are being presented.

Throughout its history, the use of the VSL approach has been quite supportive of meaningful risk regulation policies. Thus, not only is it the correct economic approach, but it also places a much more substantial value on the lives that will be saved than previous measures such as the present value of lost earnings. Although some have proposed using no dollar values, given the emphasis on showing that the benefits of regulation exceed the value of the costs, the practical consequence of this approach will not be to elevate their value but to diminish their importance in regulatory policy making. Rather, treating some risk reductions as 'priceless' may make them 'worthless'.

NOTES

1. This chapter draws on a related longer paper, W. Kip Viscusi (2010). 'Policy Challenges of the Heterogeneity of the Value of Statistical Life', *Foundations and Trends in Microeconomics*, **6** (2), 99–172.
2. This chapter was prepared as a paper for the CREATE – DHS Conference, Washington, DC, September 23–24, 2010. It draws on a related longer paper, Viscusi (2010).
3. See Viscusi and Aldy (2003) for a tabulation of the different estimates. To this day, the Thaler–Rosen estimates remain at the very low end of estimated values of the labor market.
4. See Viscusi and Aldy (2007) and Aldy and Viscusi (2007, 2008).
5. My 1982 estimates used in this analysis were just over $3 million per expected life saved.
6. The highest risk levels analyzed in the literature were in early studies that used the risk information from the Society of Actuaries, for which the average annual risk of fatality is 1/1000. These risk values are available by broad occupational group, not also by industry. The large risk value is misleading, however, because the data do not distinguish the occupation-specific risk but rather reflect the overall mortality risk from all causes associated with people in particular occupations. For example, in these data, actors have a particularly high risk.

REFERENCES

Aldy, J.E. and W.K. Viscusi (2007). 'Age differences in the value of statistical life: revealed preference evidence', *Review of Environmental Economics and Policy*, **1** (2), 241–260.

Aldy, J.E. and W.K. Viscusi (2008). 'Adjusting the value of a statistical life for age and cohort effects', *Review of Economics and Statistics*, **90** (3), 573–581.
Covey, J., A. Robinson, M. Jones-Lee and G. Loomes (2010). 'Responsibility, scale, and the valuation of rail safety', *Journal of Risk and Uncertainty*, **40** (1), 85–108.
Dorsey, S. and N. Walzer (1983). 'Workers' compensation, job hazards, and wages', *Industrial and Labor Relations Review*, **36** (4), 642–654.
Hersch, J. and W.K. Viscusi (2010). 'Immigrant status and the value of statistical life', *Journal of Human Resources*, **45** (3), 749–771.
Kniesner, T.J., W.K. Viscusi and J.P. Ziliak (2006). 'Life-cycle consumption and the age-adjusted value of life', *Contributions to Economic Analysis and Policy*, **5** (1), 1–34.
Kniesner, T.J., W.K. Viscusi and J.P. Ziliak (2010). 'Policy relevant heterogeneity in the value of statistical life: new evidence from panel data quantile regressions', *Journal of Risk and Uncertainty*, **40** (1), 15–31.
Leigh, J.P. and R.N. Folsom (1984). 'Estimates of the value of accident avoidance at the job depend on the concavity of the equalizing differences curve', *Quarterly Review of Economics and Business*, **24** (1), 56–66.
Magat, W.A., W.K. Viscusi and J. Huber (1996). 'A reference lottery metric for valuing health', *Management Science*, **42** (8), 1118–1129.
Moore, M.J. and W.K. Viscusi (1988). 'The quantity-adjusted value of life', *Economic Inquiry*, **26** (3), 369–388.
Mrozek, J.R. and L.O. Taylor (2002). 'What determines the value of life? a meta-analysis', *Journal of Policy Analysis and Management*, **21** (2), 253–270.
Olson, C.A. (1981). 'An analysis of wage differentials received by workers on dangerous jobs', *Journal of Human Resources*, **16** (2), 167–185.
Posner, E. and C. Sunstein (2005). 'Dollars and death', *University of Chicago Law Review*, **72** (2), 537–598.
Shepard, D.S. and R.J. Zeckhauser (1984). 'Survival versus consumption', *Management Science*, **30** (4), 423–439.
Thaler, R.H. and S. Rosen (1975). 'The value of saving a life: evidence from the labor market', in N.E. Terleckyj (ed.), *Household Production and Consumption*, New York: Columbia University Press, pp. 265–300.
Van Houtven, G., M.B. Sullivan and C. Dockins (2008). 'Cancer premiums and latency effects: a risk tradeoff approach for valuing reduction', *Journal of Risk and Uncertainty*, **36** (2), 179–200.
Viscusi, W.K. (1978). 'Labor market valuations of life and limb: empirical evidence and policy implications', *Public Policy*, **26** (3), 359–386.
Viscusi, W.K. (1979). *Employment Hazards: An Investigation of Market Performance*, Cambridge, MA: Harvard University Press.
Viscusi, W.K. (1981). 'Occupational safety and health regulation: its impact and policy alternatives', in J.P. Crecine (ed.), *Research in Public Policy Analysis and Management*, Vol. 2, Greenwich, CT: JAI Press, pp. 281–299.
Viscusi, W.K. (1993). 'The value of risks to life and health', *Journal of Economic Literature*, **31** (4), 1912–1946.
Viscusi, W.K. (2003). 'Racial differences in labor market values of a statistical life', *Journal of Risk and Uncertainty*, **27** (3), 239–256.
Viscusi, W.K. (2009). 'Valuing risks of death from terrorism and natural disasters', *Journal of Risk and Uncertainty*, **38** (3), 191–213.

Viscusi, W.K. and J.E. Aldy (2003). 'The value of a statistical life: a critical review of market estimates throughout the world', *Journal of Risk and Uncertainty*, **27** (3), 239–256.

Viscusi, W.K. and J.E. Aldy (2007). 'Labor market estimates of the senior discount for the value of statistical life', *Journal of Environmental Economics and Management*, **53** (3), 377–392.

Viscusi, W.K. and J. Hersch (2001). 'Cigarette smokers as job risk takers', *Review of Economics and Statistics*, **83** (2), 269–280.

Viscusi, W.K., J. Huber and J. Bell (2008). 'Estimating discount rates for environmental quality from utility-based choice experiments', *Journal of Risk and Uncertainty*, **37** (2–3), 199–220.

Viscusi, W.K. and R.J. Zeckhauser (2003). 'Sacrificing civil liberties to reduce terrorism risks', *Journal of Risk and Uncertainty*, **26** (2–3), 99–120.

Viscusi, W.K. and R.J. Zeckhauser (2005). 'Recollection bias and the combat of terrorism', *Journal of Legal Studies*, **34** (1), 27–55.

Viscusi, W.K. and R.J. Zeckhauser (2006). 'National survey evidence on disasters and relief: risk beliefs, self-interest, and compassion', *Journal of Risk and Uncertainty*, **33** (1–2), 13–36.

5. Dealing with safety in UK public sector project appraisal

Michael Jones-Lee

INTRODUCTION

It is an inescapable fact of life that virtually every activity that we undertake carries some risk of death or injury. It is also the case that in most situations risk can be reduced, but only at a cost. That is, safety can usually be improved, but only by using up scarce resources that could otherwise have been devoted to alternative beneficial uses. This means that if society's resources are to be allocated efficiently and to greatest advantage, then in public sector decisions concerning the provision of safety in the form of a public good rather than a marketed product, some means must be found to place a value on safety improvement so that benefits can be compared directly with costs.

But how is the value of safety to be defined and estimated in practice? Until 1988 monetary values for the prevention of fatal and non-fatal injuries used by the UK Department of Transport – which was the first UK public sector agency to employ explicit monetary values of safety in cost–benefit analysis – were derived on the basis of the so-called 'gross output' approach. Under this approach the cost of a premature fatality or non-fatal injury is defined essentially as the loss of current and future output resulting from the victim's death or injury. The value of preventing death or injury is then treated as the cost avoided.

However, it is almost certainly the case that most people value safety principally because of their aversion to the prospect of their own and others' death and injury per se, rather than as a result of their desire to preserve current and future levels of output and income. If this is so, then according to the principles of conventional welfare economics the values of safety should be defined so as to reflect people's 'pure' preferences for safety as such, rather than in terms of effects on output or income as under the gross output approach. But in order to define and estimate values of safety in this way it is clearly necessary to have some means of measuring people's preferences for safety and, more particularly, their strength of preference, and the question is then how this can best be achieved.

Arguably, the most obvious and natural measure of the extent of a person's preference for a good or service is the maximum amount that they would be willing to pay for it. This reflects not only the person's valuation of the good or service relative to other potential objects of expenditure, but also their ability to pay, which is itself a reflection of society's overall resource constraint. Thus, under what has naturally come to be known as the 'willingness to pay' (WTP) approach to the valuation of safety, the aim is first to determine the maximum amounts that those affected would individually be willing to pay for (typically small) improvements in their own and others' safety. These amounts are then simply aggregated – possibly with distributional weights applied – across all individuals to arrive at an overall value for the safety improvement concerned. The resultant value is thus a clear reflection of what the safety improvement is worth to the affected group relative to the alternative ways in which individuals in the group might have spent their limited incomes. It is also worth noting that this way of defining values of safety effectively mimics the operation of market forces in circumstances in which markets typically do not exist, given that such forces can be seen as vehicles which allow individual preferences to interact with relative scarcities and production possibilities in determining the allocation of society's scarce resources.

In order to standardize the values of safety that emerge from the WTP approach and render them comparable with values derived under other approaches (such as gross output), the concept of prevention of a 'statistical' fatality or injury is employed. To illustrate this concept, suppose that a group of 100 000 people enjoy a safety improvement that reduces the probability of premature death by some cause during a forthcoming period by, on average, 1 in 100 000 per person for each and every member of the group. As a result, the expected number of fatalities within the group during the forthcoming period will be reduced by precisely one, and the safety improvement is therefore described as involving the prevention of one statistical fatality.

Now suppose that individuals in the affected group of 100 000 people are, on average, each willing to pay £v for the reduction in the risk of death afforded by the safety improvement. It follows that aggregate willingness to pay will be £v x 100 000 and this figure is therefore naturally referred to as the WTP-based value of statistical life (VSL) for the cause concerned.

Clearly, in the above example average individual willingness to pay for the risk reduction is a reflection of the rate at which people in the affected group are willing to trade-off wealth against risk 'at the margin' in the sense that the trade-offs typically involve small variations in wealth and small variations in risk. Empirical work on the valuation of safety therefore tends to focus on these individual marginal rates of substitution of wealth for risk.

All of this having been said, it is extremely important to appreciate that defined in this way the VSL is not a value (or price) of life in the sense of a sum that the typical individual would accept in compensation for the certain prospect of their premature death; for most of us no finite sum, however large, would suffice for this purpose, so that in this sense life is literally priceless. Rather, the VSL is aggregate willingness to pay for typically very small reductions in individual risk of premature death which, in reality, is what most safety improvements actually provide at the individual level.

Following adoption of the WTP-based approach to the valuation of safety by the Department of Transport in 1988, various other UK public sector and related agencies have since followed suit, so that the WTP approach is now widely used in UK public sector decision-making. In the remainder of this chapter some of the key questions encountered in the practical application of WTP-based values of safety in decision-making in different UK public sector and related agencies will therefore be considered in more detail. In particular, the questions to be addressed will include the following:

- How, in practice, should individual willingness to pay for a safety improvement be aggregated across those affected by the improvement in order to arrive at an overall value? Or equivalently, what constitutes the appropriate central-tendency measure of individual willingness to pay taken over a large group of people?
- How, in practice, should empirical estimates of individual willingness to pay be obtained?
- Should different VSLs be applied in different contexts to reflect differing degrees of dread, baseline risk, control or the possibility of accidents involving large-scale loss of life?
- How can cost–benefit analysis involving WTP-based values of safety best take account of the requirements set by predetermined safety standards and regulations?
- How should safety-related issues such as social disruption or types of environmental damage, for which monetary values are not yet available, be dealt with in the allocative and regulatory decision-making process?
- Should WTP-based values of safety be used in decisions related to potentially catastrophic events such as natural disasters or terrorist attacks? That is, do such values have any direct relevance

for government agencies such as the Environment Agency, Home Office and Ministry of Defence in the UK, or the Department of Homeland Security in the USA?

AGGREGATE WTP AS A MEASURE OF SOCIAL BENEFIT

Given the basic ethical precept that public sector decisions should reflect citizens' preferences, and given economists' mid-twentieth-century 'empiricist' aversion to interpersonal comparisons of utility, it is not surprising that early work on the definition and estimation of WTP-based values of safety tended to rely on the hypothetical compensation test (HCT) as its ethical foundation. Essentially, the HCT specifies that an adjustment to the way in which a society's scarce resources are utilized is justified if those who gain as a result of the adjustment do so to a sufficient extent to be able to compensate those who lose and still remain better off than before the adjustment.

However, some would argue (this author included) that since compensation is rarely, if ever, actually paid to those who lose as a result of an allocative decision, reliance on the HCT as an ethical defence for the application of aggregate WTP-based benefit measures is effectively a philosophical sleight of hand. In fact, it would appear that what is actually being assumed when social values are defined in terms of aggregate WTP is that the marginal social welfare of income (or wealth) is constant. Since many people find that condition morally objectionable, there has therefore been a tendency (at least implicitly) to define values in terms of the distributionally weighted aggregate of individual WTP amounts. This is effectively what happens when the VSL is based on a national average of WTP, with the same value being applied whatever the income level of the subgroup actually affected by a safety improvement. The alternative, suggested recently by the author and others (see Baker et al., 2008) is to replace the 'constant marginal social welfare of income' assumption with the condition that the marginal social welfare of survival probability should be treated as constant. It then transpires that values of safety should be based not on the arithmetic mean of individual WTP, but on the harmonic mean augmented by a premium that reflects the nature of the taxation arrangement that is used to finance the safety improvement concerned. However, and perhaps most significantly, it also turns out that if the safety improvement is financed by a tax that increases with income (or wealth) at roughly the same rate as the individual valuation of safety (as might reasonably be expected to be the case), then the harmonic mean, augmented by the appropriate premium, will differ very little from the arithmetic mean.

HEDONIC PRICING OR CONTINGENT VALUATION?

Viewed from an international perspective, two broad avenues of approach have been applied in the empirical estimation of WTP-based values of safety, namely the 'hedonic pricing' (or revealed preference) approach – typically based on labour market wage risk trade-offs – and the 'contingent valuation' (or stated preference) approach. Both approaches have clear strengths and weaknesses and are, in the author's view, more appropriately seen as complementary rather than competing estimation procedures. However, whereas the hedonic pricing approach has been the principal means of obtaining empirical estimates of the VSL in the USA, the main focus in the UK has been on the stated preference approach. This occurred, at least in part, as a result of the fact that some members of the UK Department of Transport (which was the first UK government agency to commission work aimed at estimating WTP-based values of safety) were initially somewhat sceptical about the ability of members of the public to comprehend the key concepts underpinning WTP-based values and, as a result, pressed for a direct investigation of the public's understanding via direct questioning in a sample survey-based study.

In comparing the two approaches it must be said that the obvious advantage of the hedonic pricing approach is that it is based on actual rather than hypothetical choices. However, the approach presupposes that workers are well informed about job risks and that market forces, rather than union pressure, are the main determinant of wage rates. The approach also requires the application of fairly complex statistical procedures to disentangle the wage–risk trade-off from the many other factors that are likely to influence wage rates, such as job skills, job location, unionization, industrial context and so on. In addition, the hedonic pricing approach would appear to be incapable of providing any information concerning the rates at which those employed in 'safe' occupations (such as lawyers or teachers) or, indeed, those not in paid employment (such as housewives/husbands), are willing to trade income or wealth for risk.

In the case of the stated preference approach, its great advantages are that it allows the researcher to focus on the wealth–risk trade-off directly; to ensure that the sample on which the analysis is based is adequately representative of the population as a whole; and to deal with a wide variety of different types of risk, rather than just those arising in a labour market context. The disadvantages of the approach are, however, equally obvious and include the fact that it is inevitably dealing with hypothetical rather than actual choices; that it presupposes that respondents understand the questions that are being put to them; and that they will provide truthful and carefully considered answers.

Indeed, one of the most serious limitations of the stated preference approach when applied to the valuation of safety is almost certainly a consequence of respondents' limited understanding of the questions and their resultant provision of spontaneous responses that are insufficiently carefully thought out. This typically takes the form of what is referred to as 'scope insensitivity' and occurs when a respondent either gives exactly the same WTP for two different risk reductions or gives amounts that do not differ to the extent that might reasonably be expected.

In fact, one of the earliest and starkest examples of scope insensitivity in response to WTP questions related to safety improvement is embodied in the results of a UK national sample survey carried out in 1982 and reported in Jones-Lee et al. (1985) and Jones-Lee (1989). In particular, in a representative sample of over 1000 respondents, roughly 35 per cent of the sample gave the same non-zero WTP for a reduction of 5 in 100 000 in the annual risk of being killed in an automobile accident as for a 2 in 100 000 reduction. In addition, the sample mean response for the larger risk reduction was less than 50 per cent more than the mean response for the smaller risk reduction, rather than being, as one might reasonably have expected, in the region of double that figure.

Various approaches have been adopted in an attempt to mitigate the problems associated with the stated preference approach to estimating WTP-based values of safety. For example, in a number of studies carried out by the author and colleagues it has been found that the most effective way in which to communicate the concept of, for example, an *n* in 100 000 risk is by showing the respondent a piece of graph paper (or grid) with *n* out of 100 000 squares blacked out. As far as the elicitation of truthful and carefully thought-out responses is concerned, it has been found to be most effective, prior to asking willingness to pay or other types of preference-elicitation questions, to provide respondents with a clear and careful explanation of why such questions are being put to them and the importance of providing reliable and carefully considered answers. In particular, emphasis is placed on the fact that the aim of the survey is to provide the government agency concerned with a clear indication of the nature and strength of the public's preferences and attitudes so that the agency can take full account of these in its allocative and regulatory decision-making. It has also been found to be useful, once a respondent has answered the various WTP questions, to draw their attention to any apparent anomalies or inconsistencies and to ask for confirmation and/or a brief explanation of the response concerned. For these reasons, and in order to ensure that the respondent is actually giving careful thought to the questions being asked, in the author's experience it has generally proved to be more effective to conduct interviews on a face-to-face basis, rather than over the Internet or by post, though it has to be admitted that there have been some surprising exceptions; see, for example, Covey et al. (2010).

In addition to these procedural adjustments to the methods of preference elicitation, more fundamental conceptual developments have also been undertaken. In particular, the UK Department for Transport's current WTP-based VSL was estimated using the so-called 'chained approach' under which respondents are not required to make a direct trade-off between wealth and risk of death, but are instead asked first about their willingness to pay for the certainty of a complete and quick cure for a non-fatal injury of lesser severity, and their willingness to accept compensation for the certainty of suffering the injury. From these 'certainty' responses it is then possible, on the basis of plausible assumptions, to derive an estimate of the respondent's willingness to trade-off wealth against the risk of suffering the non-fatal injury. By establishing the respondent's willingness to trade-off risk of the injury against risk of death via an appropriately framed 'standard gamble' question, it is then possible to estimate their willingness to trade-off wealth against risk of death by chaining together the wealth–risk of injury and risk of injury–risk of death trade-off rates. For a more detailed account of this approach, see Carthy et al. (1998).

Another possible approach aimed at dealing with limited scope sensitivity (on which the author is currently working) relies on recognition of the fact that an individual's WTP will increase strictly in proportion to the magnitude of risk reduction only if their underlying utility of wealth function is linear. If, as seems very much more likely to be the case, the utility of wealth function is strictly concave, then theory indicates quite clearly that WTP will also be a strictly concave function of risk reduction. In fact, it then turns out that any degree of scope insensitivity, other than complete insensitivity, can be accommodated by appropriate specification of the key underlying parameters of the utility of wealth function. For example, assuming that the utility of wealth function conditional on survival takes the homogeneous form, then it turns out that an individual whose WTP response for a 1 in 100000 reduction in the risk of immediate death is, say, £10 and whose WTP response for a 1 in 1000 reduction is only £20 would in fact have a marginal rate of substitution of wealth for risk of immediate death of £1.98 million. Thus, whereas the standard reaction to responses such as those specified in this example would be to regard them as displaying a high degree of scope insensitivity, thereby raising serious doubts about their credibility and reliability, the new procedure is quite capable of accommodating them as perfectly rational responses from someone with highly non-linear but basically conventional preferences. However, it must be admitted that this approach appears to be subject to two potentially serious limitations. In the first place, while in principle it can accommodate any degree of non-zero scope sensitivity even if this is very limited, it cannot deal with complete insensitivity, that is, a situation in which a respondent reports precisely the same willingness to pay for two different risk reductions. In addition, it is important to appreciate that the magnitude of the estimated values of safety produced by this approach is highly sensitive to the degree of scope sensitivity actually displayed by a respondent.

DIFFERENT VSLS FOR DIFFERENT CAUSES AND DIFFERENT CONTEXTS?

There is, by now, extensive empirical evidence confirming the intuitively plausible hypothesis that for most people the prospect of premature death by some causes is viewed with a considerably greater degree of fear or 'dread' than others (see, e.g., Slovic et al., 1981). Thus for many people the prospect of dying in a fire while trapped in a public building, or as the result of cancer, is regarded as being considerably worse than sudden death in a road accident or dying while asleep. Not surprisingly, therefore, many have argued that the VSL for more highly dreaded causes can be expected to stand at a significant premium in relation to the corresponding figure for less fearsome cases; see, for example, Sunstein (1997). However, recent work by the author and others suggests that although some causes of premature death are indeed considerably more highly dreaded than others, in most cases dread effects are to all intents and purposes largely offset by the impact of baseline risk, in that more highly dreaded causes typically present lower levels of baseline risk for the majority of people.

More specifically, in the analysis reported in Chilton et al. (2006) the 'dread effect' for a given cause B relative to the 'reference' cause A (chosen to be a pedestrian fatality) was defined as the respondent's indifference 'risk–risk' ratio for A relative to B, with baseline risk and cause clearly identified for both A and B, divided by the corresponding ratio with only the baselines risk (and not cause) for A and B being specified. The overall dread effect for the sample as a whole was then computed as the geometric mean of individual dread effects. In the event, the dread effect for an automobile driver or passenger fatality (relative to a pedestrian fatality) was 1.54:1; for death in fire in a public place 5.80:1; and for death in a rail accident 8.65:1. However, in a separate study the arithmetic mean WTP-based VSL for fire in a public place relative to the figure for an automobile driver or passenger fatality was only 0.96:1, while that for rail accident fatality relative to automobile driver or passenger fatality was 1.003:1; see Chilton et al. (2002) for the post-Ladbroke Grove rail accident follow-up study results. Given that for most people in the UK the risks of dying in a fire in a public place or in a rail accident are both less than 5 per cent of the risk of being killed in an automobile accident, it would seem that in these cases the effect of dread was, to all intents and purposes, completely offset by the influence of baseline risk.

Thus, it would appear that for the more common situations involving immediate death – rather than cases involving protracted periods of pain and suffering prior to death (such as heart disease or cancer) – there is a fairly powerful argument in favour of applying a common VSL. In light of this, those UK public sector and related agencies that employ WTP-based VSLs have recently elected to use a common value (at least for causes of immediate death) equal to the roads figure that the Department of Transport originally adopted in 1988 to replace its earlier 'gross output'-based value.

There was, however, one notable exception. In particular, although the rail industry chose to employ the roads VSL in the case of single-fatality rail accidents, it applied a figure roughly three times as large in the valuation of safety projects aimed at preventing multiple-fatality accidents. Furthermore, until relatively recently the UK's principal safety regulatory agency, the Health and Safety Executive (HSE), argued in favour of placing a premium on the prevention of multiple-fatality accidents, claiming that 'society has a greater aversion to an accident killing 10 people than to 10 accidents killing one person each' (HSE, 2001). Indeed some people have argued – and the HSE appeared to endorse the position, at least in the early 2000s (see, e.g., Hirst and Carter, 2002) – that the value of preventing an accident involving n fatalities should be an increasing, strictly convex function of n, or more specifically, proportional to n^a with $a > 1$; see, for example, Okrent (1981).

But in spite of this widely held position concerning the value of preventing multiple-fatality accidents, evidence from each of four separate studies conducted by the author and others over a period of more than ten years appears to run counter to the 'differential valuation' position (see Jones-Lee and Loomes, 1995; Chilton et al., 2002; Covey et al., 2010). In particular, in all four studies results clearly indicate that a majority of respondents did not believe that the prevention of a given number of fatalities in a multiple-fatality accident of the type that might occur on, say, the railways should be accorded a higher value than prevention of the same number of fatalities in separate single-fatality accidents. In light of this and in response to political pressure from those who argued against the application of a scale premium to the VSL, the UK rail industry has recently revised its position and now applies a single VSL in assessing all rail safety projects. In addition, the HSE now recommends using a single VSL in all cases except cancer risks, for which a figure equal to twice the standard VSL is currently applied.

However, as a result of concerns about the appropriateness of the 'cancer premium', the HSE has recently commissioned research (to be carried out by the author and a colleague) to review the matter. The first phase of this research project, which was completed in October 2010, was largely exploratory and aimed simply at examining the extent to which theory and existing empirical evidence might shed light on the extent to which the 'latency' delay associated with work-related cancer risks might be expected to offset the high degree of dread with which many people view the prospect of cancer. In particular, work to date has indicated that even though the effects of baseline risk and dread can certainly be expected to drive the VSL for cancer risks to a level that is significantly higher than that for, say, road risks, the latency period for work-related cancer risks (which typically involves a delay of several years before the adverse health effects resulting from exposure to carcinogenic conditions actually materialize) appears to work in the opposite direction; see, for example, Cropper et al. (1994) or Hammitt and Liu (2004). Indeed, preliminary work drawing on the multiperiod theoretical framework set out in Jones-Lee (1989), and empirical evidence concerning the VSL–age relationship, suggests that in the case of work-related cancer risks the latency effect will effectively cancel out the baseline risk/dread effect, at least for a latency period in excess of ten years, as is apparently typically the case for work-related cancer risks.

All things considered, therefore – and contrary to what most economists (including the author) expected would be the case when work started on the empirical estimation of the VSL for different causes of premature death – there would appear to be reasonable grounds for applying a more or less common VSL to virtually all causes of death and all contexts that might be expected to feature in public sector safety decisions. However, as noted below, it is as yet not clear whether this would be justifiable in the case of decisions aimed at reducing the risk of a catastrophic accident caused by a natural disaster or terrorist attack.

VALUATION OF SAFETY IN UK PUBLIC SECTOR DECISION-MAKING

Health and Safety Executive

In enforcing the Health and Safety at Work Act 1974 (HSWA), the Management of Health and Safety at Work Regulations 1992 (MHSW) and the Railways (Safety Case) Regulations 1994, the UK HSE imposes an upper bound on the fatality risk to which members of the public and those in the workplace may be exposed. In particular, in specifying its 'tolerability of risk' (TOR) framework (which it has applied since the 1980s), the HSE sets an upper bound above which fatality risks are regarded as being unacceptable or 'intolerable' and, save in exceptional circumstances, must be reduced whatever the cost, even if this means discontinuing the activity giving rise to the risk.

Although in its most recent publications the HSE does not give a precise specification of the level at which the upper bound should be set (HSE, 1999), there are indications that, broadly speaking, the HSE continues to endorse its earlier recommendation that for fatality risks the upper bound should be 1 in 10 000 per annum for individual members of the public, and 1 in 1000 per annum for workplace risks (HSE, 1992, paras 169–175; HSE, 1999, paras 117–121).

But the application of safety standards per se still leaves open the question of what decision-makers are expected to do before the HSE upper bound is reached. In fact the answer is provided by the TOR regulatory framework itself. Thus, in addition to setting an upper bound on tolerable risk, the so-called 'TOR Triangle' also involves a lower bound below which risks are treated as being 'broadly acceptable' and are generally regarded as being insignificant (this is treated as being in the region of one in a million per annum). But this then leads on to what is, from a practical point of view, arguably the most significant feature of the TOR framework, namely the stipulation that, between the upper and lower bounds of the TOR Triangle, risks are viewed as being 'tolerable' provided that they have been reduced to levels that are 'as low as reasonably practicable' (ALARP) or equivalently 'so far as is reasonably practicable' (SFAIRP).

As far as 'reasonable practicability' is concerned, the courts have ruled that this term should be interpreted as requiring that a safety improvement must be undertaken provided that the costs of implementing the improvement are not disproportionate to the resultant risk reduction. Thus, in the Court of Appeal in *Edwards v National Coal Board (1949) IKB 704*, Lord Justice Asquith's judgment was to the effect that:

> 'Reasonably practicable' is a narrower term than 'physically possible' and seems to me to imply that a computation must be made by the owner, in which the quantum of risk is placed on one scale and the sacrifice involved in the measures necessary for averting the risk (whether in money, time or trouble) is placed on the other; and that if it be shown that there is a gross disproportion between them – the risk being insignificant in relation to the sacrifice – the Defendants discharge the onus on them.

The issue of reasonable practicability was also considered by the House of Lords in *Marshall v Gotham Co Ltd (1954) AC 360*, the headnote of which states:

> The test of what is (reasonably practicable) is not simply what is practicable as a matter of engineering, but what depends on the consideration, in the light of the whole circumstances at the time of the accident, whether the time, trouble and expense of the precautions suggested are not disproportionate to the risk involved, and also an assessment of the degree of security which the measures suggested may be expected to afford.

Although these two rulings clearly indicate that in reaching a decision concerning 'reasonable practicability' it is appropriate to weigh the costs of implementing a risk reduction against the resultant benefits, the fact that the first judgment refers to 'gross disproportion', while the second stipulates only that costs should not be 'disproportionate' to the risk reduction, has – perhaps not surprisingly – raised serious questions that are essentially unresolved. Thus, in its document *Reducing Risks, Protecting People* (R2P2; HSE, 1999, p. 73), the HSE focuses on the 1949 *Edwards v National Coal Board* 'gross disproportion' judgment and stipulates that 'when weighing risks against costs . . . at least, there is a need to err on the side of safety in the computation of safety costs and benefits', and in a more recent document (HSE, 2001) that:

> we believe that the greater the risk, the more that should be spent in reducing it, and the greater the bias on the side of safety. This can be represented by a 'proportion factor', indicating the maximum level of sacrifice that can be borne without it being judged 'grossly disproportionate'.
>
> Although there is no authoritative case law which considers the question, we believe it is right that the greater the risk, the higher the proportion may be before being considered 'gross'. But disproportion must always be gross.

Similarly, the Rail Safety and Standards Board (2007) notes that:

> HMRI guidance on ALARP for its inspectors [Section 3.2] stated that 'factors of disproportion' should be applied to the VPF to introduce an imbalance between costs and risks. The factors were:

(i) low baseline individual risk and no societal risk, disproportion factor 1–2
(ii) low baseline individual risk and societal risk applies, disproportion factor 3
(iii) high baseline individual risk, disproportion factor 3–10 depending on the level of individual risk.

In connection with the HMRI guidance, it should be noted that the term 'societal risk' – or as it is now more commonly referred to in UK public sector safety documents, 'societal concern' – is intended to capture the wider issues related to public safety, such as social disruption, the impact on public anxiety and the possibility of large-scale loss of life.

In spite of all this, several recent reports call into question the appropriateness of the 'gross disproportion' interpretation of the ALARP condition; see for example RSSB (2005) or House of Lords Select Committee on Economic Affairs (House of Lords, 2006). In particular, what does 'gross disproportion' really mean? Admittedly in the case of the rail industry, as noted above, the HMRI guidance provides a broad indication, but in practice this offers little more than a rough rule of thumb. And how are decision-makers to proceed in other contexts? But arguably the fundamental issue is that even if, as in the case of the HMRI guidance, the disproportion factor is actually quantified, what defence is there for setting it at any level greater than one, given that the ethical principles underpinning standard social cost–benefit analysis will recommend adoption of a project only if its benefits (appropriately defined) exceed its costs?

Given all of this, it seems fair to say that the current weight of opinion in the UK seems to be in favour of basing safety policy on the more specific and less extreme 'disproportion' (rather than 'gross disproportion') interpretation of the ALARP condition, with this requirement being treated as equivalent to the standard cost–benefit criterion. Indeed, in some of its recent publications, the HSE itself recommends the application of what would appear to be standard cost–benefit analysis. For example, in its document *The Tolerability of Risk from Nuclear Power Stations*, the HSE states that: 'in pursuing any further safety improvements to demonstrate ALARP account can be taken of cost. It is in principle possible to apply formal cost–benefit techniques to assist in making decisions of this kind' (HSE, 1992, para 35), and in its more recent publication, *Reducing Risks, Protecting People*, that 'cost–benefit analysis (CBA) offers a framework for balancing the benefits of reducing risk against the costs incurred in a particular option for managing risks' (HSE, 1999, Annex 3, para 8).

Furthermore, in *Managing Risks to the Public: Appraisal Guidance*, HM Treasury argues that in relation to decisions affecting health and safety, 'Once a range of options has been created, they should be assessed by estimating their costs and benefits, and/or by their cost effectiveness' (HM Treasury, 2005, para 4.1).

In view of all this, it is therefore not surprising that the techniques of social cost–benefit analysis, cost-effectiveness analysis and, more recently, decision theory have come to feature centrally in the public and private sector safety decision-making process.

All of this having been said, as argued below in the section 'Dealing with the Consequences of Public Sector Safety Decisions for Which Monetary Costs and Values are Not Available', few (if any) advocates of the use of cost–benefit analysis in UK public sector decision-making would regard the results of cost–benefit analysis as the sole criterion by which to judge the desirability of undertaking a safety project, and would recommend that a variety of other factors currently not quantifiable in monetary terms may need to be weighed in the decision-making process. As such, it might reasonably be argued that the standard position does, after all, lie closer to the 'gross disproportion' end of the spectrum of possible interpretations of the ALARP condition.

Department for Transport

The Department for Transport – originally referred to as the Department of Transport – was the first UK public sector agency to employ a WTP-based VSL. In fact the department had, since the 1950s, employed output-based values for the prevention of fatal and non-fatal injuries in its appraisal of proposed road safety projects, but in the late 1970s it was persuaded to commission a pilot study to assess the feasibility of conducting a questionnaire-based national sample survey to estimate a WTP-based VSL for road safety project appraisal. The results of the pilot study are reported in Hammerton et al. (1982). In light of the findings of the pilot study, which were in the main encouraging, the Department of Transport then commissioned a full-scale contingent valuation study based on a national sample survey, which was carried out in June–July 1982 by National Opinion Polls Ltd (NOP). The results of the main study are reported in Jones-Lee et al. (1985).

Given that the results of the 1982 study pointed towards a VSL based on mean WTP in excess of £1 million and on the median in the region of £500 000, and given that the Department of Transport's gross output-based figure at that time was well below £200 000 (although it had been subject to an upward revision to £286 000 pending a review of the valuation procedure), there was an understandable reluctance to move too rapidly to a change from the gross output to the WTP methodology. Nonetheless, following an extensive review of the then existing literature (see Dalvi, 1988), and in light of the findings of the 1982 study, the Department of Transport finally abandoned the gross output approach in 1988 and adopted a WTP-based VSL at the lower end of the range of estimates: £500 000 in 1987 prices.

This figure was then updated annually in line with inflation and growth of gross domestic product (GDP) per capita until its revision (involving an increase of about 10 per cent) in 1999 following a sample survey carried out as part of a study jointly commissioned by the HSE, the Department of the Environment, Transport and the Regions (DETR), the Home Office and HM Treasury, using the so-called 'chained approach' (see Carthy et al., 1998) which, as noted above, was designed to break the wealth–risk trade-off down into a number of simpler and more manageable steps than are inevitably involved in questions asking directly for a respondent's WTP for a given reduction in the risk of premature death. This figure, together with WTP-based values for the prevention of non-fatal road injuries estimated in a stated preference study carried out in 1991 (see Jones-Lee et al., 1995), has been updated in line with inflation and growth of GDP per capita and currently stands at roughly £1.6 million in 2009 prices, although the Department for Transport has recently commissioned a study to be carried out by the author and colleagues to review all of its values of safety.

The Rail Safety and Standards Board (RSSB)

In the UK, although the train operators are private sector companies, the rail system itself (including railway lines, signalling systems and stations) is essentially a public sector agency, known as Network Rail, having been nationalized a few years ago. In spite of this diversity of ownership and management, safety for the railway system as a whole, including lines and trains, is overseen by the RSSB under the ultimate regulatory authority of the Office of Rail Regulation (ORR) and, until 2006, by Her Majesty's Railway Inspectorate (HMRI).

Essentially, the RSSB operates according to the ALARP criterion, applying standard cost–benefit analysis in the assessment of all safety improvements, subject to the HSE's upper bound on 'tolerable' risks. As noted earlier, until recently, the RSSB employed two distinct VSLs: one equal to the Department for Transport figure for single-fatality accidents, and the other equal to roughly three times the Department for Transport figure for situations involving the possibility of a multiple-fatality accident. However, in light of political pressure and the findings of work carried out by the author and others that indicated that members of the public do not, in the main, endorse the prioritization of the prevention of large-scale rail accidents relative to the prevention of small-scale accidents involving the same number of fatalities, the RSSB recently abandoned its higher 'multiple-fatality' VSL and now applies the Department for Transport figure in all cases.

However, it is perhaps also worth noting that since the majority of rail fatalities in the UK are in fact trespassers, suicides or others behaving illegally or irresponsibly, the RSSB recently commissioned research to be carried out by the author and others to investigate the public's attitude to the appropriateness, or otherwise, of applying the same VSL in the appraisal of projects aimed at preventing such fatalities as is applied in the case of passengers or others who are behaving responsibly and in accordance with the law. In the event, the results of this research indicated that if account is taken of public opinion, the implied VSL for the case of adults behaving illegally or irresponsibly should be set at about 50 per cent of the 'standard' figure, though this discount did not apply in the case of children (see Covey et al., 2010). However, partly as a result of doubts concerning the appropriateness of applying such discounts from a legal point of view, the RSSB has decided to take the conservative approach of maintaining a common VSL in all cases.

Department for Environment, Food and Rural Affairs (Defra)

Given that the principal adverse health impacts of air pollution are reductions in life expectancy and the exacerbation of respiratory and cardiovascular disorders, in 1999 the UK agency responsible for environmental protection (then the Department of the Environment, Transport and the Regions, DETR; now Defra) commissioned a study to be carried out by the author and colleagues to estimate WTP-based values for the prevention of these adverse health effects. In the event the study, carried out in late 2002 to early 2003, was based on a nationally representative sample survey that produced just over 500 useable interviews. On the basis of responses to direct WTP questions concerning gains in life expectancy of one month, three months and six months, the value of a life year (VOLY) was estimated to be approximately £30 000 in 2003 prices, and this is the value, appropriately updated for inflation and growth in GDP per capita, that Defra currently applies. As noted below, this figure is broadly in line with the VOLY used in the UK health sector, which was itself derived directly from the Department for Transport VSL.

The National Institute for Health and Clinical Excellence (NICE)

In the UK the decision about whether a medical treatment or drug is sufficiently cost-effective to be provided free of charge to the patient by the

National Health Service ultimately rests with NICE. In reaching such decisions, NICE has specified the VOLY in such a way that the cost of providing a patient with a treatment that generates a health improvement equivalent to a one-year gain in life expectancy in full health must be less than or equal to the VOLY in order to qualify for approval. In fact NICE determined the level at which to set the VOLY that would apply in this decision-making process simply by dividing the Department for Transport VSL by average remaining life expectancy in the UK (about 40 years), thereby obtaining a figure in the region of £40 000 in current prices.

The initial response to this way of obtaining an estimate of the VOLY was somewhat sceptical, given that it appears, prima facie, to rely on the assumption that the value that the typical individual places on continued survival is simply the sum of equally valued future life years, which is clearly of somewhat doubtful validity. However, research by the author and others (see Mason et al., 2008) has shown that if a gain in life expectancy is generated by a reduction in the risk of death that applies only in the current period, then aggregate WTP over a large group of individuals will in fact be closely approximated by the VSL for that group divided by the mean remaining life expectancy within the group. By contrast, the same model (which is based on the standard expected utility maximization assumptions) implies that if the gain in life expectancy is instead generated by a proportionate reduction in hazard rates over the whole of each affected individual's remaining lifetime (as is currently believed to be the principal result of a reduction in air pollution), then the VOLY is given by the mean, over the age range of the affected group of individuals, of the rate at which the VSL increases with life expectancy. Clearly if, as would appear to be the case, the VSL is an increasing but strictly concave function of remaining life expectancy, then the VOLY defined in this way will be strictly less than the corresponding figure obtained by dividing the VSL by mean remaining life expectancy, as is the case with the NICE figure.

DEALING WITH THE CONSEQUENCES OF PUBLIC SECTOR SAFETY DECISIONS FOR WHICH MONETARY COSTS AND VALUES ARE NOT AVAILABLE

Few, if any, of those who advocate the use of cost–benefit analysis in public sector project appraisal would regard the results of such analysis as constituting the sole criterion by which the desirability or otherwise of undertaking a safety project should be judged. Rather, there may be a variety of wider societal issues for which monetary costs and values are not available, but which nonetheless need to be weighed in the decision-making process and will therefore require the application of well-informed and balanced judgement. Examples of such issues are the possibility of social disruption following a major accident, or the adverse environmental impact of traffic routes designed to relieve congestion and reduce accident rates.

In the UK, so-called 'multi-criteria decision analysis' (MCDA) is being increasingly used in parallel with cost–benefit analysis as a means of dealing with such judgemental issues in the decision-making process (see, e.g., Phillips and Stock, 2003; Morton and Fasolo, 2009). Essentially, MCDA aims to assist the decision-maker, or decision-making panel, to reach a decision concerning the appropriate way in which to achieve a given set of objectives in a well-informed, structured and consistent manner. In order to do this, the MCDA process first requires the decision-making panel (typically with the assistance of MCDA advisors) to establish a 'value tree' that specifies:

- the objectives that the panel wishes to achieve;
- the options available to meet those objectives; and
- the characteristics or attributes of the options that the panel considers to be the criteria relevant to an assessment of the effectiveness of the options in meeting the objectives.

For each available option the decision-making panel is then required to score or 'value' each of the criteria on a scale from 0 to 100 in terms of the degree or extent to which the characteristic or attribute associated with that criterion is provided by the option concerned. The panel is then required to assign a weight to each criterion to reflect its relative importance in meeting the panel's objectives. This weighting task – which is typically viewed as the most demanding aspect of the MCDA process – is usually undertaken in one of three ways:

- Simply by making a judgement concerning relative importance.
- 'Swing weighting', which involves comparing and quantifying the relative value of a move from a score of 0 to a score of 100 on each of the various relevant criteria.
- 'Trade-off weighting', which requires the panel to determine the score, x, such that a swing from a score of 0 to a score of x on the criterion judged to be the most important is regarded as being equally desirable as a swing from 0 to 100 on the criterion concerned.

The final stage in the MCDA process then involves computing a weighted sum of the scores of the criteria for each of the different options available, with the option having the highest weighted sum of scores being regarded as the most desirable. Notice that in this process an 'undesirable' criterion such as cost would be scored so that the least costly option was awarded a score of 100 and the most costly a score of 0.

DECISIONS RELATED TO POTENTIALLY CATASTROPHIC EVENTS AND NATIONAL SECURITY

In the UK the government agencies principally responsible for safety decisions related to potentially catastrophic events are the Health and Safety Executive (for industrial and nuclear accidents), the Home Office (for crime), Defra and the Environment Agency (for natural disasters and floods) and, in the case of terrorist attacks, the Ministry of Defence. In the USA the corresponding agencies clearly include the Environmental Protection Agency and the Department of Homeland Security.

While it is certainly the case that in the UK these agencies rely to some extent on formal analytical procedures including MCDA and cost–benefit analysis in their allocative and regulatory decision-making, and in some cases also apply WTP-based values of safety, it seems equally clear that in the case of hazards that could result in potentially catastrophic consequences involving extensive loss of life, material damage and social disruption, it will inevitably be necessary to proceed along the lines suggested by the precautionary principle and rely to some degree on informed and balanced judgement, as well as formal analytical procedures. In addition, it seems likely that some of the more challenging questions faced by these agencies will relate to specification of the nature of the possible adverse consequences of a potentially catastrophic event and their likelihood of occurrence.

Thus, while clearly specified values for the prevention of death and injury will no doubt constitute useful inputs to the decision-making process, it seems unlikely that they will shed a great deal of light on some of the more difficult questions faced by the government agencies concerned. It is perhaps also worth noting that, at least in the UK, empirical evidence concerning the public's attitude to accidents involving large-scale loss of life is, thus far, essentially limited to cases in which the number of fatalities is considerably smaller than that which might be expected to result from a major catastrophe of the type that occurred in the 9/11 attacks in the USA, or in the recent Japanese earthquake and tsunami. So while there are clear indications that as far as the UK public is concerned the prevention of, say, 30 fatalities in a multiple-fatality rail accident should be accorded roughly the same value as the prevention of 30 statistical fatalities in separate single-fatality accidents, at present little if anything is known about the UK public's relative valuation in the case of a catastrophic accident that could result in hundreds or even thousands of fatalities.

MAIN CONCLUSIONS

The main conclusions arising from the discussion presented in this chapter are as follows:

- Even if the hypothetical compensation test (or, equivalently, the assumption of constant marginal social welfare of wealth or income) is abandoned as the ethical basis of the social cost–benefit analysis of safety and replaced by the 'constant marginal social welfare of survival probability' condition, the VSL will still be well approximated by the population mean marginal rate of substitution of wealth for risk of death, provided that a safety improvement is financed by taxes that have roughly the same income elasticity as the individual valuation of safety.
- In spite of very substantial differences in dread, baseline risk and latency effects of premature death across different contexts, UK evidence suggests that in virtually all cases so far considered, these effects are to all intents and purposes largely offsetting, thereby justifying the application of a 'common' VSL across all contexts, including roads, rail, fires in public places, work-related cancer and so on.
- There is by now extensive empirical evidence indicating that as far as members of the UK public are concerned, there is no ethical justification for setting the VSL applied to the prevention of a fatality in a multiple-fatality accident of the type that might occur on, say, the railways at a premium in relation to the figure used in the single-fatality case.
- Although the results of a cost–benefit analysis are undoubtedly treated as an important input in public sector allocative decision-making in the UK, they are certainly not regarded as being the sole determinant of whether a particular project should be undertaken, particularly in the case of investment decisions aimed at safety improvement. Instead, factors such as potential social disruption, inconvenience and the possible impact on the public's choice of transport mode will typically also be weighed in the decision-making

process. In particular, during recent years, multi-criteria decision analysis has also been increasingly used alongside cost–benefit analysis in the decision-making process as a means of encouraging the careful and balanced weighing of factors that, as yet, have not been quantified in monetary terms and therefore cannot be entered directly in cost–benefit analysis.

- While empirical evidence concerning the UK public's preferences and attitudes would appear to provide a fairly persuasive case in favour of applying a common VSL in assessing the benefits of preventing single- and multiple-fatality accidents of the type that might occur on the railways, there is as yet no corresponding evidence concerning the UK public's attitude to the prevention of loss of life on the sort of scale that might occur in a major catastrophe.

With reference to the last point, it is perhaps worth noting that in contrast to the situation in the UK, work carried out so far in the USA does provide some insights into the question of the appropriate magnitude of the VSL to apply in the case of potentially catastrophic events. In particular, the results of a stated preference study using person trade-off questions reported in Viscusi (2009) indicate that while respondents placed roughly the same value on the prevention of a fatality in a terrorist attack as in the case of a single-fatality traffic accident, in the case of natural disasters the value was only about half the traffic figure. It should, however, be noted that the maximum level that the number of fatalities was allowed to reach in the person trade-off questions was 250, so that one is bound to wonder whether similar conclusions would have emerged if the scale of loss of life in the trade-off questions had been allowed to rise to substantially higher levels in the case of a natural disaster or terrorist attack.

Another stated preference study, reported in Smith et al. (2009), suggests that members of the US public would be prepared to contribute substantial amounts – via federal income taxes or gasoline prices – to reduce the risk of terrorist attacks on commercial aircraft, though the study does not provide explicit estimates of the implied VSL.

Finally, further insights into the question of relative valuation in the USA are also provided in Robinson et al. (2010). While the argument presented contains no new empirical evidence and is based entirely on further analysis of existing data, it does suggest that there are grounds for believing that when a more substantial body of empirical evidence becomes available, this may well point towards a VSL for catastrophic events that substantially exceeds the figures currently being used for more 'everyday' cases.

It would therefore appear to be a matter of some importance for both the UK and USA that empirical research is set in motion as soon as possible with a view to shedding further light on the public's attitude to the prevention of loss of life on the sort of scale that might be expected to occur in a major catastrophe.

REFERENCES

Baker, R., S. Chilton, M. Jones-Lee and H. Metcalf (2008). 'Valuing lives equally: defensible premise or unwarranted compromise?' *Journal of Risk and Uncertainty*, **36**, 25–138.

Carthy, T., S. Chilton, J. Covey, L. Hopkins, M. Jones-Lee, G. Loomes, N. Pidgeon and A. Spencer (1998). 'On the contingent valuation of safety and the safety of contingent valuation: Part 2 – the CV/SG "chained" approach', *Journal of Risk and Uncertainty*, **17** (3), 187–213.

Chilton, S., J. Covey, L. Hopkins, M. Jones-Lee, G. Loomes, N. Pidgeon and A. Spencer (2002). 'Public perceptions of risk and preference-based values of safety', *Journal of Risk and Uncertainty*, **25** (3), 211–232.

Chilton, S., M. Jones-Lee, F. Kiraly, H. Metcalf and W. Pang (2006). 'Dread risks', *Journal of Risk and Uncertainty*, **33**, 165–182.

Covey, J., A. Robinson, M. Jones-Lee and G. Loomes (2010). 'Responsibility, scale and the valuation of rail safety', *Journal of Risk and Uncertainty*, **40**, 85–108.

Cropper, M., S.K. Aydede and P.R. Portney (1994). 'Preferences for life-saving programs: how the public discounts time and age', *Journal of Risk and Uncertainty*, **8**, 243–265.

Dalvi, M.Q. (1988). *The Value of Life and Safety: A Search for a Consensus Estimate*, London: Department of Transport.

Hammerton, M., M.W. Jones-Lee and V. Abbott (1982). 'The consistency and coherence of attitudes to physical risk', *Journal of Transport Economics and Policy*, **16**, 181–199.

Hammitt, J.K. and J-T. Liu (2004). 'Effects of disease type and latency on the value of mortality risk', *Journal of Risk and Uncertainty*, **28** (1), 73–95.

Health and Safety Executive (HSE) (1992). *The Tolerability of Risk from Nuclear Power Stations*, London: HMSO.

Health and Safety Executive (HSE) (1999). *Reducing Risks, Protecting People*, London: Health and Safety Executive.

Health and Safety Executive (HSE) (2001). *Principles and Guidelines to Assist HSE in its Judgements that Duty-holders Have Reduced Risk as Low as Reasonably Practicable*, London: Health and Safety Executive.

Hirst, I.L. and D.A. Carter (2002). 'A "worst case" methodology for obtaining a rough but rapid indication of the societal risk from a major accident hazard installation', *Journal of Hazardous Materials*, **A92**, 223–237.

HM Treasury (2005). *Managing Risks to the Public: Appraisal Guidance*, London: HM Treasury.

House of Lords (2006). *Government Policy on the Management of Risk*, London: Stationery Office.

Jones-Lee, M.W. (1989). *The Economics of Safety and Physical Risk*, Oxford: Basil Blackwell.

Jones-Lee, M.W. and G. Loomes (1995). 'Scale and context effects in the valuation of transport safety', *Journal of Risk and Uncertainty*, **11**, 183–203.

Jones-Lee, M.W., M. Hammerton and P.R. Philips (1985). 'The value of safety: results of a national sample survey', *Economic Journal*, **95**, 49–72.

Jones-Lee, M.W., G. Loomes and P.R. Philips (1995). 'Valuing the prevention of non-fatal road injuries: contingent valuation vs standard gamble', *Oxford Economic Papers*, **47**, 676–695.

Mason, H., M. Jones-Lee and C. Donaldson (2008). 'Modelling the monetary value of a QALY: a new approach based on UK data', *Health Economics*, **18**, 933–950.

Morton, A. and B. Fasolo (2009). 'Behavioural decision theory for multi-criteria decision analysis: a guided tour', *Journal of the Operational Research Society*, **60**, 268–75.

Okrent, D. (1981). 'Industrial risks', *Proceedings of the Royal Society*, A 376, 133–149.

Phillips, L. and A. Stock (2003). 'Use of multi-criteria analysis in air quality policy', report to Department for Environment, Food and Rural Affairs.

Rail Safety and Standards Board (RSSB) (2005). 'The definition of VPF and the impact of societal concerns', Rail Safety and Standards Board Report T 430.

Rail Safety and Standards Board (RSSB) (2007). *Safety Decisions Programme: The Route to 'Taking Safe Decisions*', London: Rail Safety and Standards Board.

Robinson, L.A., J.K. Hammitt, J.E. Aldy, A. Krupnick and J. Baxter (2010). 'Valuing the risk of death from terrorist attacks', *Journal of Homeland Security and Emergency Management*, **7** (1), Article 14 (online).

Slovic, P., B. Fischoff and S. Lichtenstein (1981). 'Perceived risk: psychological factors and social implications', in F. Warner (ed.), *The Assessment and Perception of Risk*, Proceedings of the Royal Society, Vol. 376, London: Royal Society, pp.17–34.

Smith, V.K., C. Mansfield and L. Clayton (2009). 'Valuing a homeland security policy: countermeasures for the threats from shoulder mounted missiles', *Journal of Risk and Uncertainty*, **38** (3), 215–243.

Sunstein, C.R. (1997). 'Bad deaths', *Journal of Risk and Uncertainty*, **14** (3), 259–282.

Viscusi, W.K. (2009). 'Valuing risks from terrorism and natural disasters', *Journal of Risk and Uncertainty*, **38** (3), 191–213.

6. A comparison of key benefit estimation issues for natural hazards and terrorism: *ex ante*/*ex post* valuation and endogenous risk

Scott Farrow

Many decision analytic tools can be used to inform public investments in terrorism response. Among them are multi-objective approaches, cost-effectiveness and benefit–cost analysis. At the core of all of them is the concept of someone's preferences, whether citizen, terrorist or decision-maker, from which behavior and values are derived. This chapter focuses on usable similarities or contrasts in behavioral choices between natural hazard and terrorism settings. Although neither term is defined precisely here, events such as floods, fires, earthquakes, wind, drought, pests and epidemics may most often be considered natural hazards, while acts of violence for political purposes aimed typically against civilians is a common definition of terrorism. Terrorism has the element of human intention that many analysts believe distinguishes terrorism from natural hazards. Other acts of violence against civilians such as crimes may differ from terrorism in their purpose and attributes, but can be seen as related behaviors.

This chapter focuses on how to value hazardous events avoided and the behavioral similarities and differences in prevention, avoidance and mitigation that individuals may choose in response to natural hazards or terrorism. The first topic is the valuation of hazardous events. What may be identified as a standard analysis focuses on damages if an event occurs, and then considers the probability of that event happening (Farrow and Viscusi, 2011). That approach, however, can omit the effect on value of altering the variability of outcomes, which is key to risk aversion and the *ex ante* approach. Contrasting these two approaches will be the focus of the first few sections. The second topic concerns the endogeneity of the probability of attack, specifically that the attacker alters behavior in response to defensive actions. For each topic, recommendations are provided for further research that could improve the analysis of anti-terrorism investments.

VALUING HAZARDOUS EVENTS

Standard practice in both applied natural hazard and terrorism analysis is to seek measures of 'surplus' or opportunity cost and, if there is uncertainty, to compute the expected value. Estimation often involves a replacement cost or price times quantity lost with its probability estimated from realized data as done typically in the case of natural hazards, or in the case of terrorism from a subjective probability or as a residual analysis (e.g. FEMA, 2008; Willis and LaTourette, 2008). Farrow (2007) generalizes this approach to a number of expenditure-constrained social cost models applied to terrorism in which the key empirical value to be determined is the marginal expected social cost avoided, the benefit. The social cost avoided allows for changes in both probability and consequence as a result of a policy or investment. This standard approach focuses on the probabilistically weighted dollar outcome of the loss, which has been the subject of debate regarding whether an *ex post* or *ex ante* approach should be used to value governmental policies (Arrow and Lind, 1970; Freeman, 1990; Graham, 1981; Smith, 1986).

More advanced practice distinguishes between valuation based on the conditional value of an outcome an individual somehow knows will occur, an *ex post* approach, and the value an individual might express prior to an event occurring, an *ex ante* approach (Smith, 1986). The differences between these two approaches can, but need not, be substantial precisely for the type of outcomes that seem to worry both natural hazard and terrorism managers, namely events that are small in probability but of high consequence. In that sense, the *ex post/ex ante* approach does not distinguish between natural and terrorism hazards if their probabilities and outcomes are the same, but could distinguish non-linearly between small-probability and high-consequence events and events that are lower in either dimension. The following discussion is based on Freeman (1989, 2003) and work by Farrow and Scott (2013) applying the concepts to willingness to pay (WTP) for flood prevention and mitigation.

EX ANTE AND *EX POST* VALUES FOR REDUCING CONSEQUENCES

Consider two models of valuing consumer behavior in a risky situation where a bad event may occur, A^*, or not, 0; with probability q and $1-q$. What has been labeled the *ex post* approach (e.g. Freeman, 1989) is based on a risk-neutral consumer valuing a certain outcome and then weighting by its probability of occurrence. Policies may alter either outcomes or probabilities (for a discussion of the importance of these separate elements, see Farrow and Shapiro, 2009). The *ex ante* approach evaluates how much an individual would pay prior to the event occurring to achieve the same utility as the random occurrence of the event but without the variation.

More formally, based on Freeman (1989, 2003), the *ex post* WTP identifies the payment with given income M and indirect utility function V, such that utility is equalized in either state of the world:

$$V(M, A^*) = V(M - WTP, 0). \tag{6.1}$$

The expected *ex post* cost for total avoidance assumes that this WTP is weighted by the probability of its occurrence, q^*WTP, equivalent to a risk-neutral approach to decision-making. Freeman also investigates the marginal value of a small change in A^* and the amount of money one would give up to maintain utility. The *ex post* marginal willingness to pay, $MWTP_P$ (the subscript signifies *ex post*) is obtained by totally differentiating equation 6.1, equating the differential to zero, and weighting by probability to yield the following:

$$MWTP_p^* = dM/dA^* = -qV_{A^*}/V_{M^*} \tag{6.2}$$

The $MWTP_p$, *ex post*, is seen to be a function of the expected marginal utility value, V_{A^*}, converted to monetary value by the marginal utility of money given that the event occurs.

The alternative *ex ante* approach seeks a monetary payment to also maintain utility, but one that takes into account the probability of outcomes in determining a state independent payment. Formally, the expected utility-maximizing consumer seeks to find an option price (OP), as in Smith (1983), that generates the same expected (indirect) utility with and without the payments and so solves:

$$E(V) = qV(M, A^*) + (1 - q)V(M, 0) = qV(M - OP, A^*) + (1 - q)\, V(M - OP, 0). \tag{6.3}$$

A marginal expression similar to equation (6.2) can be derived by totally differentiating the left-hand side with respect to q, M and A^*; setting dq equal to zero and dA^*equal to zero for A^* equal to zero, such that the *ex ante* marginal willingness to pay ($MWTP_A$) is:

$$MWTP_A = \frac{[\partial E(V)/\partial A^*]}{[\partial E(V)/\partial M]} = \frac{dM}{dA^*} = -\frac{qV_{A^*}}{[qV_{M^*} + (1 - q)\, V_{M^0}]}. \tag{6.4}$$

When equations (6.2) and (6.4) are combined, Freeman derives the difference between the *ex ante* and *ex post* measures as in equation (6.5):

$$\text{Proportional difference} = \frac{MWTP_A - MWTP_p}{MWTP_A} = (1-q)-(1-q)\frac{V_{M^0}}{V_{M^*}}. \tag{6.5}$$

Note that equation 6.5 can be solved for the *ex ante* value as a function of the *ex post* value and derivatives of the indirect utility function, the approach used later for estimation. The difference between the two measures is seen to hinge on the difference in the marginal utility of income in the different states of the world. If that utility is state-independent or changes very little, then the measures are equal or nearly equal and the distinction between *ex ante* and *ex post* is not important. In contrast, if the marginal valuations are distinctly different then large differences in MWTP can exist. There are important subtleties in how the marginal values may differ. It is possible that the indirect utility function models behavior such that damages associated with the bad event, A^*, are equivalent to financial damages in the sense that they are fully replaceable at market price. In that case, the *ex ante* value will exceed the *ex post* value. In contrast, some or all of the damages may not be replaceable in the same way, which can also be defined with a different specification of the indirect utility function and an index of irreplaceability (Cook and Graham, 1977; Smith, 1984). The marginal willingness to pay *ex post* may then exceed the *ex ante* measure. Further complications arise when distinguishing changes in outcome, the focus of the above discussion, from changes in probability (Freeman, 1989).

Consequently, the *ex ante* and *ex post* marginal values can differ in important ways that are under-researched in the case of either natural hazards or terrorism. It may be that the building structure to which standard flood insurance often applies is effectively replaceable, and similarly for some aspects of damage from terrorism attacks. Alternatively, there may be other damage, perhaps more associated with indirect or non-use aspects of terrorism attacks, which may be viewed as irreplaceable losses. Total damage may ultimately include differing proportions of the two types of damage. Consequently, the following recommendation may be viewed as identifying the types of damage and preferences of people who are subject to those types of damages:

Recommendation 1: Investigate evidence or conduct research regarding preferences and their relation to types of damage caused by terrorism events, including whether terrorist events induce 'replaceable' or 'irreplaceable' losses or in what proportion.

The following quantitative development focuses on preferences that model 'replaceable' values in the sense that *ex ante* measures are expected to be larger than *ex post* measures, and is consequently a bounding type of analysis. Freeman investigated several different risk-averse specifications of the indirect utility function, V, assuming the damage losses are replaceable, and concluded that the difference between *ex ante* and *ex post* is largest precisely where probabilities were low but potential losses were high. For instance, an event leading to a loss of 50 percent of income with a probability of 0.001 yielded a difference between the *ex ante* and *ex post* values that was ten times higher than that with a probability of 0.9. The error an analyst might make using *ex post* values instead of *ex ante* values rose from a 6 percent error in the latter probability case (0.9) to about a 65 percent error in the former case (0.001).

Within the class of utility functions modeling damage to replaceable assets, Freeman generated a set of data points measuring the proportional error (Freeman, 1989, Tables 1A-1C). Those data points measuring proportional error are used here as the dependent variable in a second-order regression response surface with independent variables risk (q), degree of risk aversion, and damage as a proportion of wealth or income.[1] The resulting response surface visually demonstrates Freeman's findings; a large proportional damage outcome with a small probability can lead to the *ex ante* measure exceeding the *ex post* by more than a factor of two, as illustrated in Figure 6.1.

The analysis can become less transparent when there are many or an infinite number of damage outcomes. While small-probability, high-consequence combinations may be more heavily weighted as in Figure 6.1; the probability of such events also enters directly into the expected value of an *ex ante* measure. Whether or not the distinction between *ex post* and *ex ante* measures is important can be affected by the form of a damage function and the associated probabilities (Farrow and Scott, 2013). The potential policy significance from using *ex ante* values leads to the following recommendation:

Recommendation 2: Conditional on findings regarding Recommendation 1, consider using ex ante *values in place of* ex post *values, perhaps simulating over various preference models, using a response surface summary from a set of utility functions, or integrating over multistate outcomes.*

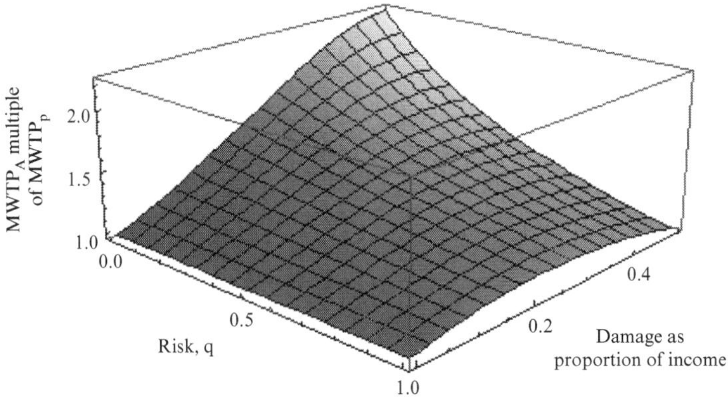

Figure 6.1 *Response surface:* ex ante *multiple of* ex post *value for varying risk and damage levels, risk aversion equal to 2*

Changes in Probability

The previous section addressed changes only in consequence or outcome. Freeman (and other authors to be discussed in more detail below) also addresses valuing changes in the probability of an event from both an *ex ante* and an *ex post* perspective. Although Freeman derives results that compare *ex ante* and *ex post* valuation approaches to changes in probability, the sign of the change appears more ambiguous for the range of values investigated. The proportional error in using the *ex post* value is often relatively smaller than that for the change in consequence, but the sign can change as well. Taking both changes in consequence and probability together, Freeman concludes that *ex post* measures in general are an ambiguous indication of the *ex ante* WTP. Hence investigating Recommendations 1 and 2 may focus effort on the area where new information may be most valuable to guide valuation.

Implementation of the *Ex Ante* Approach to the Benefit–Cost Analysis of Terrorism

There are, of course, challenges in adapting a conceptual *ex ante* valuation approach to an applied setting when the consequence or the probability or both are changing. Farrow and Scott (2013) applied the replaceable approach to *ex ante* WTP for flood protection that changes the consequence. This might be appropriate, for instance, if building code changes implemented as part of the National Flood Insurance Program in the USA reduce damage associated with a flood of a given probability.

Four implementation challenges are apparent in applying the *ex ante* approach to floods that may have implications for terrorism applications. The first is whether to consider the conditional damage to be known to individuals based on their location in the hazard zone. If so, that substantially reduces the pool of those with WTP. However, in the case of terrorism, such specific conditional knowledge does not seem reasonable, so what is a possible issue in the flood context is less relevant in the terrorism setting. The second challenge is determining the appropriate (indirect) utility function. One approach is a kind of model averaging where a regression is fit to the data outcomes for several utility functions, as discussed with regard to Figure 6.1. An alternative approach could simulate from a set of utility functions, effectively creating a different kind of model averaging for which the literature on Bayesian model averaging may be appropriate.

The third challenge is that the definition of the wealth or income over which the individual is averse can significantly affect results (Meyer and Meyer, 2006). For instance, Freeman developed his approach using income. His maximum damage as a share of income is 50 percent. For major events such as floods or terrorism, some individuals may well suffer losses significantly exceeding 50 percent of annual income, although some specific forms of utility functions become undefined if the loss exceeds total income. Many authors use measures of wealth, which can be more difficult to obtain but which are then consistent with some of the functional forms.

The fourth challenge lies in developing the expected value of the *ex-ante* WTP, which requires information about the probability distribution of damages. Although some program analyses may focus on an event of a particular size, for instance, the US National Flood Insurance Program focuses on the 100-year flood or the US Department of Homeland Security (DHS) focuses on events the size of September 11, 2001; more typically a whole distribution of consequences may occur with various probabilities. Farrow and Scott (2013) use the Federal Emergency Management Agency (FEMA) (2008) Hazus model to develop a damage function in a region for multiple flood levels. The probability density function is developed based on the complementary cumulative probability that a flood of a given size will be exceeded in the next time period. A parallel approach in terrorism, in which information about probabilities is notoriously difficult, is to consider methods that model exceedance probabilities similar to those used in flooding. In that case, the question is not 'What is the probability of another September 11 event in the next N years?'; the question is 'What is the probability that an event that size or larger will occur in a given time span?' While still difficult to answer, framing probabilities in exceedance terms provides an approach to the relative size and occurrence of events. These challenges to empirical implementation in flooding lead to the following recommendation:

Recommendation 3: Consider implementation issues in ex ante *valuation such as the appropriate measure of income or wealth and developing the probabilistic information necessary to assess the expected value of the* ex ante *measure.*

Non-expected Utility Behavior

As is well known, human behavior in risky situations appears to differ, sometimes in systematic ways, from that modeled by expected utility theory. Consistent with the literature, which finds that characteristics of an event alter our perceptions and possibly our values, Viscusi (2009) recently found that valuation of a statistical life was significantly higher for avoiding death through terrorism than through a natural disaster, and about the same as that for death avoided in a traffic accident. In the situation with natural hazards, it has been suggested that individuals go through several states of risk understanding prior to and after various events (Kunreuther and Pauly, 2006). Such reactions to relatively rare events may also be relevant for terrorism, as may risk models that distinguish characteristics of an event such as its 'dread' or lack of control of exposure. Although these factors are potentially relevant to terrorism, it may be useful to develop basic results using expected utility such as those discussed above and then seek to augment the basic results with behaviorally based adaptations. For instance, Farrow and Scott (2013) compare results using a cumulative prospect theory approach with those from expected utility.

INTELLIGENT ADVERSARIES AND ENDOGENOUS RISK

It is frequently and correctly said that terrorism policy and investments involve consideration of the responses of intelligent adversaries. At first glance it may appear that natural hazards, such as floods and earthquakes, are distinctly different, because nature may be considered to exogenously generate the probability of an event. Further consideration suggests that 'human-caused' catastrophes may have a natural initiating event but the extent of the damage depends significantly on interaction with the human system. Among other examples are the damage associated with Hurricanes Katrina and Sandy that appear interrelated with the design of

Table 6.1 Probability and consequence representations for natural hazards and terrorism

Model	Natural hazards	Terrorism
Basic	$P^*C(e) + u$	$P(e)^*C(e) + v$
Both endogenous	$P(e)^*C(e) + u$	$P(e)^*C(e) + v$

the built environment and response plans in New Orleans and New York; and a sequential dam failure in China in 1975 involving scores of dams that led to more than 75 000 fatalities. Economists, in fact, have been concerned about the endogeneity of risks in macroeconomic, and natural and environmental hazard settings (e.g. Kydland and Prescott, 1977; Kousky et al., 2006; Shogren and Crocker, 1991; Quiggin, 1992). Such natural hazard models and their concern for endogenous valuation may be similar to those of terrorism where the risk may more obviously be considered endogenous.[2] The endogenous risk literature suggests the usefulness of modeling the behavioral or dynamic response of the system as part of the analysis of benefits or costs.

The following discussion begins with concepts based on expected value in place of expected utility. This is perhaps closer to implementation practice (and is consistent with the Arrow and Lind, 1970 *ex post* approach to public decisions under uncertainty) but will also connect to risk aversion, expected utility or other variants.

Consider heuristic modeling of the differences in the expected cost of a natural hazard event or a terrorism event. The key elements in the expected cost are the determinants of probability (P), consequence (C), and some error associated with each expected value, either u in the case of a natural hazard or v in the case of a terrorism event. Policy implementation takes place through expenditures, e. Table 6.1 heuristically presents a basic and a more endogenous comparison between the two types of hazards. The first row represents the basic or standard view that probability is exogenous for natural hazards and endogenously dependent on expenditures for terrorism, while the consequence is endogenous (chosen) in both cases. The second row reflects the more complex view that both probabilities are endogenous and are a function here of expenditures. Further, it may well be that the pure uncertainty for terrorism, v, is substantially larger than that for a natural hazard. If P and C are also considered random variables, the uncertainty surrounding terrorism may be larger than that for natural hazards, but the difference in the advanced case is more one of degree than of kind. The distinctions in Table 6.1 can be used to illustrate similarities and differences in the expected value analysis of the two types of events.

Current US DHS practice for terrorism-based regulatory benefit–cost analysis frequently seeks a breakeven probability for benefits to exceed costs, with an implicit assumption about how the regulation affects consequences (Farrow and Shapiro, 2009). In that sense, current practice at times is like the natural hazard basic model in Table 6.1. However, other research considers probability to be endogenous. A variety of expected value, antiterrorism models that allow both probability and consequence to be a function of expenditures are presented in Farrow (2007). Left unresolved in such theoretical models are the empirical behaviors that might be altered by expenditures affecting the probability of being attacked. For instance, the conceptual environmental literature is concerned with the endogenous government response when individuals put themselves into risky situations, such as building on flood plains (Shogren and Crocker, 1991; Quiggin, 1992). There is some empirical literature related to the subject, such as the varying responses to risk following a hurricane, as in Smith et al. (2006). Regarding terrorism, the parallel issue is the choice made by attackers in choosing their targets, which may well depend on the nature of the defensive expenditures. These issues are at the frontier of both natural hazard and terrorism research.

The game theory literature on antiterrorism can also be viewed as explicitly modeling how attacker behavior changes with investments, and so modeling the endogeneity of probability as a function of defensive expenditures (e.g. Zhuang and Bier, 2007 and references therein). Further, antiterrorism analysts have frequently discussed threat, vulnerability and consequence (or criticality) as part of their analysis. Those components of an event can be viewed as a sequence of conditional probability statements such that expenditures may affect the threat, the vulnerability and the consequence, all of which may affect the attack probability at a site.[3] In a related area of study, consumers take a variety of self-protection measures against crime, environmental and natural hazard risks that may affect probability or outcomes. People choose to locate in areas or choose jobs in part based on the probability of various events. They may invest in safety devices, alter the construction of their homes or buy insurance. Although the prevailing view seems to be that such costs, whether actually paid or revealed through opportunity cost, represent the lower bound to *ex ante* WTP, some debate remains (Shogren and Crocker, 1991; Quiggin, 1992). Consequently, the similarity in considering how the endogenous probability of an event depends on expenditures leads to the following recommendation:

Recommendation 4: Systematically study the behavioral response of attackers to model, even if incompletely, how expenditures may alter probabilities.

The final modeling heuristic identified in Table 6.1 is the error term, initially though not necessarily modeled as additive to the expected value. The ability to model events can vary significantly from application to application and a model may provide a significantly worse prediction for terrorism than, say, for a hurricane. Elsewhere, Farrow (2012) has argued that where analysts are primarily generating forecasts with limited or missing historical data (in contrast to regression analysis models), then a pure error term such a u or v is frequently omitted. That omission may misrepresent the precision of the analysis and cause further confusion about the distinction that may exist between modeling various risky events. Although perhaps unknowable in a classical sense, analysts no doubt believe their model captures some proportion of the total variation in the dependent variable they would like to explain, whether it is damage from a terrorist attack or from a natural hazard, or some other outcome. Farrow develops a method to augment simulation models with a subjective estimate of goodness of fit, the coefficient of determination or R^2, to generate an estimate of the variance of the pure error term.

The approach was developed for applications such as benefit–cost analysis where historical data are not available for the dependent variable, compared to the regression analysis case where such data are available. In the regression analysis case, estimates of the error term and its variance are obtained based on differences between observed and forecast data. Lacking observed values of the dependent variable in a benefit–cost analysis, analysts typically assume there is zero random error even if simulations might be carried using uncertain parameters and conditioning factors. Farrow (2012) notes that it is possible to invert the usual analysis of variance definition linking the error variance to R^2. The usual definition of R^2 is based on the ratio of the explained sum of squares divided by the total sum of squares (e.g. Wooldridge, 2006, p. 42). The mean square error, a common estimate for the variance of the error term σ^2, can be extracted from this ratio and solved for as a function of R^2:

$$\hat{\sigma}^2 = \left(\frac{1 - \hat{R}^2}{\hat{R}^2}\right)\frac{SSM}{N} \tag{6.6}$$

where SSM is the model sum of squares and N is the number of observations. Lacking data for the measure of fit, the analyst may use Bayesian methods or other sources of information for an estimate of R^2 while the model sum of squares can be obtained from simulations. Quantifying the variance of the error term may make explicit another of the differences between natural hazard and antiterrorism analysis where the presumption is likely to be that the error variance for terrorism is larger than that for many natural hazards. The final recommendation follows:

Recommendation 5: In simulation models that forecast impacts, consider an error term that is essentially a sensitivity analysis about the accuracy of the model, and convey to the decision-maker a quantitative measure of uncertainty that includes an augmented variance estimate.

CONCLUSION

This chapter suggests that the benefit–cost modeling of terrorism compared with natural hazards is more a matter of degree than of kind. Further, several tools sometimes used in the benefit–cost analysis of environmental issues may be adapted for use in the analysis of terrorism. The following similarities and differences have been identified:

- *Ex ante* versus *ex post* valuation. The concept appears relevant in both natural hazard and terrorism analysis even if the typical starting point for analysis is the *ex post* expected value. Related recommendations are as follows:

Recommendation 1: Investigate evidence regarding preferences and their relation to types of damage caused by terrorism events and whether terrorist events induce 'replaceable' or 'irreplaceable' losses or in what proportion.

Recommendation 2: Consider using ex ante *values constructed from* ex post *values, perhaps simulating over various preference models, using a response surface summary of sets of utility functions, or integrating over multistate outcomes.*

Recommendation 3: Consider implementation issues in ex ante *valuation such as the appropriate measure of income or wealth and developing the probabilistic information necessary to assess the expected value of the* ex ante *measure.*

- Endogenous probability. In the context of terrorism, this concern is about an intelligent adversary but a similar issue arises in domestic public policy with individual location and self-defensive behavior that may induce a governmental response. In addition, both natural hazard and terrorism models are abstractions from reality with less than a perfect 'fit' to the problem. However, it may well be that our knowledge of antiterrorism models is significantly worse than our models of natural hazards. Consequently, although both types of models may currently omit a pure error term, the variance for anti-terrorism models is likely to be larger than that for natural hazard models.

Recommendation 4: Systematically study the behavioral response of attackers to try to model, even if incompletely, how expenditures may alter probabilities.

Recommendation 5: In simulation models which forecast impacts, consider an error term that is essentially a sensitivity analysis about the accuracy of the model, and convey to the decision-maker a quantitative measure of uncertainty that includes an augmented variance estimate.

NOTES

1. Regression results are available from the author. As a 'forecast' equation for the proportional error, the adjusted R^2 was 0.86.
2. It may be interesting to consider what a terrorist strategy would be if defenses are such that the marginal social costs of an attack are equalized across locations. The resulting pattern of attack may appear as random since an attack at any location would have an equal expected pay-off to the attacker.
3. A rich debate exists on the limitations of the threat, vulnerability and consequence framework; see for example Cox (2008) and Ezell et al. (2010).

REFERENCES

Arrow, K. and R. Lind (1970). 'Uncertainty and the evaluation of public investment decisions', *American Economic Review*, **60** (3), 364–378.

Cook, P. and D. Graham (1977). 'The demand for insurance and protection: a case of irreplaceable commodities', *Quarterly Journal of Economics*, **92**, 143–156.

Cox, L. Jr. (2008). 'Some limitations of "Risk = Threat × Vulnerability × Consequence" for risk analysis of terrorist attacks', *Risk Analysis*, **28** (6), 1749–1761.

Ezell, B., S. Bennett, D. von Winterfeldt, J. Sokolowski, and A. Collins (2010). 'Probabilistic risk analysis and terrorism risk', *Risk Analysis*, **30** (4), 575–589.

Farrow, S. (2007). 'The economics of homeland security expenditures: foundational expected cost-effectiveness approaches', *Contemporary Economic Policy*, **25** (1), 14–26.

Farrow, S. (2012). 'A missing error term in benefit–cost analysis', *Environmental Science and Technology*, **46** (5), 2523–2528.

Farrow, S. and M. Scott (2013). 'Comparing multi-state expected damages, option price and cumulative prospect measures for valuing flood protection', *Water Resources Research*, **49** (5), 2638–2648.

Farrow, S. and S. Shapiro (2009). 'The benefit–cost analysis of homeland security expenditures', *Journal of Homeland Security and Emergency Management*, **6** (1), 1–20, http://www.bepress.com/jhsem/vol6/iss1/25/.

Farrow, S. and W.K. Viscusi (2011). 'Toward principles and standards for the

benefit–cost analysis of safety', *Journal of Benefit–Cost Analysis*, **2** (3), Article 5 (online).
Federal Emergency Management Agency (FEMA) (2008). 'HAZUS® MH estimated annualized earthquake losses for the United States', FEMA report 366, http://www.fema.gov/library/viewRecord.do?id=3265, accessed July 28, 2011.
Freeman, M., III (1989). 'Ex-ante and ex-post values for changes in risks', *Risk Analysis*, **9** (3), 309–317.
Freeman, M., III (1990). 'Welfare measurement and benefit–cost analysis of projects affecting risk', *Southern Economic Journal*, **58** (1), 65–76.
Freeman, M., III (2003). *The Measurement of Environmental and Resource Values*, 2nd edn, Washington, DC: RfF Press.
Graham, D. (1981). 'Cost–benefit analysis under uncertainty', *American Economic Review*, **71**, 715–725.
Kousky, C., E. Luttmer and R. Zeckhauser (2006). 'Private investment and government protection', *Journal of Risk and Uncertainty*, **33**, 73–100.
Kunreuther, H. and M. Pauly (2006). 'Rules rather than discretion: lessons from Hurricane Katrina', *Journal of Risk and Uncertainty*, **33**, 101–116.
Kydland, F. and E. Prescott (1977). 'Rules rather than discretion', *Journal of Political Economics*, **85** (3), 473–491.
Meyer, D. and J. Meyer (2006). *Measuring Risk Aversion*. Hackensack, NJ: World Scientific.
Quiggin, J. (1992). 'Risk, self-protection and ex-ante economic value – some positive results', *Journal of Environmental Economics and Management*, **23** (1), 40–53.
Shogren, J. and T. Crocker (1991). 'Risk, self-protection, and ex-ante economic value', *Journal of Environmental Economics and Management*, **20**, 1–15.
Smith, V.K. (1983). 'Option value: a conceptual overview', **49** (3), 654–668.
Smith, V.K. (1984). 'A bound for option value', *Land Economics*, **60** (3), 292–296.
Smith, V.K. (1986). 'Benefit analysis for natural hazards', *Risk Analysis*, **6** (3), 325–334.
Smith, V.K., J. Carbone, J. Pope, D. Hallstrom and M. Darden (2006). 'Adjusting to natural disasters', *Journal of Risk and Uncertainty*, **33** (1–2), 37–54.
Viscusi, W.K. (2009). 'Valuing risks of death from terrorism and natural disasters', *Journal of Risk and Uncertainty*, **38**, 191–213.
Willis, H. and T. LaTourette (2008). 'Using probabilistic terrorism risk-modeling for regulatory benefit–cost analysis: application to the Western Hemisphere Travel Initiative in the land environment', *Risk Analysis*, **28**, 325–329.
Wooldridge, J. (2006). *Introductory Econometrics*, 3rd edn, Mason, OH: Thomson-Southwestern.
Zhuang, J. and V. Bier (2007). 'Balancing terrorism and natural disasters-defensive strategy with endogenous attacker effort', *Operations Research*, **55** (5), 976–991.

PART III

Adaptation and economy-wide effects

7. Urban adaptation to low-probability shocks: contrasting terrorism and natural disaster risk

Matthew E. Kahn

INTRODUCTION

All United States metropolitan households and firms face trade-offs in choosing whether to locate in the city center or the suburbs. More and more of these decision-makers are choosing to suburbanize. Suburban locations offer cheaper land prices and a newer, more efficient building stock. Although in the past transportation costs to access the productive city center posed a significant cost of suburbanization, improvements in transportation such as highways and information technology diffusion have dramatically reduced this cost (Baum-Snow, 2007). Starting in the 1960s through the early 1990s, city center quality of life decline introduced a new 'push factor' encouraging suburbanization. Major cities suffered from high taxes per dollar of government services, poor inner city public schools, pollution, urban poverty, racial discord and crime (Mieskowski and Mills, 1993).

City center terrorism risk represents another push factor encouraging suburbanization. The pursuit of individual self-interest suggests that fear of terrorism will accelerate metropolitan area suburbanization. If individuals and firms increasingly suburbanize, in part because of salient terrorism risk, then a re-enforcing 'chicken and egg' dynamic will play out as more households and jobs suburbanize. This chapter examines whether this intuitive logic is likely to play out in the USA's major cities and evaluates the economic consequences of such a trend. I argue that city center terrorism risk will not lower metropolitan area productivity. As a result of recent improvements in city center quality of life, I predict that increased city center terrorism risk will not accelerate suburbanization.

Cities are the growth engine of capitalism because they facilitate trade, specialization, learning and innovation. Those cities that can attract and retain the skilled are most likely to prosper. Today, there are hundreds of major cities for households and firms to choose from in the United States. Our modern and technologically savvy society has unprecedented access to information about each city's opportunities and challenges.

The modern urban empirical literature has emphasized the agglomeration benefits of cities as workers and firms learn, specialize and trade (Glaeser et al., 1992; Dumais et al., 2002; Rosenthal and Strange, 2004). If terrorism erodes such agglomeration spillovers, then adaptation to terrorism risk could impose large social costs. This view is argued by Abadie and Dermisi (2008) who document evidence of an increase in vacancy rates in downtown Chicago commercial office spaces in the aftermath of the September 11, 2001 attacks.

Fear of city center terrorism could certainly encourage both population dispersion and job sprawl. Paul Krugman and I anticipated this point immediately after the September 11 attacks. In the days following the September 11 attacks, I wrote a draft of an editorial that was never published, titled 'Will Wall Street leave Wall Street?' This editorial built on my current work at the time on the causes and consequences of employment suburbanization (Glaeser and Kahn, 2001, 2004). But Dr Krugman authored a far better piece in his *New York Times* column. An excerpt from the October 3, 2001 opinion piece 'Reckonings: an injured city' is worth reprinting here:

> Will the terror attack permanently damage New York's position as America's economic capital?
>
> After all, America's pre-eminent city owes its position to historical accident. The natural advantages of New York – its fine harbor, its location at the terminus of the only possible canal route to the Great Lakes – were real enough during the city's rise. But those natural advantages have long since ceased to be important to the city's economy. What keeps New York a great city is circular causation; people and businesses locate there because of the opportunities created by the presence of other people and businesses.
>
> And because the city's economy is sustained by circular causation, a sufficiently large blow to that economy could in theory do permanent damage. If enough businesses and people leave, for whatever reason, the local economy could fall below critical mass and enter a downward spiral in which businesses leave because other businesses are leaving.
>
> The beneficiaries of such an exodus would probably not be other great cities; instead, businesses would move out into the endless sprawl. I was not the only person in suburban New Jersey who, somewhat to my shame, felt perfectly safe on Sept. 11: there are millions of people living and working nearby, but no obvious targets, because there's no there here [*sic*].
>
> The question is how large a blow would be needed to start such a spiral? How robust are cities, anyway? (Krugman, 2001)

This chapter elaborates on Krugman's themes. Could cities such as New York City be 'knocked out' by further terrorist threats? If Manhattan suffers from such a perception, will the greater New York City metropolitan area suffer, or do geographical areas within the same metropolitan area compete via a 'zero-sum game' for such economic activity as hedge fund trading?

Fortunately for the mayors and land owners in center cities, there are counterveiling 'consumer city' trends occurring at the same time that terrorism risk lurks. City center crime is falling, pollution problems are improving and people are rediscovering the joys of city center living. These trends should allow city center stake holders to sleep soundly at night as they recognize that their new 'golden goose' is fusion of cuisine and leisure activity rather than Goldman Sachs.

In addition to facing elevated terrorism risk, coastal cities also face the risks posed by climate change. I compare and contrast how urbanites and their greater metropolitan areas will adapt in the face of two distinct, low-probability but potentially very costly threats: namely terrorism and climate change. There are valuable lessons to be learned by comparing how we individually and collectively respond to a passive, semi-predictable opponent (Mother Nature in the case of climate change) versus our responses to an active and less predictable opponent engaging in 'intelligent design' (terrorists).

The Productivity Advantages of Metropolitan Areas

Many of society's most talented and ambitious people live and work in dense center cities. An open question is whether this fact is due to 'selection' or 'treatment'. Do superstars who would have had a great career regardless of where they lived (think of Donald Trump) seek to live in exciting vibrant places (this would be the selection effect)? Or do such individuals become superstars because they live and work in these cities (this would be the treatment effect)? Modern urban economics makes the case that both effects are likely to matter. In this section, I focus on the 'treatment effect' hypothesis that posits that working in a dense economic area causes a person to be more productive.

When people live and work in close physical proximity, they economize on the costs of trading and interacting with each other. Consider the opposite case of Robinson Crusoe living alone on an island. Crusoe knows that he is alone and thus must be a 'jack of all trades' because he cannot trade with anyone. In contrast, cities offer ample trading possibilities and thus allow individuals and firms to narrowly specialize in their comparative advantage. Such specialization, given learning by doing, allows such firms to become even better at their core tasks as they purchase through markets all other inputs they need. Excellent law firms in a big city do not need to have an excellent in-house cafeteria when great restaurants are close by. This example broadly generalizes.

In densely populated center cities, firms are located in close physical proximity. Such proximity encourages random interactions. Urbanists such as Jane Jacobs celebrated such chance encounters as a source of learning and experimentation. Firms that know they could improve their production process seek out advice and new strategies. Other firms thinking that they could improve their product by shifting its attributes (think of fashion) have strong incentives to learn and copy from others' success. Such spillover effects are much more likely to take place in bustling cities. It is important to note that these productivity gains are likely to be greater for individuals with more human capital and in cases where their neighbors also have more human capital. In this sense, social interaction in superstar cities such as New York City is likely to raise overall income inequality.

Another productivity advantage of cities is called labor pooling. Every firm is subject to demand shocks. In an area featuring just one firm, unemployment will rise when that firm has a negative demand shock. Now consider a city featuring many firms which experience idiosyncratic demand shocks such that at any point in time some firms experience reduced demand while other firms experience increased demand. By having many firms located in the same city, workers face less unemployment risk because they can move from one firm to another without moving their family to a new home and new social network.

Given current intercity transportation technology such as cars, buses and subways, a person can live miles from a workplace and still be a dependable worker. This means that regardless of a household's preference for housing size or local schools, the workers in the family can choose among a large number of potential urban employers and be well matched with a specific firm.

The political leaders of cities will recognize that investments in public goods, such as good transportation infrastructure and safe streets, encourages agglomeration. After all, if a downtown is difficult to travel to then less economic activity will cluster there.

Terrorism Will Not Erode the Productivity Advantage of Metropolitan Areas

Across all major US cities, there has been an ongoing decentralization of activity (Mieszkowski and Mills, 1993). After World War II, the population suburbanized and commuted to the city center workplaces. Over the last 40 years, there has been a sharp growth in suburban employment

(Glaeser and Kahn, 2001). Given that time is our scarcest asset, workers will have a high demand to live close to employment centers. As a result, the majority of US workers now live and work in suburban areas. These workers commute using private vehicles and move at higher speeds than those who use public transit to commute downtown (Glaeser and Kahn, 2004). These suburbanites live a life that would be quite familiar to the New Jersey residents who Paul Krugman's quote alluded to in the introduction. Such suburbanites face little terrorism risk even though they live in New York City's metropolitan area.

Terrorism could accelerate this suburbanization trend. Urban centers face the greatest risk from terrorism because by definition they feature the highest population density and offer the most victims per terrorist action. Center cities receive more media coverage than suburban locations, and this further amplifies the effect of a terrorist attack and the likelihood that an attack would take place there.

In anticipation of this risk, each centrally located firm such as Goldman Sachs on Wall Street must evaluate its optimal location choice. Although city center locations offer attractive social and entertainment options for commuting workers, rents tend to be higher for their employers. Each individual firm will choose its optimal location decision by comparing its own private benefits and costs of remaining in the city center. No individual firm has an incentive to internalize the spillover effects its location choice has on other companies.

If a given major city now faces increased terrorism risk, could this erode the metropolitan area's overall productivity? The logic chain underlying such a claim is built on the belief that beneficial agglomeration externalities are maximized in the densest part of the metropolitan area and that such benefits are lost if economic activity decentralizes. However there is nothing intrinsic about city center locations such as Chicago's Loop or Wall Street that guarantees that a firm that locates in the city center will experience increased productivity. Instead, this observed fact that city center firms are more productive is due to a 'selection effect' (the set of firms which can afford the expensive downtown rent are not a random sample) and a 'treatment effect' (the central business district, or CBD, has traditionally solved a coordination problem). Thomas Schelling's famous example of coordination focuses on two strangers who must meet each other somewhere in New York City. Both will individually gravitate to Grand Central Station because each knows that the other is seeking such a focal point. A similar effect happens in the case of the CBD. In this case, a type of self-fulfilling prophesy unfolds. The CBD is productive because it attracts the best and brightest to locate there, and this snowball effect comes into play. In order to become successful, emerging firms must relocate to regions of high activity and productivity, such as the CBD. This logic indicates that central locations matter, but there is no explanation as to why downtown is a unique epicenter of productivity.

As suburbanized employment continues, new employment centers will emerge. If Goldman Sachs moves to the New Jersey suburbs, 'pilot fish' firms will follow it and a new agglomeration will emerge. Although the downtown land owners and the mayor who presides over this physical area will bemoan this trend, it is unlikely that the overall regional economy will suffer. Only a handful of industries benefit from very close physical proximity (that is, walking distance) to other firms. One example is the advertising industry. Arzaghi and Henderson (2009) find that the productivity benefits enjoyed by one advertising firm fall sharply as its distance to other advertising firms increases. In general, the major agglomeration force across industries is the need for labor pooling. Workers want to live and work in cities that feature multiple employers because this leads to thick local labor markets and a lower risk of unemployment. Because of the high percentage of car ownership, suburban workers are able to commute to many different suburban locations to work. The new metropolitan area of San Jose, California, is an example of a highly productive sprawled metropolitan area. In lower-density cities such as San Jose, people can drive at higher speeds and cover more ground to increase their range of employment opportunities.

To make the claim that terrorism considerably diminishes industrial productivity, one would need to make a credible case that suburban employment centers are not productive places. The suburban corporate campuses of both Google and Microsoft represent counter-examples. The hedge fund traders clustered in Greenwich, Connecticut offer another example of productive, highly skilled people working and thriving far from a dense urban center. In all fairness to the 'costs of terrorism' view, emerging firms and start-ups will have to work hard to mingle and 'be in the loop' in a suburban employment setting. Unlike a publicly accessible city street, Google can control its security and create a buffer around its own buildings. In such a privatized corporate campus setting featuring little walking and much driving from suburban location to suburban location, serendipitous interactions between strangers are less likely to take place. While urbanists such as Jane Jacobs would bemoan this point, it remains an open question whether less social learning will take place. If new start-up firms believe that they are 'out of the loop' then new institutions such as hotel networking meetings and 'social hours' would evolve to help connect companies to exploit gains to trade.

The Rise of the Consumer City Center Will Offset the Terrorist Threat

Although employment suburbanization suggests that terrorism will weaken the city center, the rise of center cities as 'consumer cities' represents an offsetting trend. Today, large center cities are regaining their 'groove' thanks to declining city center crime and less pollution. Since the early 1990s, crime has fallen sharply (Reyes, 2007). Regardless of whether the cause is legalized abortion, efficient policing or the decline in leaded gasoline, the effect is the same: a large reduction in the murder rate. In 1990, there were 2245 murders in New York City, while in 2008 there were roughly 500 murders.[1] Recently reverse commuting has grown sharply, such that people live downtown and commute to suburban jobs.

These facts support the claim that the future of dense urban cities will become the epicenter of consumer living (Glaeser et al., 2001). The greening of the city center especially in port cities such as New York City and Boston, has led to the rise of the 'consumer city', which has strengthened the core. The attractive and unique cultural and historical amenities existing downtown cannot be reproduced in the suburbs. Incidentally, the wealthy can afford the higher cost of living and price premium of such a desirable environment. Wealthy people living downtown in major cities such as San Francisco, London and New York City express a purchasing power that creates an endogenous gentrification (Guerrieri et al., 2010; Waldfogel, 2008) such that the demand for upscale commercial stores and restaurants fuels desirable conditions for those businesses to prosper.

In my own research, I have studied the causes and consequences of the ongoing 'greening' of center cities in the developed world (Kahn, 2006). The decline of city center manufacturing has offered an environmental silver lining. Cities such as New York City and London have lost hundreds of thousands of manufacturing jobs. An unintended benefit of the transition from manufacturing to a services and tourism economy is sharp improvements in air, noise and water pollution. Recognizing these gains, cities such as Boston have invested in major 'greening' projects such as the Big Dig to develop green spaces with easy access to the waterways.

The rise of the consumer city center such as New York City suggests that city center terrorism risk can be offset by local quality of life improvements. Mayors are well aware that tourism is a 'golden goose' for cities. City center quality of life improvements during a time of elevated terrorism risk discourage sprawl. The extremely high home prices in major US cities today, ranging from New York City to Chicago to Boston and San Francisco, highlights that successful people are betting that center cities will continue to be in strong demand.

Cross-metropolitan Area Competition in an Age of Terrorism

Common sense and hedonic pricing research pinpoints the 'best cities in America'. These tend to be coastal cities in attractive, temperate climates featuring sophisticated cultural opportunities. Albouy's (2008) top nine amenity cities are San Francisco, Santa Barbara, Monterey, Honolulu, San Diego, New York City, Los Angeles, San Luis Obispo and Boston. Seattle ranks 12th, Portland ranks 19th and Houston ranks 74th. Hedonic researchers identify such cities using revealed preference logic. If a city features relatively high home prices and offers relatively low wages and suffers low outmigration, then it must offer a high quality of life.

Changes in city-specific terrorism risk could shake up this ordering of 'America's best cities to live and work'. Terrorism risk is another spatially tied attribute that is capitalized into cross-city and within-city real estate pricing gradients. Workers and firms not only choose where to locate within a metropolitan area but also which metropolitan area to locate in. There are over 300 metropolitan areas in the United States. In an open system of cities, workers and firms will conduct a two-stage location: choose a metropolitan area and then choose a location within the metropolitan area. Those cities and neighborhoods deemed to be risky will experience a reduction in real estate pricing. The owners of such assets will bear the incidence of this 'new news'. Although real estate values would decline in cities deemed to be increasingly at risk, other cities could actually experience a windfall. For example, Boston and New York City are rough substitutes. If New York City is perceived to be at elevated risk from terrorism, this could displace economic activity both to its suburbs and to downtown Boston. In this case, rents could rise in downtown Boston because of demand displaced from the New York City market. Given that downtown areas are built up and thus there is an inelastic supply of durable real estate, any 'new news' that lowers demand to locate there will translate into falling real estate prices.

Time Trends in Urban Concern about Terrorism as Revealed by Google Searches

The goal of terrorism is to disrupt the status quo and throw a society into a state of chaos. 'Terrorism is a form of "psychological warfare", in which individuals or groups (whether by intimidation, torture and/or mass attacks) seek to "invoke pervasive fear in a civilian population by personalizing the threat so that everyone feels vulnerable"' (Maguen et al., 2008).

The residents of major cities such as New York City should express the greatest terrorism concerns. Such concern can feed on itself through social

Figure 7.1 National television news stories in which terrorism is mentioned

interactions. When the media covers a story, this raises the likelihood that people are talking about the issue and the event can take on a life of its own. It is easy to imagine there being multiple equilibria, whereby a population can become highly concerned about terrorism, and interaction with like-minded friends and colleagues reinforces this worldview. Consider a simple bandwagon model (see Becker, 1991) in which your interest in a subject increases if your friends are also interested in the subject. For example, one's concern about terrorism may decline if one's peer group's interest declines. From an empirical perspective, terrorist shocks represent an exogenous shock that ultimately reduces concern through both individual and peer-group effects.

Figure 7.1 provides some facts about the national television coverage of terrorism. Using the Vanderbilt Television Archives, I graphed the aggregate count of network news stories counted by the search engine that mentioned 'terrorism' reported that year. As shown in the graph, the terrorist attacks of 2001 and 2005 lead to sharp increases in coverage, but after 2001 there is a clear pattern of declining media attention.

A second way to look at public interest in terrorism is to use Google Trends. Google Insights is a publicly available online tool for tracking aggregate Google search activity over time for specific geographic areas such as states.[2] Recent research shows that Google search terms are a powerful tool to predict public health epidemics and economic activity. Here I tracked weekly Google searches from January 2004 onwards for the entire United States and for New York City to study trends in search activity for 'murder' and 'terrorism'. To provide a sense of the role of

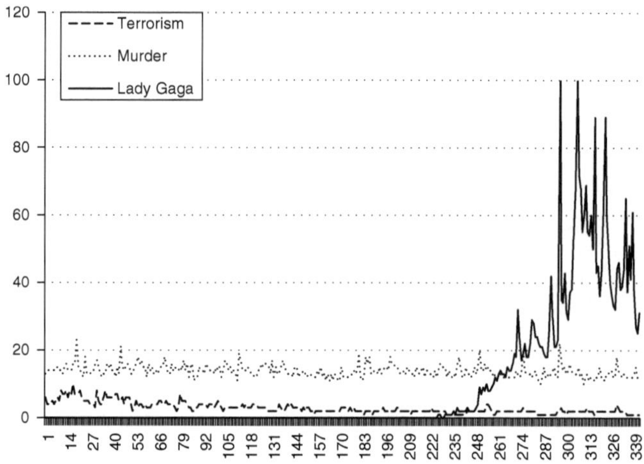

Figure 7.2 Weekly scaled Google searches in the United States from January 2004 until August 2010

fads, I contrasted these searches with interest in the popular music sensation Lady Gaga. The data available on Google Insights is not the actual number of keyword searches, but rather a scaled variable that enables relative comparisons of trends through time within a keyword and also between keywords. Figure 7.2 graphs the data for the entire United States. Figure 7.3 presents the search activity trends for the New York City metropolitan area. These results suggest that concern about terrorism is on a downward trend in the USA. Does this mean that people are letting their guard down? Or does this declining Google Search activity indicate an increasing trust in the Department of Homeland Security's ability to protect the public?

Contrasting Urban Adaptation to Terror and Natural Disaster Risk

Coastal superstar cities such as London and New York City face low probability but potentially dangerous risk from both terrorism and climate change. In this section, I contrast the terrorism and climate change fat tail uncertainty. By definition, there is 'intelligent design' behind terrorist attacks, while Mother Nature does not throw her punches with the intent of causing harm. In the case of natural disasters, there is more likely to be a clear temporal and spatial pattern concerning where the risks are most likely to take place (flood zones) and the time of year (hurricane season). This predictability enhances adaptation possibilities. The reoccurring

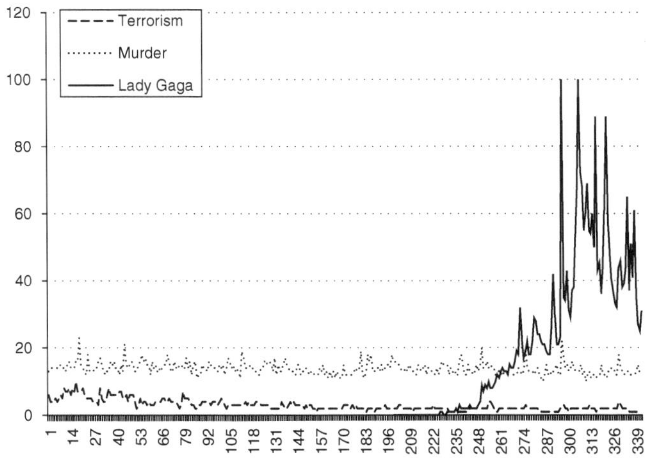

Figure 7.3 Weekly scaled Google searches in New York City from January 2004 until August 2010

seasonal cycles of disasters (for example 'hurricane season') help keep it fresh in the mind and make it easier to adapt to because we do not forget about the risk.

Anticipating that natural disasters will pose repeat challenges for specific geographical areas induces innovation that will help us adapt to climate risks (Kahn, 2010). Thom Mayne of the University of California, Los Angeles (UCLA) is designing floating homes that will face less flood damage in the event of another disaster. Although examples of similar innovations, such as structures that can withstand flooding or earthquakes, are easy to think of, it is more challenging to generate optimistic examples of how capitalist innovation can protect us from urban terrorism risk. Improved airport scanners are an obvious transportation example but could such 'remote sensing' be used at public transit stations and group sporting events?

Although climate modeling is both an art and a science, climate scientists have made progress in forecasting climatic conditions that provide an early warning system against anticipated disasters. Such information triggers short-term migration responses as people move to higher ground, and this lowers the damage caused by a shock. In contrast with terrorism, the Department of Homeland Security (DHS) has introduced its color-coded system. It remains an open question whether such information changes individual behavior and in aggregate protects us from the impact of a terrorist attack.

In the case of terrorist attacks, the attacks are much less likely to be concentrated in specific locations (the coast) or at specific times (hurricane season). The strategic terrorist who recognizes the beefed-up security at airports will attempt to identify other targets. This pessimistic logic suggests that past history is much less useful for predicting terrorist attacks on cities than in predicting natural disaster patterns. It is true that the highest population density parts of cities are highly correlated over time and remain a tempting target for terrorists, but the mode of attack is less predictable.

Household income plays a role in protecting people from natural disaster risk. Richer people consume higher-quality products and live in better, safer neighborhoods. The net effect of this population sorting is that the poor face greater risk from natural disasters. In contrast, this logic is less likely to apply in the case of terrorist attacks because they are concentrated in workplace communities. In a world where people work downtown and the majority live in the suburbs, terrorism is more likely to affect above-average income people. Conversely, in Israel, terrorist attacks on public transit are more likely to affect lower-income victims because richer people travel by private car.

Are government and individual efforts to protect the populace complements or substitutes? The social benefits of DHS measured in terms of protecting the population from terrorist risk hinge on the ability and willingness of the public to take self-protective action. In both instances, there is an issue of 'crowding out' that arises. If one has faith in the success of the Department of Homeland Security, each household is less likely to suburbanize, which actually increases the possible victim count from a given terrorist attack. After all, if the population is uniformly distributed across a given area, then an attack will cause less damage than if an intelligently designed attack focuses on a densely populated area.

The same point arises in the case of defending cities such as New Orleans from a future Hurricane Katrina. As the federal government builds better sea walls around New Orleans, then a trusting public is more likely to remain in New Orleans. If the public did not trust the government, then fewer people would live in areas at risk. In this sense, public investment in risk reduction lures more people to live in at-risk places. Economists call this the 'crowd-out' effect: public investment and regulation diminish private household investment in self-protection (Viscusi, 1984). The empirical relevance of this point in the case of the homeland security and adaptation to climate change is an important research topic.

CONCLUSION: RISK IN CITIES

Major coastal cities such as New York City and London face threats from terrorism and climate change. Other cities such as Detroit and Manchester, UK, are unlikely to face significant threats from either terrorism or climate change. Cities such as New York City and London are disproportionately at risk because they are coastal, dense, media centers with considerable downtown employment and a dense public transit infrastructure.

Although Manhattan is likely to continue to be a prime terrorist target, the good news for Manhattan land owners is that city center living has made a major comeback. Urban crime has been falling since the early 1990s. Most major US center cities are greener, cleaner and more peaceful than they have been historically. These prosperous diverse cities attract tourists, which helps fuel a gentrification snowball featuring high-end stores and restaurants and the celebration of culture.

This chapter has argued that the rise of consumer center cities will protect them against the dispersion threat of terrorism. Although fear of terrorism may lead some economic activity to migrate away from center cities, the overall metropolitan areas will not suffer a productivity loss because of this suburbanization trend. Close proximity facilitates trade and learning, but these interactions can take place in the suburbs. It is relevant to note that this is a long-run perspective. It is important to acknowledge that a major terrorist strike at a city center would cause significant short-run disruption. The capital stock cannot be rebuilt overnight. But, an optimist would point to how the Northeast has responded to Hurricane Sandy. The recovery period can be relatively short.

The unintended social consequences of self-protective strategies for minimizing terror risk will remain an active research topic. Although I do not believe that a metropolitan area's productivity will be lowered by suburbanization, I am concerned about a different local learning phenomena. The social capital literature (see Costa and Kahn, 2003) has emphasized the distinction between 'bridging' and 'bonding' social capital. The former relates to making friends with people who are less familiar, while it is human nature to interact with people of similar backgrounds. Major cities contain increasingly diverse pockets of immigrant groups. If fear of terrorism causes the population to stratify by socio-economic group, then 'bridging' social capital is harder to achieve. Building up trust in such cases will be harder, and this will affect our ability to engage in collective action.

A final thought about the geography of terror risk merits mentioning. Throughout this chapter, I have assumed that the city center is the epicenter of a terrorist attack. An alternative scenario is that a highly populated metropolitan area is downwind from the attack site. Given the geography of nuclear plants in the Northeast United States and the densely populated areas nearby, millions of victims could be exposed to radiation from an attack on a nearby nuclear reactor. In choosing where to invest more of its resources, DHS might consider investing more in protecting at-risk sites for which there are a greater number of victims downwind.

NOTES

1. Gould and Stecklov (2009) argue that fighting terrorism offers spillover benefits of reducing crime. Their results are consistent with a stronger deterrence effect produced by an increased police presence after a terror attack. A higher level of policing is likely to catch more people trespassing and, at the same time, reduce the number of property crimes.
2. Google Insights is available at http://www.google.com/insights/search/#. For a public health example of how Google Insights has been used in past research, see Pelat et al. (2009).

REFERENCES

Abadie A. and S. Dermisi (2008). 'Is terrorism eroding agglomeration economies in central business districts? Lessons from office real estate markets in downtown Chicago', *Journal of Urban Economics*, **64**, 451–463.
Albouy, D. (2008). 'Are big cities really bad places to live? Improving quality-of-life estimates across cities', University of Michigan Working Paper.
Arzaghi, M. and V. Henderson (2009). 'Networking off Madison Avenue', NBER Working Paper.
Baum-Snow, N. (2007). 'Did highways cause suburbanization?' *Quarterly Journal of Economics*, **122** (2), 775–805.
Becker, G.S. (1991). 'A note on restaurant pricing and other examples of social influences on price', *Journal of Political Economy*, **99**, 1109–1116.
Costa, D.L. and M.E. Kahn (2003). 'Civic engagement and community heterogeneity', *Perspectives on Politics*, **1** (1), 103–111.
Dumais, Guy, Glenn Ellison, and Edward L. Glaeser (2002). 'Geographic concentration as a dynamic process', *Review of Economics and Statistics*, **84** (2), 193–204.
Glaeser, E. and M. Kahn (2001). 'Decentralized employment and the transformation of the American city', No. w8117, National Bureau of Economic Research.
Glaeser, E.L. and M.E. Kahn (2004). 'Sprawl and urban growth', in J.V. Henderson and J.F. Thisse (eds), *Handbook of Regional and Urban Economics*, 1st edn, Amsterdam: Elsevier, pp. 2481–2527.
Glaeser, E.L., H.D. Kallal, J.A. Scheinkman, and A. Shleifer (1992). 'Growth in cities', *Journal of Political Economy*, **100** (6), 1126–52.
Glaeser, E., J. Kolko and A. Saiz (2001). 'Consumer city', *Journal of Economic Geography*, **1** (1), 27–50.

Gould, E. and G. Stecklov (2009). 'Terror and the costs of crime', *Journal of Public Economics*, **93**, 1175–1188.
Guerrieri, V., D. Hartley, and E. Hirst (2010). 'Endogenous gentrification and housing price dynamics', *Journal of Public Economics*, **100**, 45–60.
Kahn, M.E. (2006). *Green Cities: Urban Growth and the Environment*, Washington, DC: Brookings Institution Press.
Kahn, M.E. (2010). *Climatopolis: How Our Cities will Thrive in the Hotter Future*, New York: Basic Books.
Krugman, P. (2001). 'Reckonings: an injured city', *New York Times*, October 3, available at http://www.nytimes.com/2001/10/03/opinion/reckonings-an-injured-city.html?ref=paulkrugman (accessed February 2014).
Maguen, S., A. Papa, and B.T. Litz (2008). 'Coping with the threat of terrorism: a review', *Anxiety, Stress, and Coping*, **21** (1), 15–35.
Mieszkowski, P. and E. Mills (1993). 'The causes of metropolitan suburbanization', *Journal of Economic Perspectives*, **7** (3), 135–147.
Pelat, C., C. Turbelin, A. Bar-Hen, A. Flahault, and A. Valleron (2009). 'More diseases tracked by using Google trends', *Emerging Infectious Diseases*, **15**, 1327–1328.
Reyes, J.W. (2007). 'Environmental policy as social policy? The impact of childhood lead exposure on crime', *B.E. Journal of Economic Analysis and Policy*, **7**, Article 51 (online).
Rosenthal, S. and W.C. Strange (2003). 'Geography, industrial organization, and agglomeration', *Review of Economics and Statistics*, **85** (2), 377–393.
Viscusi, W.K. (1984). 'The lulling effect: the impact of child-resistant packaging on aspirin and analgesic ingestions', *American Economic Review*, **74** (2), 324–327.
Waldfogel, J. (2008). 'The median voter and the median consumer: local private goods and population composition', *Journal of Urban Economics*, **63** (2), 567–582.

8. Macroeconomic consequences of terrorist attacks: estimation for the analysis of policies and rules[1]

Adam Rose

INTRODUCTION

The design of policies and rules to reduce the risk of terrorist attacks should ideally be evaluated according to an objective decision-making framework such as benefit–cost analysis (BCA). Although BCA is straightforward in principle, it often involves many serious complications when applied to the area of terrorism. Direct costs of interdiction are straightforward in terms of enumerating expenditures on equipment and manpower. However, complications arise here, because tactics such as increased screening and surveillance cause significant spillover effects, including inconvenience, delays and congestion, as well as potentially positive or negative changes in the overall business environment. Direct benefits of risk reduction are the avoided losses. These losses begin with direct property damage and direct business interruption, as well as injuries and deaths, though the measurement of the latter can be quite controversial. More difficult to assess are the indirect impacts that spread through a regional or national economy. The estimation of losses is further complicated by some unique considerations relating to terrorism in the realms of resilience and behavioral responses.

The majority of chapters in this book focus primarily on the direct costs and the spillover aspects of policies and rules to be implemented by government agencies such as the US Department of Homeland Security. This chapter focuses on the benefits side, with an emphasis on macroeconomic considerations. There are two major approaches to benefit estimation at the macroeconomic level. The first and most popular might be termed the welfare economics approach, in which benefits, including general equilibrium effects, are measured in terms of consumer surplus. This approach typically takes into account many subtleties. In the case where an event has not actually taken place, one important distinction is between *ex ante* and *ex post* analysis. The former includes uncertainty, and therefore the welfare concept is defined so as to hold expected utility constant. If society is risk-neutral, and when event probabilities are applied, then this is the same as the expected economic loss. The *ex post* case assumes the event has taken place and estimates compensation that would be required to avoid losses. This would ideally be a Hicksian willingness to accept concept and would hold utility constant. There is also the further problem of estimating the range of events at risk, including probabilities (*ex ante*) in losses and consequences (*ex post*). In general, traditional BCA would not consider economic impacts as losses if they simply represent reallocations of resources. However, cases where some economic activity is lost forever and not simply displaced would be considered losses. These circumstances need to be carefully specified in performing a macro consequence analysis.

The second approach to benefit estimation might be termed the 'macroeconomic indicator' approach. It expresses benefits in terms of such variables as output, income and employment. This approach is more prevalent in research on the economic consequences of disasters and in macroeconomic policy analysis. It omits many of the subtleties of the welfare economics approach, but offers results in terms more familiar to policy makers. However, output measures, such as gross domestic product (GDP), are typically not equal to the consumer surplus component of BCA. Of course, the two approaches are not mutually exclusive in terms of modeling. For example, computable general equilibrium (CGE) analysis, emphasized as a preferred approach in this chapter, is capable of yielding both sets of measures. It can generate macro-indicator impacts as well as welfare measures emanating from the model's utility functions (see, e.g., Rose et al., 2011). Moreover, it can incorporate many of the subtleties of an ideal welfare economics approach (see, e.g., Klaiber and Smith, 2011).

This chapter begins with a summary of the evolution of economic consequence analysis leading to the development of a comprehensive analytical framework. I then provide some insight into the variability of potential consequences that makes it difficult to apply 'benefit transfer' methods as a shortcut. Next I describe how CGE modeling by itself and in conjunction with supplementary analysis is able to estimate features that complicate the loss estimation picture. I then discuss the expanded framework of analysis in more detail. I conclude with some observations about future research needs.

THE EVOLUTION OF ECONOMIC CONSEQUENCE ANALYSIS

The modern terminology in terrorist studies for the focus of this chapter is economic consequence analysis. It stems from two threads. First is the physical damage from terrorist attacks, which has been the purview of natural science and engineering in evaluating such phenomena as the blast capability of improvised explosive devices (IEDs), the epidemiological implications of the denotation of a radiological dispersion device (RDD) or the dispersal of anthrax spores. Economists enter the picture by translating the property damage, loss of life or lost workdays into direct economic loss estimates. Aside from the controversy over the value of human life, this is a straightforward process.[2]

The analysis of broader, often termed 'indirect', effects stems from the field of economic impact analysis. This dates back to the first operational models capable of examining the workings of the entire economy, that is, Keynesian models and input–output (I-O) models tracing back to the 1930s. Typical applications were to broad-based initiatives, such as fiscal policy, war build-ups and strategic bombing campaigns (see, e.g., United States Strategic Bombing Survey, 1945; Baran and Galbraith, 1947). More focused were economic impact studies examining the opening of a new mine or closing of a factory. Most of these studies were more appropriately undertaken at the regional level, where simple approaches, such as economic base or I-O models, could readily be constructed (see, e.g., Isard, 1960; Leontief, 1966). The relative stability between the indirect effects and direct effects was often very straightforward and was congealed into 'impact multipliers'. The field was streamlined even further by the publication of tables of output, income and employment multipliers for the US or its various regions (Kim, 1985; Cartwright et al., 1981). It became well established that one could use rules of thumb for such analyses, for example, that the multiplier effects for a medium-sized city or small state would be on the order of 1.5 to 2.0, and that a large city or medium-sized state would have an overall multiplier between 2.0 and 2.5, and so on.[3]

Features of these two threads merged into hazard loss estimation in the 1990s, typically applied to natural events (see, e.g., West and Lenze, 1994; FEMA, 1997;[4] Shinozuka et al., 1998). Another feature was added: that of resilience, or the ability to mute the economic impacts of disasters by more efficient utilization of remaining resources and by accelerating the pace of recovery (Rose et al., 1997).[5] Rose (2004, 2007) has proposed a straightforward definition of resilience as the avoided losses resulting from implementing a given resilient tactic divided by the maximum potential losses for a given event in the absence of that tactic. Rose et al. (2009) measured the resilience of the New York Metropolitan Area economy to the 9/11 attacks at 72 percent as a result of business relocation as a resilient response. This stemmed from the fact that 95 percent of the businesses, comprising 98 percent of the employment, in the World Trade Center area did not shut down but rather relocated their operations, mainly in the New York Metro Area (the losses are simply due to the time lags in the relocation). Simulation studies for resilient consumer responses (for example, conservation, input substitution) to hypothetical water and power disruptions caused by terrorist attacks in Los Angeles indicated a potential resilience effectiveness exceeding 80 percent (Rose et al., 2007). The major option here is 'production recapture', or the ability of firms to turn on their production lines or otherwise open for business as soon as water and power services are restored and to make up for lost production.[6]

In the past decade, the major extension of economic consequence analysis has been to include behavioral considerations. A prime example is the 'fear factor', which refers to changes in risk perception that translate into changes in economic behavior. Gordon et al. (2007) pointed this out in an assessment of the man-portable air-defense systems (MANPADS) tactic to reduce the terrorist threat to commercial aviation, citing the experience following 9/11, which resulted in a nearly two-year downturn in air travel and related tourism in the US. Rose et al. (2009) refined the analysis of the post 9/11 attack by detrending for the effect of the ongoing recession in 2001 but found even the adjusted consequence was as high as $45 billion, which accounted for over 80 percent of the estimated direct business interruption losses stemming from the event. A recent study by Giesecke et al. (2012) of a potential RDD ('dirty bomb') attack on the financial district of Los Angeles would lead to social amplification of risk and stigma effects (see Kasperson et al., 1988; Burns and Slovic, 2010) that could exceed the conventional 'resource loss' effects by several fold.

A schematic of a broadened loss estimation framework developed by Rose (2009) is presented in Figure 8.1. It shows the inclusion of resilience and behavioral linkages in the overall economic consequence analysis picture. It also includes two other aspects that need to be included in the overall picture, the implications of which are often misinterpreted. The first is remediation, which is typically not part of traditional economic impact analysis and has a conventional role in hazard loss estimation as simply repair and reconstruction. In the case of a terrorist attack, this can take on a much larger role, especially if the attack is caused by an insidious chemical, biological or radiological agent. For example, Rose (2008) found that the cost of remediation for a radionuclide attack on a reservoir

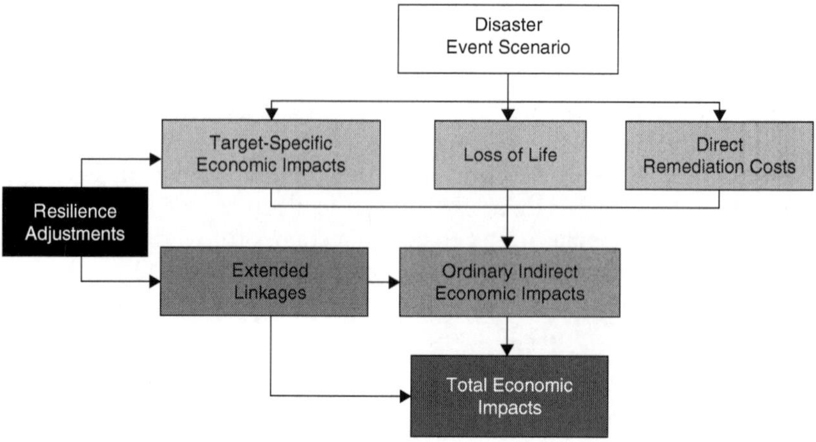

Figure 8.1 Economic assessment framework overview

of a small city of 100 000 was equal to the sum of the property and business interruption losses.

The cost of mitigation tactics also enters the picture of a comprehensive economic consequence framework in its move toward a full-blown BCA. The interesting consideration here is the interpretation by many that remediation and mitigation have benefits stemming from their direct expenditures alone (aside from the standard benefits of avoided losses). This ignores the basic principle that resources are expended in the course of implementing remediation or mitigation, and that these resources typically must be diverted from productive use elsewhere. This mistake is more easily made by the use of I-O models, which do not include resource constraints or price adjustments.[7] I discuss further below how more advanced models, such as CGE analysis, can sort out these issues and more accurately assess the impacts on gross domestic (or regional) product.

One final note is that economic consequence analysis, especially at the macro level, is usually measured in terms of national account categories such as income, GDP or gross output. This is in contrast to welfare measures (for example, consumer surplus proxied by equivalent or compensating variation), which are more standard in microeconomic analysis. For an excellent analysis of the use of welfare measures in CGE analysis in particular, and the complexity of measurement issues in general, the reader is referred to Klaiber and Smith (2011).

THE VARIABILITY OF CONSEQUENCES OF TERRORIST ATTACKS

The presence of resilience and behavioral responses imparts significant variability to the economic consequences of terrorism in relation to attack mechanisms and targets. Simple rules of thumb cannot be used as in the relatively mundane area of economic impact analysis. The situation makes benefit transfer relatively more difficult for application to terrorist attacks as well.

This is illustrated by simulation results for terrorist attacks on six targets as presented in Table 8.1. The first four cases were estimated with the use of an I-O model supplemented by regression and benefit transfer methods to incorporate resilience. The last two cases were estimated primarily with the use of a CGE model, which required relatively fewer ancillary techniques because of this model form's relative superiority in incorporating resilient actions and the behavioral consequences of changes in risk perceptions. Details of the simulations can be found in Rose et al. (2008) and Lee et al. (2008).

Losses are divided according to major impact categories of loss of life, ordinary business interruption (BI), behavioral linkages and resilience. In fact, although all six cases are caused by a bioterrorist agent, the size of the various components varies enormously across cases.[8]

Table 8.1 Summary of economic consequences of bioterrorism attacks (gross output losses, in billions of 2007 dollars)

Type of attack	Loss of life	Ordinary business interruption (BI)	Behavioral linkage	Resilience	Total gross output[a]
Stadium	−57.2	−0.5	−16.2	8.5	−65.4
Urban center	−2.2	−8.2	[b]	4.4	−6.0
Airport	−1.0	[c]	−220.0[d]	119.5[e]	−101.5
Lettuce	−0.054	−0.024	[b]	[b]	−0.078
Foot and mouth	[c]	−46.2[f]	[b]	4.2[f]	−42.0
Water service	[b]	−27.3	−2.6	26.7	−3.2

Notes:

a Total does not include stimulus from remediation.
b Not measured.
c Less than $100 million.
d Adjusted for background economic conditions.
e Recent estimate added to the analysis.
f Resilience via substitution is considered to offset domestic consumption loss, such that ordinary BI estimates represent only the decrease in export sales.

A brief summary of the results indicates the following:

1. Stadium attack. This event results in limited property damage, but a potentially huge loss of life because of the crowding of people in a confined location. The BI is small because it involves loss of activity in a single venue. Future sporting events can be moved to other locations. Extended linkages are large because fear of similar attacks reduces attendance elsewhere. At the same time, resilience is significant, as people substitute other leisure activities for sporting events.
2. Urban center attack. This event is less likely to have a concentrated impact on people as the previous case but will have a relatively larger impact on ordinary BI, though this effect is significantly offset by business relocation and other resilience measures. Behavioral linkages were not measured in this case, but further research presented below in the section on 'CGE Modeling of Special Features of Terrorist Consequences' indicates that this could be the dominant loss component.
3. Airport attack. This event would result in a limited loss of life and property damage, as well as BI in terms of lost flights for a short duration. However, as in the case of the 9/11 attacks, it could lead to a fear of flying and hence a large related reduction in tourist or business-trip activity.
4. Lettuce crop attack. This event would cause a minimal loss of life because the population would be much less concentrated than in the other cases and because health warnings would be issued quickly. Also, there are ready substitutes for agricultural products.
5. Foot and Mouth Disease attack. This event would lead to minimal loss of life but sizeable business activity reductions from the slaughtering of animals and decrease of export sales. Resilience would be significant in terms of the increase in consumption of chicken and fish as substitutes.
6. Municipal water system attack. This event would likely cause minimal loss of life. BI would be sizeable, and behavioral linkages would be significant through the shutdown of neighboring water systems for testing. Resilience would be especially large because of the strength of the resilient actions, such as production rescheduling.

Although the component estimates in Table 8.1 may at first appear random, some patterns do emerge, and I offer the following factors that most influence the results. Several of these causes of variation are technical in nature, but several others are highly dependent on public policy and private sector decisions before and after the attack. The explanations can be summarized in the following categories:

- lethality of the biological agent;
- concentration of people and their ability to escape;
- vulnerability/security of the target;
- duration of the event;
- fear of replication on this or related targets;
- perceived ability to mitigate future attacks; and
- resilience.

The results indicate that several components having the greatest influence are behavioral rather than technical. This should help policy makers pinpoint strategies for reducing losses from bioterrorism.

COMPUTABLE GENERAL EQUILIBRIUM ANALYSIS

This section assesses the capability of CGE modeling to estimate the losses of a terrorist attack. It includes a discussion of advantages and disadvantages of CGE in general and in the context of the economics of terrorism. It elaborates on recent advances by the author and others to overcome CGE model limitations with respect to disequilibria, parameter specifications and behavior. It emphasizes the ability of CGE modeling to address three aspects of consequence analysis that have typically been neglected (at least quantitatively) in nearly all studies of disasters, both human-made and natural. The first of these is the full range of indirect, macroeconomic or general equilibrium impacts, which have the potential to greatly increase the size of loss estimates. The second is individual business and market resilience, or the inherent ability of businesses and markets to cushion themselves against shocks, which have the potential to lower these loss estimates. The third is the inclusion of behavioral considerations especially relevant to terrorism that affect risk perceptions and translate into additional costs.

Basic Considerations

A layman's definition of CGE is a model of the entire economy based on decisions by individual producers and consumers in response to price signals, within limits of available capital, labor and natural resources. CGE is thus a comprehensive model with behavioral content that mimics the workings of markets under explicit constraints (see, e.g., Shoven and Whalley, 1992).

CGE is the state of the art in regional economic impact analysis (Partridge and Rickman, 2010). It has been applied extensively to such topics as simulating the impacts of a change in sales tax rates, developing new oil or gas fields, examining industrial targeting and assessing air quality regulations. It also has a more than 20-year history in fields closely related to the economic impacts of terrorism, such as natural hazards and climate change. The first economy-wide modeling of related topics was a CGE analysis of climate change damage by Kokoski and Smith (1987), with a significant emphasis on the sensitivity of the results to the value of key parameters. Brookshire and McKee (1992) provided an overview of advantages and disadvantages of CGE modeling to the application of natural hazards, while Boisvert (1992) provided a simple example of a CGE model applied to a utility service disruption following an earthquake. His model used Cobb–Douglas production functions, which require that the elasticity of substitution between all factors of production is assumed to equal unity. Unfortunately, this simple and early standard approach in CGE modeling, used in great part because data on key parameters are lacking, yields an overly flexible response for short-run phenomena. Early simulations by Rose (1998) indicated that these Cobb–Douglas production functions would estimate that a regional economy suffering an outage of electricity of, say, 50 percent might suffer a reduction of output (totally apart from resilience other than input substitution) of only 2 or 3 percent. Note, however, that the use of Cobb–Douglas elasticities is less of a problem when one examines long-term phenomena such as climate change damage or reconstruction following a terrorist attack, because of the longer period that the economy has to adjust to equilibrium.[9]

One consideration especially important in the context of terrorist attacks is the fact that economic activity is not uniformly distributed throughout a region. Moreover, the major feature that distinguishes terrorist attacks from natural hazards is the deliberate intent of the former, which, rather than being random, are focused on targets that can generate the greatest direct and indirect damage. This leads to relatively greater concentrations of property damage and production disruption among economic sectors. Rose and Guha (2004) developed a methodology to differentiate disruptions of utility lifeline services across customers. Together with the use of more realistic elasticities of substitution, their model yielded reasonable results for a major earthquake simulation in the Memphis, Tennessee region.

Several major advances were made by Rose and Liao (2005), some of which are discussed at greater length below. These include operational ways of linking real-world resilience options to key parameters of a constant elasticity of substitution (CES) production function, an algorithm for recalibrating key production function parameters to empirical or simulation data, and a method for separating partial equilibrium from net general equilibrium impacts. These methodological refinements were successfully applied to an analysis of a water service disruption in Portland, Oregon in the aftermath of a hypothetical earthquake.

To assess the worthiness of CGE for the analysis of the consequences of terrorist threats to the economy, I identify specific considerations and how the modeling framework can address them. In the course of the discussion, I also compare CGE with the other two approaches typically used to analyze economic impacts of disasters: I-O and macroeconometric models. These considerations include the following:

1. Specific targets. This is a relative advantage of CGE models because the basic unit of analysis is an individual firm or household; moreover, these are often grouped into sectors and socio-economic classes, respectively. Other 'multisector' modeling approaches like I-O and even highly disaggregated econometric models are not specified below the 'meso' scale (sector groupings). Individual targets can be pinpointed in all these modeling approaches through a geographic information system (GIS) overlay, but their separate identity is easier to maintain in a CGE model (Rose and Liao, 2005).
2. Individual behavior. Here again CGE has distinct advantages in the ability to model both normal behavior and the broader category often referred to as bounded rationality, which includes non-maximizing objectives, myopia and fear. I-O models lack any behavioral content, and the behavioral content of econometric models is typically limited to optimization. See also the discussion in the following section on behavioral effects.
3. Market behavior. In CGE models, prices provide signals to allocate resources. Prices are absent in I-O models, and their role is more indirect in econometric models. The resilience of communities is greatly aided by the workings of markets, but this has been an oft-neglected aspect of disaster studies.
4. Stock and flow losses. CGE models can estimate the effects of terrorist attacks in terms of both property damage and business interruption. The former is especially relevant in the case of terrorism, where just a 'threat' can cause losses from business closure or population evacuation. Most I-O models lack the matrix of capital coefficients necessary to evaluate the former. CGE models are superior to econometric models in analyzing the pattern of decisions to rebuild the capital stock and its ability to influence business interruption losses.

5. Non-market considerations. Many terrorist attacks are intended to have a symbolic impact in addition to business impacts. Such targets would include environmental and iconic cases such as the Grand Canyon and the Statue of Liberty, respectively. Another example of non-market impacts would be infrastructure, including highways, electric and water utilities and communication networks. These are obvious economic entities, but their provision of services is not often accomplished through the market, so prices must be inferred. Recent advances in CGE analysis have extended its capability to include non-market considerations (see, e.g., Oladosu, 2000; Smith and Carbone, 2007; as well as the discussion below on non-market feedback effects). Non-market impacts have been incorporated into I-O models extensively (see, e.g., Duchin and Lange, 1992), though not in relation to any surrogate markets that might influence changes in their value if they are damaged or if economic conditions change. Non-market values have been much less frequently incorporated into macroeconometric models.
6. Economic resilience to terrorist attacks. Given the relative flexibility of consumer and producer responses, CGE models are especially adept at incorporating resilience. Failure to incorporate individual and market resilience is likely to lead to overestimation of negative impacts. Non-linearities and the ability to substitute inputs are major aspects of resilience that are inherent in CGE models but nearly impossible to incorporate in I-O models. They are also somewhat difficult to incorporate into econometric ones. However, econometric models are to date superior in modeling the role of inventories.
7. Recovery processes. Recovery from major terrorist attacks may take a long time, and there is a dynamic adjustment process that would ideally be modeled. CGE models have been extended to a dynamic form, including incorporation of changing conditions and adaptations, to trace the entire time path of adjustment (Dixon et al., 2011). This is more difficult with I-O models. Though it is a somewhat standard feature of econometric models to trace a time path, it is relatively more difficult to incorporate changing conditions.
8. Economic disequilibria. A shock to the system from a terrorist attack will cause the economy to be out of sync, and its return to equilibrium may take some time. As discussed at length below, CGE models can be adapted to take into account various disequilibria with respect to labor markets, government budgets, trade balances and input availabilities. I-O models by their very nature cannot accommodate disequilibria, and it is difficult to do so in econometric models as well.

9. Macroeconomic repercussions. This would include the range of effects, beginning with more basic multiplier effects, then general equilibrium impacts and then broader, less tangible macro effects, including synergies. I-O models can only include basic multiplier processes, while CGE can include a broader range of general equilibrium effects and some synergies, as can econometric models. However, econometric models have an edge over CGE models to date in dealing with matters relating to interest rates and financial markets (I-O models are incapable of taking these factors into account at all). The reason for the advantage of econometric models may not, however, be due to inherent capabilities, but simply to their relatively longer existence and their much more prevalent application to these areas.
10. Distribution of impacts across socio-economic groups. Economic losses are unlikely to be evenly distributed, and any equivalent loss will have a more adverse effect on low-income populations. All three modeling approaches (if the social accounting matrix extension of I-O models is considered) are adept at addressing these impacts. CGE and econometric models have the advantage of being able to incorporate differences in behavior across socio-economic groups.
11. Spatial diffusion of the economic impacts. Space and location can be incorporated into CGE models applied to disasters in a straightforward manner. Distance is typically effectively handled by a transportation cost variable. When roads, bridges, railroads and ports are damaged, these transportation costs can be adjusted accordingly.[10] Another key dimension relates to the spread of the impacts of disaster over space. A terrorist attack in one location spreads throughout the economy of a region and often beyond to other regions and nations. Moreover, there is likely to be some feedback effect in the target region as well. I-O and econometric models are more advanced in terms of their interregional application, but again this is probably more a matter of modeling experience than any inherent inability of CGE models. It should, however, be noted that because of their complexity it is relatively much more difficult to conceptually design and obtain the data for an interregional CGE model, though recent advances have been made (see, e.g., Dixon et al., 2007).

Although this summary has emphasized the superiority of CGE to its two major competitors, both of them deserve credit for facilitating the construction and enhancing the abilities of CGE models (see, e.g., Rose, 1995). Nearly all CGE models have at their core the production of intermediate goods, the data for which almost always come from I-O tables, as do basic data on primary factors of production and on government revenues and expenditures. Broader account balances relating to savings and investment, as well as imports and exports, are usually obtained from social accounting matrices. Econometric specification of CGE model parameters is considered to yield more accurate estimates than the standard practice of data transfer and calibration. Also, both I-O and CGE models by themselves have no forecasting ability, so 'conjoining' them with econometric models is desirable for long-run analyses. Finally, the relatively lower complexity of I-O models makes it easier to conjoin them with other types of models in an integrated system (see, e.g., Gordon et al., 2005; Sohn et al., 2004).

CGE MODELING OF SPECIAL FEATURES OF TERRORIST CONSEQUENCES

Resilience in the Context of CGE Models

The production side of the standard CGE model is composed of a standard, nested (multitiered), CES production function for each sector (see, e.g., Rose and Liao, 2005; Dixon et al., 2011; Giesecke et al., 2012). The production function is normally applied to aggregate categories of major inputs of capital, labor, energy and materials, with subaggregates possible for each (for example, the energy aggregate is often decomposed by fuel type – electricity, oil, gas, and coal – and the labor input can be distinguished by occupational category). This production function represents a type of hierarchical or sequential decision-making process. For a given level of output, the firm's manager first chooses the optimal combination of capital and energy. The manager next juxtaposes that combination to labor to determine the optimal choice of inputs in the third tier, and so on. In the top tier, input decisions are made regarding the previous aggregate combination and material inputs (intermediate goods). Materials are often modeled in terms of fixed input coefficients, but special provision can be made for substitution possibilities for select types (see, e.g., Rose et al., 2009).

Many types of inherent resilience are already built into CGE models, including input and import substitution, use of inventories, and relocation (implicitly through interregional trade changes). Adaptive resilience refers to the instances where these outcomes are enhanced through ingenuity or learning. Examples are increased input or import substitution possibilities or increased inventory levels. These require parameter changes. Rose and Liao (2005) developed algorithms to solve for the necessary changes in elasticities of substitution in CES production functions. Essentially, this required empirical or simulation data on an input limitation and of the corresponding output levels attained under stress. The algorithm then solves for the increased elasticity values as the dependent variables. Given the complexity of the problem, however, a definitive analytical solution is not possible, and numerical methods had to be used. An algorithm for changing the productivity parameter of the production function for changes in the adaptive resilience tactic of increased conservation of scarce inputs was also developed by Rose and Liao. This, however, is a simpler problem and can be solved analytically.

Other major resilience strategies include technological change and production recapture (making up lost production after business activities have stabilized). At this time, the former is addressed by ad hoc methods such as replacement or adjustments of a production function with external data. In the case of the latter, some 'recapture factors' have been developed (Rose and Lim, 2002; FEMA, 2014) that simply represent scalars to adjust lost production. The cost of implementing this resilience tactic is rather small (overtime pay, but only in some instances) and so is usually not incorporated into the analysis, though it readily could be via a change in the wage rate.[11]

Behavioral Effects

Up to this point, our discussion has focused on what might be termed resource loss effects. I now turn to the economic ramifications of behavioral effects. Fischhoff et al. (1981) did some of the pioneering work on perceived risk associated with various types of hazards, finding that perceptions are mainly driven by uncertainty and dread. Slovic (1987) suggested that hazardous events signaled some increased future risk. Kasperson et al. (1988) proposed a framework relating to the 'social amplification of risk' through the interaction of psychological, institutional and cultural processes. Additional research on hazard situations indicated the possibility of long-term consequences through stigma attached to the affected areas.

Moreover, these changes in risk perception can alter economic behavior in the short term and the long term. For example, employees are likely to require a premium to work at a site previously attacked or perceived to be a major target. Investors are likely to require a higher rate of return at such a site as well. Shoppers or tourists are likely to require a discount for goods, food or lodging at or near the site. These premia and discounts are likely to increase with the insidious nature of the attack. Chemical, biological and radiological agents provide little experience and are likely to incite dread on the population. Media coverage of such events will amplify the risk response. The difficulty of decontamination, and sometimes a lack of trust of government, will cause the adverse situation to linger.

Giesecke et al. (2012) recently analyzed the behavioral impacts of a hypothetical RDD, or 'dirty bomb', on the financial district of Los Angeles, and compared the effects with ordinary loss effects. This involved a GIS overlay of the model to capture unique features of economic activity in the directly affected area. Wage premia and shopper discounts were estimated through experiments and then were translated in the shift in supply demand functions in a regional CGE model. Investor premia were estimated through benefit transfer of behavioral responses to other types of hazards. The resulting values were typically in the range of 10 to 20 percent. The results indicated that short-run behavioral effects were only slightly smaller than resource loss effects. However, ordinary business interruption losses decrease to zero in a rather short time, while the persistent behavioral effects begin to add up. For just the first year, behavioral effects were 2.5 times the resource loss effects. If the stigma were to last ten years, the behavioral effects would be nearly 15 times as high as the ordinary resource loss effects, even after discounting at 5 percent.

The results have obvious policy implications relating to risk communication. Accurate and non-sensational news reporting can lower the damage from a terrorist attack, as can a thorough clean-up and adept assurances by both the public and private sectors (Elcock et al., 2004).

General Equilibrium Effects

General equilibrium effects refer to broader impacts generated through both the price and the quantity interactions of markets. I will illustrate them and their distinction from partial equilibrium (individual business or individual market) effects by summarizing modeling approaches used to estimate the costs of electricity outages. Partial equilibrium (or direct) effects of outages manifest themselves in four major ways: lost sales, equipment damage or restart costs, spoilage of variable inputs and idle labor costs. In addition, costs are incurred to reduce potential losses through the purchase of back-up generators, permanent changes in production schedules and utility capacity expansion to promote flexibility. At the margin, the cost of outages should be equal to the cost of these adaptive responses. Hence, the most popular way of measuring electricity outage losses, for example, has been tabulating expenditures on back-up generation rather than measuring damages directly (Beenstock et al., 1997). Still, measurement of just a single coping tactic or type of damage is likely to understate the direct dollar loss. Estimates of direct losses of electricity shortages range from \$1 to \$5/kWh in the US (see, e.g., Caves et al., 1992). Many regions of the US suffer outages of as many as 10–30 hours per year due to ordinary circumstances of engineering failures and severe storms.

I recommend the use of economic output losses (which can be adjusted to net or value-added terms and consequently translated into welfare measures) as a common denominator for both partial and general equilibrium effects. This facilitates the inclusion of some capital and productivity costs into the measurement. General equilibrium effects consist of the following:

1. Output loss to downstream customers of a disrupted firm through its inability to provide crucial inputs. This sets off a chain reaction beyond the first line of customers of firms who have had their electric power curtailed.
2. Output loss to upstream suppliers of disrupted firms through the cancellation of orders for inputs. Again, this is transmitted through several rounds but on the supplier side.
3. Output loss to all firms from decreased consumer spending associated with a decreased wage bill in firms directly affected by the electricity outage, as well as all other firms suffering negative general equilibrium effects.
4. Output loss to all firms from decreased investment associated with decreased profits of firms suffering the electricity outage and other firms negatively impacted by general equilibrium effects.
5. Output loss to all firms from cost (and price increases) from damaged equipment and other dislocations (including uncertainty) that result in productivity decreases in firms directly impacted.[12]

Note also that not all general equilibrium effects are negative. Some firms may benefit from the decreased prices associated with a shift in demand by other firms for various products. Several analyses indicate the existence of this possibility for several sectors, though the positive general equilibrium effects do not more than offset the negative ones. For many years, I-O models have been used to estimate the cost of utility service disruptions. These models reduce general equilibrium effects to quantity interdependencies and are typically unidirectional (for example, there are no offsetting effects through price reductions). It is not unusual for I-O models to yield multiplier effects that more than double the direct loss. General equilibrium models incorporate a broader range of interactions in the economy and more accurately measure regional economic impacts (see, e.g., Rose et al., 2007). Typically, most of these effects dampen the shock; thus 'indirect' effects are lower in CGE than in I-O models.

The calculation of equilibrium prices is a relative advantage of CGE over alternative macro impact modeling approaches, such as I-O analysis (where the calculation of price changes is separated from considerations of output changes) and macroeconometric models (which do not explicitly mimic the workings of markets in determining prices). However, the standard CGE model assumes perfect competition, though several advances allow for the incorporation of market power (see, e.g., Markusen and Robson, 1980). Many other price distortions, such as most taxes, can be evaluated in a straightforward manner in terms of reactions by producers and consumers. Other distortions, such as the effect of pollution externalities, are more problematic.

Finally, CGE models are adept at measuring market feedback effects. However, some of these effects can take place outside the market, as where a disaster generates pollution or, more broadly, where a mitigation measure may generate spillovers (for example, inconvenience or delay associated with increased airport passenger screening). If the good or service loss by the disaster makes a separable contribution to consumer preferences from the externality, then conventional CGE analysis can be applied. Smith and Carbone (2007) have offered an approximation method for evaluating these non-market feedback effects where the separability assumption does not hold.

Disequilibria

As noted above, the market system is inherently resilient to shocks and can be bolstered by various policies. All of this can best be modeled in a CGE framework. However, a fundamental shortcoming of CGE is its equilibrium emphasis. Following a major disaster, a sustained period of disequilibrium is likely to ensue. Fortunately, several refinements of CGE modeling by the author and others have moved to overcome this limitation. These disequilibria are typically related to 'closure rules' or account balance conditions.

One of the unique features of disasters is the extensive damage they cause to productive capacity. This has been modeled as a constraint on sectoral capital stock or output (see, e.g., 2004; Rose et al., 2009; Wing et al., forthcoming). The major approach has been to fix one of the previous endogenous variables, such as output levels, but that requires a like number of previous exogenous variables be made endogenous.[13] The standard procedure has been to free up the zero economic profit condition. For a situation where many sectors need to be constrained, the following complementary slackness conditions have proven effective in overcoming convexity problems including multiple equilibria (see Rose et al., 2009):

1. Upper bounds on output of the affected sectors were imposed as the base year level minus estimated direct losses from the 9/11 attack.
2. A slack price variable was introduced into the revenue equation for each sector.
3. For each sector a complementary equation was introduced that required the product of the slack price variable from (2) and the gap between actual output (X_i) and the upper bound on output (X^{up}) to be greater than or equal to zero as:

$$(X_i - X_i^{up}) \times P_{slack} \geq 0$$
$$(-\ or\ 0)(\ +, -\ or\ 0)$$

   This equation implies that revenue received by any sector could be greater than its cost (positive P_{slack}), provided that the upper-bound constraint on output is binding. However, revenues received could also be lower than the cost of production (negative P_{slack}) when actual production is lower than or equal to the upper-bound constraint. Thus, P_{slack} represents a shadow price that serves to ration the available output when the upper-bound constraint is binding, but also allows producers to reduce production and/or prices.
4. Extra revenues (or losses) are added to (or subtracted from) the affected sector's capital returns. This ensures that revenues/losses in the economy are completely distributed.
5. Since the above equation introduces disequilibrium into the model, the algorithm forces the slack variable value towards zero in relation to the objective function of the model.[14]

Other disequilibria are likely to arise in a disaster context as well, though they can be addressed by more standard modeling approaches. Examples include local government deficits (due to declines in the tax base or the need for increased post-disaster expenditures), trade imbalances (due to the need to rely more heavily on imports), and labor market imbalances (due to death and injury). The standard closure rules are to equate supply and demand in these various markets and institutions. Disequilibrium is modeled by holding a key variable fixed and allowing another to vary, or by introducing a slack variable.

Ordinarily, any gap between supply and demand is resolved by a change in price. However, it is possible in CGE modeling to fix the price of a commodity and have the supply constrained, so that potential demand exceeds actual demand. This refinement is facilitated by the development of software that uses a complementarity programming solution approach, thereby allowing for some 'slack' in the system, and hence disequilibrium. For example, Rose and Liao (2005) were able to limit the supply of water to each sector and on a differential basis. Ordinarily this would increase the price of water, but this is unrealistic given the fact that water is not priced in an ordinary market but rather under the administrative authority of a public service agency. Therefore, the price of water was fixed, essentially modeling it as a disequilibrium market. The slack was taken up by a reduction in the profit margin in the water sector (see also Rose et al., 2009).[15]

AN ILLUSTRATION OF THE OVERALL FRAMEWORK

Although this chapter is intended to be generally applicable to all human-made and natural disasters, this section focuses on a terrorist attack on a public water system using a radiological device. Details are presented in Figure 8.2. In the left-hand margin of the figure, various stages, or linkages, of the analysis are listed. Across the top margin, the level of analysis is distinguished, beginning with the water system itself and extending through to the macro level. Note also that the figure distinguishes impacts on businesses and households and includes linkages and impacts relating to decontamination/remediation and reconstruction/resettlement.

The flow of events in Figure 8.2 begins with the 'radionuclide attack' in the upper left-hand corner, which results in an actual water system contamination. However, as expressed by the dashed line in the figure, suspected water system contamination may cause a shut-down of water services or 'Do not drink/use' edicts in neighboring areas. Both the real and imagined contamination will lead to direct business interruption losses, with the suspected water system contamination working through the 'fear factor'. However, only actual water system contamination will result in deaths and injuries, which will then translate into lower effective demand for goods and services, that is, increased BI. Direct effects then cause changes in supply and demand through markets, with prices changing to achieve new equilibria (indirect BI). Evacuation and relocation can help reduce the number of deaths and injuries, but, at the same time, this results in an increase in BI as well. In fact, massive evacuations can result in larger BI than would be suffered from an actual event. In these instances policy makers place a higher premium on saving lives than on business activity. Note that resilience influences many of the aforementioned linkages. Microeconomic options for resilience include input and import

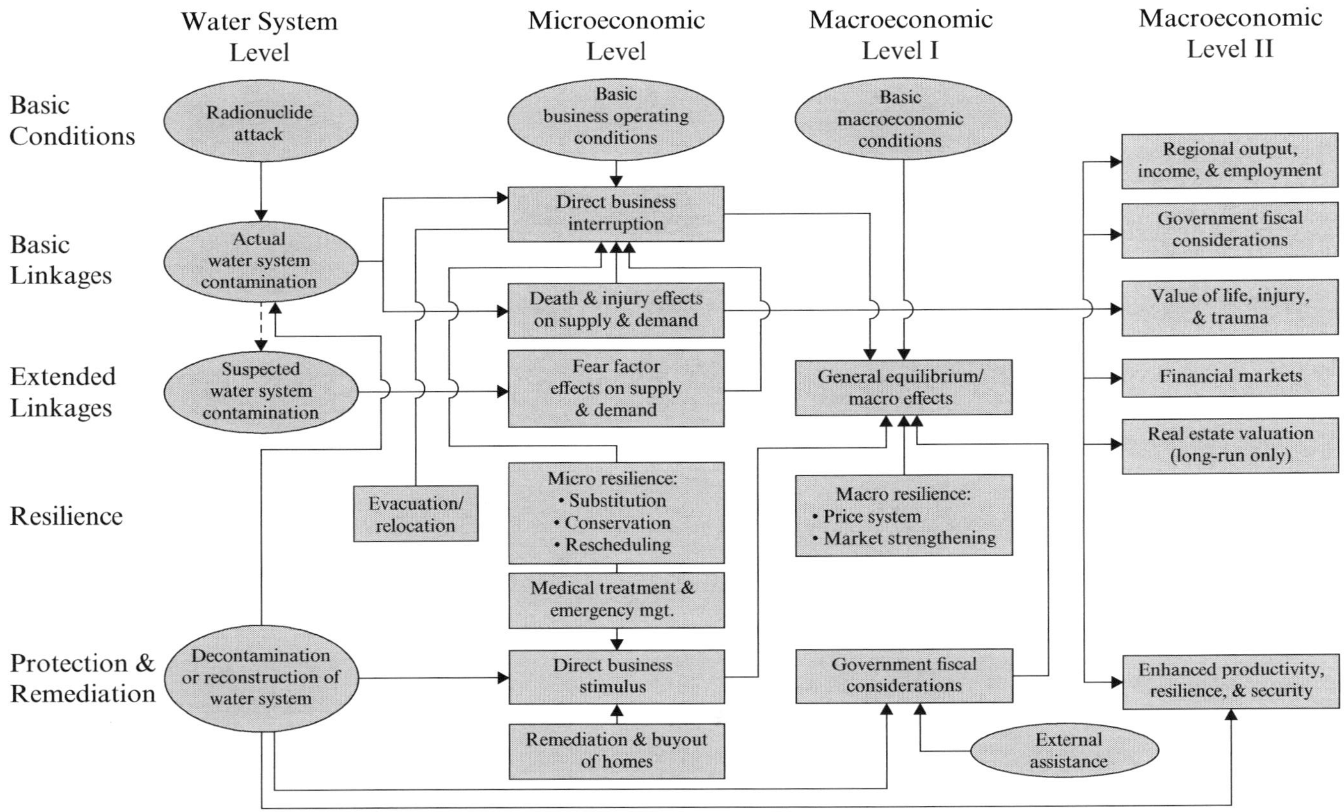

Figure 8.2 Estimating the total economic impacts of a radiological attack on a municipal water system

substitution, conservation, use of inventories and rescheduling of activities (both production and household activities that relate to well-being).

At Macroeconomic Level I, the direct BI and direct business stimulus are injected into the broader economy subject to resource constraints to capture price and quantity interactions in multiple markets. At this initial macro level, resilience relates to the rationing role of prices for goods, such as water, in short supply, as well as general signaling of relative scarcity of resources and goods for the economy as a whole.

Another layer added in Figure 8.2 is protection and remediation. Here, decontamination and reconstruction of the water system decrease the damaging agent and thus stunt the BI. In addition, decontamination or reconstruction of businesses and remediation or buy-out of homes both could stimulate economic activity at the direct level. However, they typically siphon off resources from other activities, and this combination of effects comes together at the general equilibrium level, such that the positive stimulus might be more than offset by the diversion of the necessary resources from normal (and often more productive) economic activities. Also coming into play at this level is the role of external assistance and its effect on government fiscal operations. Massive expenditures on security, either warranted or affected by the 'fear factor', would also represent an extended linkage.

The final perspective in Figure 8.2 is referred to as Macroeconomic Level II, which provides details of the overall outcome. Note, however, that these details are not additive. The bottom-line macroeconomic indicator would relate to the total production in the economy, stated in terms of gross output (total sales) or some net measure such as gross regional product, value-added or income. Employment is also listed, since it contains broader aspects of the 'human condition'. Other details would include the government-sector fiscal position (the extent to which the government incurs a deficit or finds other ways to finance the situation, and the effects of the disaster on its ability to borrow). This would also relate to matters of external aid and reduced tax payments from a deterioration of the tax base, both stock (property) and flow (sales). This final column also includes the value of death, injury and trauma to the population.

With respect to additional extended linkages, the analysis would ideally evaluate changes in real estate values, though it would include only those that continue in the long run. It would also evaluate impacts on financial markets. This would include factors such as the interest rate, which would have a major bearing on micro decisions (housing sales), fiscal considerations (government's ability to borrow) and other macro variables (money supply, exchange rates, and so on).

Finally, the last column includes aspects of enhanced productivity, resilience and security. Many of these stem from explicit policies, investments and experience, such as reconstruction and enhanced protection of the water supply, learning by businesses and households on how to cope with terrorist attacks and heightened security.

So as not to clutter the diagram, I have not displayed various non-market impacts, such as damaged ecosystems from contaminated water. This could also include a dollar value estimate of reductions in household well-being, apart from medical considerations, such as the value of household time to boil water, increased cost of purchasing alternative sources of water, and other activities to cope with the problem. Many of these are non-market impacts and pose special measurement problems (see, e.g., Rose and Oladosu, 2008; Klaiber and Smith, 2011).

CONCLUSION

This chapter has summarized a framework for analyzing the macroeconomic consequences of terrorist attacks in order to assess the benefits of policies and rules under consideration by DHS. The framework is comprehensive in its consideration of general equilibrium and non-market effects, as well as the special aspects of resilience and behavioral responses specific to terrorism. In fact, these latter two aspects can dominate the picture. Recently, Rose and Blomberg (2010) concluded that the public, rather than the perpetrators, were the major determinants of the macroeconomic consequences of the September 11, 2001 attacks. In the wake of 9/11, resilience was high, but so was fear. In addition, government policy in the form of Federal Reserve Board action and fiscal policy reduced the losses significantly. However, subsequent antiterrorist initiatives at home and abroad had major macroeconomic implications.

These complications make it difficult to apply benefit transfer approaches to evaluating the macroeconomic consequences of a terrorist attack. Although ordinary macroeconomic or general equilibrium impacts can be adapted, resilience and behavioral responses vary significantly by threat and attack target. It would be useful in this regard to identify distinct patterns and similarities across types of events. In the meantime, it will be necessary to increase the number of full-blown analyses of terrorist attacks to accurately assess the benefits of policies and rules. I have provided a rationale for the use of CGE modeling as the preferred approach.

I have omitted discussion of two major considerations that are beyond the scope of this chapter. The first is the potential of fiscal and monetary policy to offset some of the negative repercussions of a major terrorist event like 9/11. Most analysts have hypothesized that Federal Reserve actions were especially effective, but this has not been subjected to rigorous testing. Second is the macro impact of the US military response. Several analysts have suggested that this dwarfs the other impacts of 9/11. However, this claim is based on the politically contentious issue of whether the Iraq War was a direct reaction to 9/11. Political assessments such as this further complicate the already difficult area of economic consequence analysis.

I conclude by offering some suggestions for future research. In terms of basic measurement, there are still some major weaknesses. The first is that CGE models continue to be based on a single year of data and a calibration approach. Moreover, key parameters, such as elasticities of substitution, are typically adapted from locations and time periods that differ from those pertinent to the disaster event being studied. This is a general weakness of CGE but is less amenable to solution in the context of disasters, where data are rather thin for econometric estimation. In the meantime, the approach developed by Rose and Liao (2005) offers some potential for improvement.

Above, I have described an ad hoc approach developed by Giesecke et al. (2012) to incorporate behavioral effects into CGE models. Another approach is to incorporate bounded rationality (Conlisk, 1996; Giergenzer and Selten, 2002) more directly into the model through modifications of utility or production functions. This could include inserting expected utility functions with variations and standard assumptions regarding risk aversion, or, in dynamic models, including investment decision functions with limited time horizons or discount rates reflecting myopia. One fruitful area of future research is to include motivations other than maximizing behavior, including satisficing or 'minimum regrets' strategies. However, this poses both conceptual and solution problems in an otherwise equilibrium model based on traditional maximizing behavior. In addition to such conceptual advances, the major knowledge gap is the measurement of the duration of stigma effects following insidious attacks stemming from biological, chemical or radiological agents. As noted above, such long-term effects have the potential to increase consequences by more than an order of magnitude.

Finally, most of the analyses of resilience have focused on maximum potential rather than actual effectiveness, thus likely overstating the ability of resilience responses to reduce losses. Again, more case studies will be needed to estimate this gap. These studies should also be undertaken so as to identify the fundamental reasons that resilience is not applied with maximum effectiveness.

NOTES

1. The research contained in this chapter was funded by several grants from the US Department of Homeland Security, primarily under Grant # 207-ST-061–000001. This research was also supported by the National Science Foundation under Grant # SES0728934. Any opinions, findings and conclusions or recommendations in this document are those of the author and do not necessarily reflect views of the US Department of Homeland Security or the National Science Foundation.
2. Some complications arose with respect to basic conceptual issues in impact analysis and related cost–benefit analysis (CBA). One example is the valuation of labor in cases of less than full employment. Some have proposed that labor would have a zero value (cost) in this context, but others, beginning with Haveman and Krutilla (1967), have offered some excellent alternatives. Haveman and Farrow (2011) cogently summarized this literature by suggesting the best approach is to value unemployed labor at its reservation wage. They also suggest including general equilibrium effects. At the same time, *ex ante*, one cannot know precisely what proportion of workers involved will come from the ranks of the unemployed or simply change jobs. A probabilistic approach to this issue is favored but raises additional complications (see, e.g., Boardman et al., 2011).
3. Multipliers referred to here are known as 'Type II', and include indirect (or interindustry) effects plus induced effects (interactions between households' income/spending and industry production) (Miller and Blair, 2009). Note that the stability referred to stems from the fact that nearly all of these analyses assumed constancy in technology and overall economic structure (industry mix). An early exception by Isard and Kuenne (1953), which took into account patterns of industrial location, was more realistic but was rarely incorporated into subsequent impact analyses by others.
4. The Federal Emergency Management Agency sponsored the development of hazard loss estimation software known as HAZUS, which combined important features such as a building inventory for the entire US, earthquake damage functions and even a flexible I-O based indirect loss module. More recently HAZUS has been upgraded to 'multi-hazard' status by being broadened to apply to floods and wind damage as well (FEMA, 2014).
5. The focus of most loss estimation is on BI rather than property damage. Property damage takes place at a given point in time, while BI only begins at the point of the shock and then proceeds until recovery to the original or 'new normal' state has been attained. This flow measure has many advantages, including being able to factor in resilience and features of recovery policy, as well as being more compatible with the flow basis of benefit–cost analysis.
6. The cost penalty for most businesses is likely to be minimal, involving only overtime pay for workers, though some businesses, such as primary metals, could have significant start-up costs stemming from the clean-up of their production processes. Note also that the recapture potential is much greater from a terrorist attack than from a natural hazard. In the former, the terrorist targets the water or power system, leaving the remainder of the economy unscathed, while an earthquake would be indiscriminant as to its targets, thus reducing the productive capacity of all aspects of the economy.
7. This mistake is also more readily made in a regional context. It is not unusual (for example, the Northridge Earthquake) for a regional economy to actually go through a boom after a disaster because of the infusion of insurance payments, philanthropic aid and government aid. Of course, all these flows are a drain on the rest of the economy of the country. Thus, it is also best to perform economic consequence analysis in a comparative static mode by analyzing the various components individually and then adding in the outside aid flows. This provides the analyst with insight into the difference each component can make on the overall impacts. Otherwise, the impacts of a disaster itself are difficult to ascertain.

8. The influence of remediation of the attack is not included, since it is likely to be highly variable even within individual attack categories, given the bioterrorist agent, as well as being highly dependent on public policy decisions regarding timing and safety levels. For the case of a region, the results are also highly dependent on the inflow of federal government assistance.
9. An important contribution to the literature was the work by Cochrane et al. (1997) on the Federal Emergency Management Agency hazard loss estimation system, HAZUS (FEMA, 1997). The basis of the indirect economic loss module (IELM) of HAZUS is an I-O model. However, unlike the standard, linear and inflexible version of I-O, Cochrane's formulation allows for flexibility that equilibrates supply and demand imbalances through changes in imports and exports. This is similar to the handling of these trade flows in a CGE model. The major difference is that, in the CGE framework, these changes are in explicit response to prices, while Cochrane's formulation is a more mechanical equilibrating mechanism of excess demand or excess supply in the absence of price signals.
10. Another approach to transportation analysis has been the merging of a standard economic model with the transportation model. For example, Gordon et al. (2005) have developed a multiregion model for Southern California, which combines an I-O model with transportation modeling features. I-O is a crude approach that would ordinarily not be the ideal model to use; however, because of the conceptual and computational difficulties of merging a CGE model with other model types, this is currently the best of the alternatives.
11. The cost of input substitution is reflected in the adjustment process, and the negative cost (cost savings) of conservation is reflected in improved productivity of the conserved input.
12. The direct and indirect costs of electricity outages thus do not just take place during the period in which power is curtailed. Back-up generators are purchased in anticipation of outages, and the carrying cost of increased inventories of critical materials is incurred over a longer period as well. Equipment damage, spoilage and idle labor costs may translate into an immediate loss in profits, but they may not be passed through in the form of price increases until a later date. The same is true of electric utility cost and price increases that lag, even in a deregulated market. The three time periods, designated as preparatory, crisis and recovery, will vary in length depending on the context. For estimation purposes, however, they may all be simulated simultaneously in cases where there are no significant dynamic (that is, time-related) effects.
13. An alternative approach to inserting multiple constraints into a CGE model is to use the device of a 'phantom tax' (see, e.g., Dixon et al., 2011). This imposes a tax of sufficient size to stunt the demand for the input that is otherwise no longer available. The tax payments, however, evaporate, so as not to affect the government accounts.
14. The most widely used mathematical programming package for CGE analysis, General Algebraic Modeling System (GAMS) has many 'solvers', and some are based on straightforward non-linear programming algorithms (Rosenthal, 2011). This is the approach used by Rose et al. (2009). Other approaches are based on complementarity programming (some GAMS solvers and the popular MPSGE approach developed by Rutherford, 1998), where the conditions are not so dissimilar to the solution approach presented here.
15. Closely related are the ad hoc adjustments and temporary equilibria that ensue after a disaster, many of which can be incorporated through further refinement of the CGE model. Examples identified by West and Lenze (1994) include additions to the labor market in the form of outside government and non-governmental organization volunteers; examples by Cochrane et al. (1997) include households dipping deep into savings or increasing their borrowing to fund repairs; and those by Rose and Lim (2002) include businesses recapturing lost production through overtime work at a later date.

REFERENCES

Baran, P. and J.K. Galbraith (1947). 'Professor Despres on "The effects of strategic bombing on the German war economy"', *Review of Economics and Statistics*, **29**, 132–134.

Beenstock, M., E. Goldin and Y. Haitobsky (1997). 'The cost of power outages in the business and public sectors in Israel: revealed preference vs. subject evaluation', *Energy Journal*, **18**, 39–61.

Boardman, A., D. Greenberg, A. Vining and D. Weimer (2011). *Cost–Benefit Analysis*, Upper Saddle River, NJ: Prentice Hall.

Boisvert, R. (1992). 'Indirect losses from a catastrophic earthquake and the local, regional, and national interest', in *Indirect Economic Consequences of a Catastrophic Earthquake*, Washington, DC: FEMA, pp. 204–266.

Brookshire, D. and M. McKee (1992). 'Other indirect costs and losses from earthquakes: issues and estimation', in *Indirect Economic Consequences of a Catastrophic Earthquake*, Washington, DC: FEMA, pp. 267–235.

Burns, W. and P. Slovic (2010). 'Predicting and modeling public response to a terrorist strike', in P. Slovic (ed.), *The Feeling of Risk: New Directions in the Perception of Risk*, London: Earthscan Publishing, pp. 285–306.

Carbone, J. and V.K. Smith (2008). 'Evaluating policy intervention with general equilibrium externalities', *Journal of Public Economics*, **92** (5–6), 1254–1274.

Cartwright, J.V., R.M. Beemiller and R.D. Gustely (1981). *RIMS II: Regional Input–Output Modeling System: Estimation, Evaluation, and Application of a Disaggregated Regional Impact Model*, Washington, DC: US Dept. of Commerce, Bureau of Economic Analysis, Regional Economic Analysis Division.

Caves, D., J. Harriges and R. Windle (1992). 'The cost of electric power interruptions in the industrial sector: estimates derived from interruptible service programs', *Land Economics*, **68**, 49–61.

Cochrane, H., J. Steenson, H. Rose and S. Chang (1997). 'Indirect economic losses', in *Development of Standardized Earthquake Loss Estimation Methodology Vol. II*, Menlo Park, CA: RMS, Inc.

Conlisk, J. (1996). 'Why bounded rationality?' *Journal of Economic Literature*, **34**, 669–700.

Dixon, P., J. Giesecke, M. Rimmer and A. Rose (2011). 'The economic costs to the US of closing its borders: a computable general equilibrium analysis', *Peace and Defence Economics*, **22** (1), 85–97.

Dixon, P., M. Rimmer and M. Tsigas (2007). 'Regionalizing results from a detailed CGE model: macro, industry and state effects in the US of removing major tariffs and quotas', *Papers in Regional Science*, **86** (1), 31–55.

Duchin, F. and G. Lange (1992). *The Future of the Environment*, New York: Oxford.

Elcock, D., G.A. Klemic and A.L. Taboas (2004). 'Establishing remediation levels in response to a radiological dispersal event (or "dirty bomb")', *Environmental Science and Technology*, **38** (9), 2505–2512.

Federal Emergency Management Agency (FEMA) (1997). *HAZUS* (Hazards US), Washington, DC.

Federal Emergency Management Agency (FEMA) (2014). *HAZUS M-H*. http://www.fema.gov/media-library/assets/documents/1112?id=1474, accessed March 27, 2014.

Fischhoff, B., P. Slovic, S. Lichtenstein, S.L. Derby, and R.L. Keeney (1981). *Acceptable Risk*, New York: Cambridge University Press.

Giergenzer, G. and R. Selten (eds) (2002). *Bounded Rationality: The Adaptive Toolbox*, Cambridge, MA: MIT Press.

Giesecke, J., W. Burns, A. Barrett, E. Bayrak, A. Rose, P. Slovic and M. Suher (2012). 'Assessment of the regional economic impacts of catastrophic events: a CGE analysis of resource loss and behavioral effects of a radiological dispersion device attack scenario', *Risk Analysis*, **32** (4), 583–600.

Gordon, P., J. Moore II, H. Richardson and Q. Pan (2005). 'The economic impact of a terrorist attack on the twin ports of Los Angeles and Long Beach', in H. Richardson, P. Gordon and J. Moore II. (eds), *The Economic Impacts of a Terrorist Attack*, Cheltenham, UK and Northampton, MA, USA: Edward Elgar, pp. 262–286.

Gordon, P., H. Richardson, J. Moore, II, J. Park and S. Kim (2007). 'Economic impacts of a terrorist attack on the U.S. commercial aviation system', *Risk Analysis*, **27** (3), 505–512.

Haveman, R. and S. Farrow (2011). 'Labor expenditures and benefit–cost accounting in times of unemployment', *Journal of Benefit–cost Analysis*, **2** (2), Article 7.

Haveman, R. and J. Krutilla (1967). 'Unemployment, excess capacity, and benefit–cost criteria', *Review of Economics and Statistics*, **49** (3), 382–92.

Isard, W. (1960). *Methods of Regional Analysis*, Cambridge, MA: MIT Press.

Isard, W. and R. Kuenne (1953). 'The impact of steel on the New York–Philadelphia industrial region', *Review of Economics and Statistics*, **35** (4), 289–301.

Kasperson, R., O. Renn, P. Slovic, H. Brown, J. Emel, R. Goble, J. Kasperson and S. Ratick (1988). 'The social amplification of risk: a conceptual framework', *Risk Analysis*, **8**, 177–187.

Kim, U.S. (1985). 'Regional development impacts and their measurements', Fort Belvoir, Virginia, US Army Corps of Engineers, Institute for Water Resources.

Klaiber, H.A. and V.K. Smith (2011). 'General equilibrium benefits analysis for social programs', paper presented at the Annual Meetings of the American Economic Association, Denver, CO, Department of Economics, Arizona State University, Tempe, AZ.

Kokoski, M. and V.K. Smith (1987). 'A general equilibrium analysis of partial equilibrium welfare measures: the case of climate change', *American Economic Review*, **77** (3), 331–341.

Lee, B., P. Gordon and J. Moore, II (2008). 'Appendix C. Simulating the economic impacts of various hypothetical bio-terrorist attacks', in *Support for Risk and Economic Analysis for the National Biodefense Analysis of Countermeasures Center*, Los Angeles, CA: CREATE, USC.

Leontief, W. (1966), *Input–Output Economics*, New York: Oxford University Press.

Markusen, J.R. and A.J. Robson (1980). 'Simple general equilibrium and trade with a monopsonized sector', *Canadian Journal of Economics/Revue canadienne d'Economique*, **13**, 4, 668–682.

Miller, R. and P. Blair (2009). *Input–Output Analysis: Foundations and Extensions*, New York: Oxford University Press.

Oladosu, G. (2000). 'A non-market computable general equilibrium model for economic analysis of climate change in the Susquehanna River Basin', PhD thesis,

Department of Energy, Environmental, and Mineral Economics, Pennsylvania State University, University Park, PA.
Partridge, M. and D. Rickman (2010). 'CGE modeling for regional economic development analysis', *Regional Studies*, **44** (10), 1131–1128.
Rose, A. (1995). Input–output economics and computable general equilibrium models', *Structural Change and Economic Dynamics*, **6**, 295–304.
Rose, A. (1998). 'Computable general equilibrium analysis of economic losses from earthquakes', in *Proceedings of the Structural Engineers World Congress*, New York: Elsevier.
Rose, A. (2004). 'Defining and measuring economic resilience to disasters', *Disaster Prevention and Management*, **13**, 307–314.
Rose, A. (2007). 'Economic resilience to disasters: multidisciplinary origins and contextual dimensions', *Environmental Hazards: Human and Social Dimensions*, **7** (4), 383–398.
Rose, A. (2009). 'A framework for analyzing and estimating the total economic impacts of terrorist attacks and natural disasters', *Journal of Homeland Security and Emergency Management*, **6** (1), Article 6 (online).
Rose, A., J. Benavides, S. Chang, D. Lim and P. Sczesniak (1997). 'The regional economic impact of an earthquake: direct and indirect effects of electricity lifeline disruptions', *Journal of Regional Science*, **37** (3), 437–458.
Rose, A. and S.B. Blomberg (2010). 'Total economic impacts of a terrorist attack: insights from 9/11', *Peace Economics, Peace Science, and Public Policy*, **16** (1), Article 2 (online).
Rose, A. and G. Guha (2004). 'Computable general equilibrium modeling of electric utility lifeline losses from earthquakes', in Y. Okuyama and S. Chang (eds), *Modeling Spatial Economic Impacts of Natural Hazards*, Heidelberg: Springer, pp. 119–142.
Rose, A. and S. Liao (2005). 'Modeling resilience to disasters: computable general equilibrium analysis of a water service disruption', *Journal of Regional Science*, **45** (1), 75–112.
Rose, A., S. Liao and A. Bonneau (2011). 'Regional economic impacts of a Verdugo earthquake disruption of Los Angeles water supplies: a computable general equilibrium analysis', *Earthquake Spectra*, **27** (3), 881–906.
Rose, A. and D. Lim (2002). 'Business interruption losses from natural hazards: conceptual and methodological issues in the case of the Northridge Earthquake', *Global Environmental Change B: Environmental Hazards*, **4**, 1–14.
Rose, A. and G. Oladosu (2008). 'Regional economic impacts of natural and man-made hazards: disrupting utility lifeline services to households', in H. Richardson, P. Gordon and J. Moore (eds), *Natural Disaster Analysis after Hurricane Katrina*, Cheltenham, UK and Northampton, MA, USA: Edward Elgar, pp. 187–207.
Rose, A., G. Oladosu, B. Lee and G. Beeler Asay (2009). 'The economic impacts of the 2001 terrorist attacks on the World Trade Center: a computable general equilibrium analysis', *Peace Economics, Peace Science, and Public Policy*, **15** (2), Article 4 (online).
Rose, A., G. Oladosu and S. Li (2008). 'Appendix D. regional economic impacts of a bioterrorist attack on the water system of Los Angeles: a computable general disequilibrium analysis', *Support for Risk and Economic Analysis for the National Biodefense Analysis of Countermeasures Center*, Los Angeles, CA: CREATE, USC.

Rose, A., G. Oladosu and S. Liao (2007). 'Business interruption impacts of a terrorist attack on the electric power system of Los Angeles: customer resilience to a total blackout', *Risk Analysis*, **27** (3), 513–31.

Rosenthal, R.E. (2011). *GAMS – A User's Guide*, Washington, DC: GAMS Development Corporation.

Rutherford, T.F. (1998). *Economic Equilibrium Modeling with GAMS: An Introduction to GAMS/MCP and GAMS/MPSGE*, Boulder, CO: University of Colorado.

Shinozuka, M., A. Rose and R. Eguchi (1998). *Engineering Social Economic Impacts of Earthquakes: An Analysis of Electricity Lifeline Disruptions in the New Madrid Area*, Buffalo, NY: Multidisciplinary Center for Earthquake Engineering Research.

Shoven, J. and J. Whalley (1992). *Applying General Equilibrium*, New York: Cambridge University Press.

Slovic, P. (1987). 'Perception of risk', *Science*, **236** (4799), 280–285.

Smith, V.K. and J. Carbone (2007). 'Should benefit–cost analysis take account of general equilibrium effects', *Research in Law and Economics*, **23**, 247–272.

Sohn, J., G. Hewings, T.J. Kim, J.S. Lee and S. Jang (2004). 'Analysis of economic impacts of an earthquake on a transportation network', in Y. Okuyama and S. Chang (eds), *Modeling Spatial and Economic Impacts of Disasters*, Berlin: Springer, pp. 233–256.

Sue Wing, I., A. Rose and A. Wein (forthcoming). 'Impacts of the USGS ARkStorm scenario on the California economy', *Natural Hazards Review*.

United States Strategic Bombing Survey (1945). *Summary Report (European War)*, Washington, DC: US GPO.

West, C. and D. Lenze (1994). 'Modeling the regional impact of natural disaster and recovery', *International Regional Science Review*, **17**, 121–150.

PART IV

Practical implementation of policy evaluation

9. Valuing time for Department of Homeland Security projects and policies

Kenneth E. McConnell

INTRODUCTION

United States federal regulatory requirements such as Executive Order 12866[1] lead federal agencies to perform benefit–cost analysis for large rulemaking and regulatory changes. Many of these costs and benefits come in the form of time saved. These are routinely treated in benefit–cost analysis by other departments such as the Department of Transportation. Given that the Department of Homeland Security would still be regarded as a relatively new regulatory agency, the effort to impose rational methods of resource allocation faces challenges in assessing benefits and costs not confronted elsewhere. Some of the services provided involve reductions in risks to human life and domestic threats to national security, which will take analysts into relatively new territory. Costs are often more mundane, such as minor reductions in the amount of time for various travel-related tasks. Given the serious nature of Homeland Security's mandate, careful measurement of all costs and benefits is essential. The newness of the agency and the relatively high value of services provided present an opportunity for significant gains in resource allocation.

Economists have developed the logic of benefit–cost analysis as a basis for improving resource allocation. By measuring changes in resources used in terms of increases or decreases in income, we can compare rulemaking proposals with substantially different outputs in a common metric. Although there is a rigorous foundation for benefit–cost analysis[2] that is independent of the institutional structure, whether the economy is one of central planning, market or pure exchange, the basis of comparisons of income changes and public projects rests intuitively on the way producers and consumers make choices in a market economy. On the consumer side, households make choices for dramatically different services. For example, new and more expensive models of cars can reduce the risk of serious injury, given an accident. Hence households may knowingly forego reductions in risk of injury by purchasing older automobiles. In return they may use part of their income saved to purchase a larger house, access better schools for their children or pay for a weekend in Las Vegas. This series of transactions implies trading off the risk of automobile injury for some aspects of a larger house, using money as a means of making the trade-off. The ability of consumers and producers to make such trade-offs is one of the key rationales for benefit–cost analysis. In the end, the assumption that all goods and services are fungible allows analysts to convert services of quite different nature to the common metric of money. Fungibility of all goods and services by consuming households is one of the implicit assumptions that underlies all benefit–cost analysis. This applies as well to all services produced or influenced by Homeland Security.

This chapter considers the question of how to value the changes in the time that travelers incur as a consequence of changes in Department of Homeland Security rulemaking and policies.[3] Time use has for decades been recognized as a resource that is affected by policy. Economists have a long history of research on the value of time. To use this research in a policy context to evaluate the costs imposed on consumers as a result of new time requirements that might be due to a policy, it is important to consider the similarity of this new context with the ones that have been studied. The policy analyses where time costs have had a large impact are: (1) in benefit–cost analysis of transportation projects; and (2) in the development of demand models for outdoor recreation to evaluate projects or environmental policies that influence them. Transportation projects are an obvious case, where the value of saving travel time is one of the chief benefits of better roads, bridges, and so on. Road improvements, rail lines and countless other transportation-related projects are a mainstay of public sector spending, and the need for the valuing of time from projects that reduce travel time by the public is paramount. A few minutes of time incurred or saved across millions of trips amounts to many millions of dollars in costs or benefits. The travel cost demand model for recreation relies on using the travel costs, including the time costs of travel as an implicit price of a trip to a recreation site. These time costs are usually higher than the vehicle-related costs of the trip and as such are important to the estimates of consumer surplus derived from these demand models.

Waiting time is also valued depending on the mode of travel. One might consider using these findings for an application involving new time requirements for a security-related policy. For example, waiting for a visa might be considered the same as waiting in an airport, both in its discomodiousness and in the similarity of users. Other types of rules and regulations have an impact on time required of individuals as they travel, undertake border crossings, obtain new documents, or in myriad other ways. The impacts sometimes involve an increase the time required to perform the activity, as when added security documents are required. Sometimes the impacts reduce travelers' time, for example when technological advances make the electronic verification of documents faster. These changes typically come from policy proposals that have the more profound purpose of reducing risks to national security and human life. Nevertheless, altering the time required for travel creates social benefits or imposes social costs.

Benefit–cost analyses involving homeland security policies are likely to involve money and time costs that are incurred to reduce risk. As a result, understanding the derivation of measures of the opportunity cost of time and whether existing approaches are relevant for the context of security-related policies is especially important to the design of a benefit–cost methodology for these policies. This chapter surveys the approaches to valuing time and the issues that arise in doing so. After a brief description of the context for these strategies, the next section starts with the simplest form of the labor market and moves to the current research efforts that assume time is allocated in a complex labor market setting. It investigates the implications of uncertain arrival time and approaches to valuing reliability of travel. The chapter also reviews values of time as employed in the Department of Transportation, the closest to guidelines one can find in the federal government. Finally, the chapter explores some outstanding issues in the value of time and provides some recommendations for research on the value of time.

For public projects that alter the time required for the public to engage in a particular activity, the appropriate social cost of time depends on the nature of travel. In cases where the travel is for business, the social cost is the net value of production foregone. The employee is compensated for the labor effort through employer compensation, and as long as there are no non-pecuniary returns to labor, and no learning-by-doing for labor effort, the employee is indifferent to changes in the amount of travel time. Hence the loss is confined to the net value of output that could have been created during that time, but was not. In the case of personal travel, the travelers themselves suffer the loss. In this case, we need to measure the traveler's opportunity cost of time.

A simple picture of the costs or benefits of changes in time can be derived from the trade-offs represented in Figure 9.1. The demand curve is either the individual's demand for non-work activities – leisure, family visits, non-market production – or a firm's demand for the travel from the individual, based on the value of the product produced. Thus it is assumed to be derived from a marginal product curve, allocating time in either home production or for travel in a work-related activity. This would be

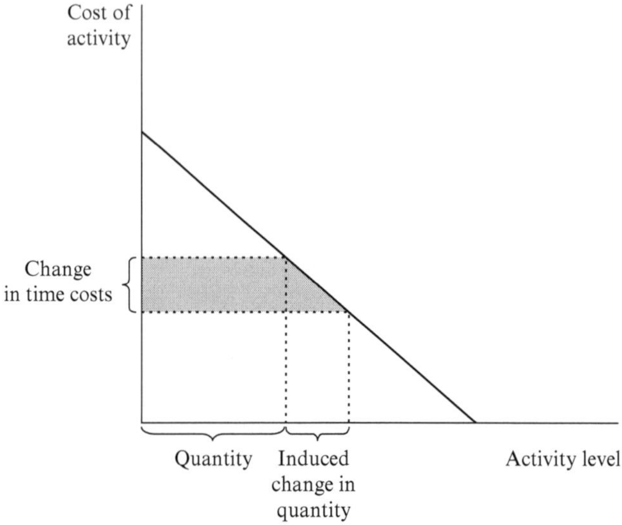

Figure 9.1 *Welfare effects of changes in time*

the derived demand for the travelers' time, and the area under the derived demand curve would be the change in the firm's profits from employing the workers.[4] The cost of the activity is its time cost, which is the product of the value of a unit of time and the amount of time required. If the demand curve were observable, then we would approximate the more exact measure of the full cost of a time increase as the change in the area under the demand curve:

$$\Delta costs\ or\ benefits = (\Delta cost) \times (quantity) + \tfrac{1}{2}(\Delta cost) \times (\Delta quantity)$$

where the quantity of activity might be measured in trips, for example. The time cost is the product of the value of time (*VOT*) and the amount of time used. If the change in the quantity of activity is assumed to be negligible ($\Delta quantity = 0$) then the appropriate measure would be:

$$\Delta costs\ or\ benefits = (\Delta cost) \times (quantity) = (\Delta time) \times VOTx(quantity).$$

One would simply multiply the value of time by the change in time requirements, and then multiply by the total number of trips that would be impacted. To illustrate, according to the regulatory assessment of the Western Hemisphere Travel Initiative (Industrial Economics, Inc., 2008), the mean daylight wait time at San Ysidro, California (the busiest port of entry in the USA) is 41 minutes. In 2004 there were 43.9 million crossings.[5] Suppose the value of time was based on Deacon and Sonstelie's (1985) natural experiment. They were able to use a mandated refund program that required dramatically lower gasoline prices at a few gas stations to estimate individuals' implicit value of time. It was based on the time people would wait in line for this low-cost gasoline. Converting their estimates to 2004 dollars implies a range from $20.48 to nearly $40 per hour. Then using the middle of this range, about $30, a six-minute reduction in the mean crossing time would be a saving of $131.7 million in 2004 dollars. This illustrates clearly the role of the value of time: changes in the value of time induce proportionate changes in the respective costs or benefits.

The analysis envisioned in this summary has treated the value of time as if it were easily known. As I show later, when the employee has flexible hours, receives a fixed wage per hour and there are no taxes, then a diagram like Figure 9.1 is easy to implement. But the general case is that an employee receives an after-tax wage that reflects the value of their time. The employer pays a before-tax wage as well as employer-provided benefits such as social security, health care and other worker benefits. These values can be quite far apart. Consider a simple case with a federal income tax rate of 25 percent, a state income tax rate of 7 percent, and the standard social security rate of 15.3 percent, half paid by the employer and half paid by the employee. Under these circumstances, the ratio of the cost of compensation per hour to the effective after-tax wage is 1.73. Assuming that the firm expects to cover the cost of compensation with the value of output and that the effective wage rate is the value of time for personal travel, we can describe this as the ratio of the value of output foregone to the value of personal time. Ratios of this magnitude can have a significant impact on the benefit–cost outcome of a proposal, so an accurate rendering of the purpose of an individual's travel is essential.

The discussion has so far focused on the value of time as a significant component of the benefits or costs of a project. The value of time is used differently in research on the demand for recreation. In this case, researchers estimate the quantity of recreational trips for recreational sites per individual as a function of the 'price' of access to the site. The price of access in this case is the effective price, typically constructed as the out-of-pocket travel costs and the cost of travel time. In its simplest form, the recreational demand function can be written as trips $= \alpha + \beta$ (effective price) where the *effective price* = *travel cost* + (*travel time to site*) $\times$ (*value of time*). In this case, systematic errors in the value of travel time have a systematic effect on the coefficient of interest, β, such that travel time that is valued below its true value will result in the coefficient being overestimated and the value of access to recreational sites being underestimated.

Since travel time is often the most significant cost, this impact can be substantial. Hence the role of the value of time is different in recreation demand estimation. It is used as an input into estimating models rather than directly in calculating benefits and costs.

The travel cost problem in recreation demand modeling is also more difficult in the sense that it involves estimating a structural model in which the valuation of time may be an endogenous outcome. In the simplest labor market structure, this works fine because the outcome of the process turns out to be exogenous. But slight complications in the labor market may make the value of time endogenous, and hence a questionable argument as a component of price in a recreational demand function. As a consequence one often finds the value of time taken simply as a proportion of the wage rate. Recognizing that economists are trying to solve several problems in estimating recreational demand functions should warn researchers to be cautious in adopting time values from this literature.

THE BECKER MODEL OF THE ALLOCATION OF TIME

In the earliest research on the value of time, researchers reasoned that individuals choose between work and leisure, and that the return for work is a constant wage. The Becker model serves as the basis of this model and most other models of the allocation of time (Becker, 1965). Figure 9.2 shows this model. Income is on the vertical axis and time on the horizontal axis. By reaching the highest indifference curve, labeled u, the individual chooses the allocation of time where the wage rate equals the (absolute value of) the marginal utility of leisure divided by the marginal utility of income. The attraction of this model is not simply that the wage rate equals the value of leisure time, but that this value of time is constant across different activities. By structuring the choice of work as continuous in hours over a defined time horizon and assuming the price of work time was constant per hour, the framework allows the value of time to be interpreted as a parameter. Further, any individual in this labor market, regardless of tastes for leisure or the composite good, would have the same value of time equal to the wage rate.

This model begins when the individual has non-wage income at the amount y_0, faces a wage rate w, and divides total time, T, between work T_W and leisure T_L so that $T_W + T_L = T$. (For simplicity y_0 is assumed to be zero in Figure 9.2.) Income is spent on a composite commodity denoted z with a price equal to one. Utility comes from composite commodity and leisure: $u(z,T_L)$. The individual's choice problem is to maximize utility

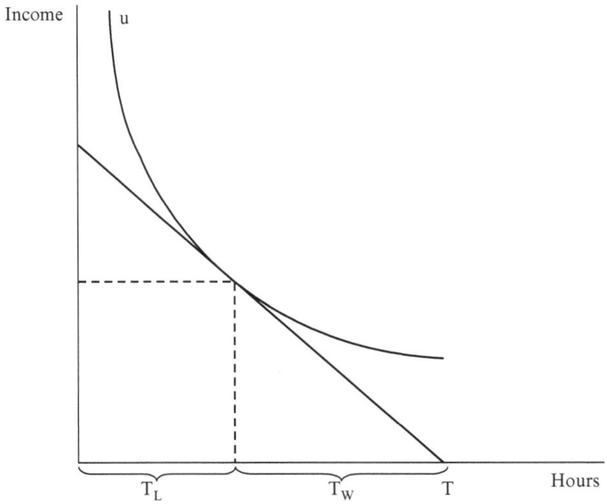

Figure 9.2 First-generation models: value of time equals wage rate

subject to the income and budget constraint, which can be collapsed to $y_0 + wT = z + wT_L$. The optimal conditions include the requirement that $(\partial u(z,T_L)\partial/T_L)/\lambda = w$ where λ is the marginal utility of income.

The assumption that utility comes from the composite commodity and leisure is standard but strong. The composite commodity assumption is innocuous, but having simply leisure provide utility implies that there will be a context-free value of time. Any leisure, no matter how it is carried out, has the same utility. In a similar way, the opportunity cost of travel, no matter what the mode or where the travel, would have the same opportunity cost. We could of course build a more complex model that would allow different types of leisure to yield different utilities, for example *u*(*x*, team sports, outdoor activities, etc.). Likewise, the model could permit different forms of employment to provide utility, some positive and some negative. This is the implicit assumption in hedonic wage models where non-pecuniary attributes are measured, and it would be uncontroversial to introduce these influences on utility in the present model.

The simple model provides the basic insight on how the labor market helps determine the value of time, and for long-run understanding about the value of time it is essential. In practice, however, there are numerous situations in which the wage rate cannot be used as a reliable measure of the value of time, or when in fact there is no 'wage rate' that can be used. A significant wedge between the value of time and the wage rate is created by taxing income. In this case, the effective wage rate becomes $w(1 - \tau)$ where

τ is the effective marginal tax rate. Considering social security and state and federal tax rates, this effective rate can be quite high. For example, if the state income tax rate is 7 percent, the federal income tax rate 25 percent and the social security rate 7.65 percent, and allowing for the deductibility of state taxes, the effective rate becomes 37.9 percent. This rate can vary substantially across individuals, depending on their federal rate and the state where they live. The after-tax wage rates can still be used as a measure of the value of individuals' personal time, however, because it is reasonable to treat the effective tax rate $w(1 - \tau)$ as a parameter.

One observation that comes from the Becker model is that there is no simple relationship between income and the value of time. In Figure 9.2, the slope of the budget constraint is the rate of change in income with respect to work. When there is no non-work income, the income–wage relationship is constant. In cases where there is non-wage income, the income–wage line is shifted up, with the slope remaining constant. In practice, researchers occasionally use the average annual income per hour worked as a measure of the opportunity cost of time. In general, the income–hours worked relationship is given by $(y_0 + wT_w)/T_a$ where y_0 is non-wage income and T_a is a fixed number of hours per year, typically chosen as 2000.[6] Even in this case, where the worker is free to choose hours, so that the value of time equals the wage rate, the ratio of income to the total of the hours worked in a year is not a measure of the value of time. Average income per hour will exceed the wage rate (and hence the VOT) when there is non-wage income and when the individual works more hours annually than T_a, the fixed work time.

SECOND-GENERATION MODELS

The institutional structure for employment offers a great many opportunities to work full-time or part-time, perhaps for different wages, and to work full-time for a salary that is independent of hours worked. Many other compensation schemes are available. Salespersons typically earn income based on a proportion of the value of their sales plus a fixed payment. University professors earn an annual salary but invest in work for expected future returns. Many professionals work for a salary plus an end-of-year bonus. One conclusion that follows from the more complex labor market settings is that the wage rate is not always a good measure of the marginal value of time, and further, the value of time may be greater or less than the wage rate. The following examples of preferences and wage schedules illustrate the gaps. These are developed under the assumption that there are no taxes or employer subsidies that create a gap between

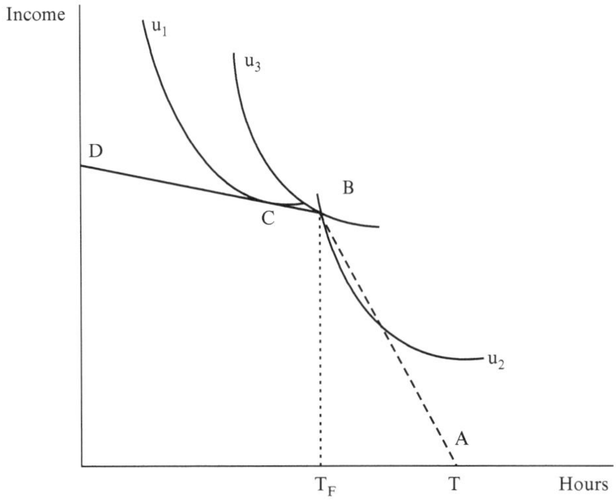

Source: Bockstael and McConnell (2006), Chapter 4.

Figure 9.3 More complex labor market conditions

the employer's compensation cost, the wage rate and the effective wage received by the worker. Tax effects would strengthen the conclusions reached here.

The shortcoming of wage as a measure of time can be seen in Figure 9.3.[7] This figure shows three types of workers with different tastes, facing the same institutional structure. The structure requires workers to work at least full-time, denoted by the point T_F on the horizontal axis. The wage rate for full-time workers is given by the slope of the dashed segment AB. A worker choosing to work overtime would complete full-time hours at the wage rate given by the slope of AB and then choose hours to locate along the budget segment BD, which has a lower wage rate. We now look at the indifference curves for three individuals with different tastes, bearing in mind that in the simplest labor markets no accounting of tastes is necessary. We ignore taxes here and look for the marginal value of time to the traveler, as opposed to the marginal cost of time to the producer. In an institutional setting where the wage is constant, all three types of workers would have the same marginal value of time, equal to the wage rate, irrespective of their preferences.

Individual 1, with indifference curve u_1, has an interior equilibrium at point C, where the value of time equals the wage rate associated with the segment DB. This individual works overtime, and has extra leisure time measured by the value of the overtime wage. Hence the overtime wage gives the VOT for small changes in time for individual 1. Individuals 2 and 3 are located at the same point, the kink on the budget constraint, but their values of time bear no relationship to the wage rate. Individual 2 is forced to work full-time by institutional constraints but has a value of time (absolute value of the slope of the indifference curve) that exceeds the wage rate (absolute value of the slope of the BD segment) and would work part-time at the full-time wage if this choice were feasible. For individual 3 the value of time is less than the wage rate for the full-time wage, segment AB, but greater than the wage rate for the part-time wage, segment BD. The wage rate equals the value of time only in the interior solution for individual 1. All workers have a monetary value of time, but it is equal to the wage rate only for type 1 workers. But all workers have a VOT determined by their tastes.

The implications of the idea that the value of time may differ from the wage rate depend on how time is being used. For example, if we consider travel time that is for non-work purposes, the appropriate concept is the foregone value of time, which is the slope of marginal utility of time normalized by the marginal utility of income. When the travel is for business purposes in these more complex settings, the wage rate seems a reasonable approximation of the value of output foregone by rulemaking that imposes increases in required travel time. In cases where the wage rate is used, it should be augmented by employer-paid benefits when the purpose of travel is for business. When travel is for personal reasons, the taxes should be subtracted from the wage.

THE FUNGIBILITY OF TIME

In the examples in the previous diagrams, the issue of whether time is fungible has been slipped into the discussion. Fungibility is a central issue in all of economics. The ability to substitute factors of a production process or goods for consumers is a critical empirical issue when we are concerned with how the economy responds to random shocks and resource shortages. It is a maintained assumption in welfare economics and benefit–cost analysis, and one that one that economists find necessary to defend, especially in cases where the services seem at first glance to be non-fungible, such as risks of fatalities and national security.

For most analysis, it is typically assumed that individuals' time is fungible. This assumption is not without its challenges, however. In recreation demand models, this challenge has long been associated with Kerry Smith.[8] This is put clearly by Palmquist et al. (2010). While time choices are:

> made continually throughout the day, they are undertaken within a defined set of constraints. Some are imposed by nature, such as hours of daylight. Others imposed by institutional constraints such as the distinction between weekdays and weekend days . . . Since decisions about time allocation are made in different contexts and with different constraints, the marginal value of time to an individual may vary, depending on prior commitments, context and the needs of the special time use. (Palmquist et al., 2010)

The key to the non-fungibility of time is the development of commitments that cannot be costlessly altered. Palmquist et al. illustrate the impact of commitments and the value of reducing commitments in a series of stated choice experiments that demonstrate individuals' increasing willingness to pay for time that comes in greater blocks. If time were completely fungible then a few minutes from a dozen different activities would be equal to the sum of these minutes from a single activity. It appears to be one of the first studies to document this important phenomenon.

The implications of this non-fungibilty for the larger question of valuing travel time are less clear. When the purpose of travel is business, it would be natural to assume that the lost product is still the employer's wage payment. However, small changes in the amount of time available for work may have a lower value than the equivalent amount of work time in a large block. For personal time, the higher value of larger blocks of time makes the time cost of longer trips greater than for shorter trips.

ATTRIBUTES OF TRAVEL

For the most part, travel time is discussed as if the context were always the same. The only difference between a plane trip from New York to Chicago and New York to Los Angeles is the approximately three-hour difference in the trip. This focus on the time of travel is a natural form of simplification made to accommodate benefit–cost analysis. Many small attributes, such as minor differences in convenience, comfort and destination, are accounted for in the price of travel. However, several travel attributes have a considerable impact on the utility of travel and the value of production foregone by changes in travel time. Here I address one attribute that has been investigated empirically: the reliability of the trip in terms of the difference between expected and actual travel time. There are many other attributes of travel. Every mode of travel has attributes that are attractive or unattractive. Some can be significant factors in people's decisions. For travel by car, the scenery can be an enjoyable aspect of the trip. The quality of the roadway itself (the absence of potholes, and so on), ease of access to rest stops, and so forth can also contribute. For air travel, attributes including the size and spacing of the seats, access to Wi-Fi, and ability to have routes without intermediate stops would be among the considerations with this mode. A careful study of attributes of travel leads to the question of whether the idea of context-free value of time makes any sense. As I will discuss below, The US Department of Transportation provides guidelines for valuing time that recognize differences across modes of travel and distances of trips.

As a first approximation, the mean travel time is a good measure of the amount of time lost per trip. In the simple models where travel time is valued at the wage rate, this measure is transformed directly into a money measure of travel. Travel time is of course unpredictable, and delays in arrival time are a vexation to the traveler. If we use an example of the time required for border crossing and ask whether existing value of time studies can be used to evaluate changes that affect time in these crossings, then there are a variety of issues to be considered. First, for a particular type of border crossing there will be a distribution of waiting times with a mean and a variance. Sometimes the crossing will take more time than expected, sometimes it will take less. If new regulations greatly increased the variance in waiting times, for a large variance there will be trips that deviate substantially from the mean travel time. It seems intuitively correct to say that large increases in travel time on one trip will not be compensated for by equally large reductions in travel time on another trip. For a small variance, deviations from mean travel will be small. It might, however, be true that many small increases in travel time on a number of trips could be compensated for by several large reductions in travel time on other trips. In the travel time literature, dispersion of travel times is called reliability. Under these circumstances, what is changing is the reliability or predictability of the time requirements to complete the task of crossing the border during a typical situation. One natural measure of unreliability is the standard deviation of travel time, which would affect travelers negatively. This measure assumes that a draw that results in a short trip would be as equally undesirable as a long trip. While a higher variance implies more late trips, it also implies more early trips. For this reason, Small et al. (2005), for example, have used the difference between the 50th and the 90th percentiles of travel time as a measure of reliability.

While it is clear that travelers on their own time have preferences for reliability, and suffer losses in utility when trips are not on time, the welfare effect when the purpose of travel is business may under some conditions be simplified. Suppose that the worker is paid a fixed salary, and is indifferent to variations in travel time. The firm also is indifferent to variations in travel time that maintain a mean expected travel time. In this simple case, then, mean preserving changes in reliability would not create social costs.

However, this simple case may be too stark. Time is not always fungible for business travelers. Work travel is after all to accomplish some tasks that are warranted for the business that authorizes the travel. It is a not a 'junket'. Often there are key meetings where all participants are needed to accomplish a task. Under these conditions decreases in reliability increase the costs of coordination. This can come in the form of allocating more time in advance of meetings to ensure all participants are present. Equally important, the effects of variation are not always symmetrical. Trips that are postponed because of travel delay are not compensated for by journeys that are completed early.

When the travel time is for personal purposes, the travelers' subjective distributions of random departures and arrivals are appropriate. Individuals make decisions based on their own expectations of travel time, and equally important, on what their subjective distributions tell them about reliability. These distributions may not approximate the empirical distributions, and may vary substantially among individuals. These distributions are not recoverable empirically. Yet the idea that subjective distributions of travel time that drive individual choices is critical in understanding behavior and behavioral anomalies.

Empirical evidence on individuals' willingness to pay to avoid unreliability has been gathered in a variety of studies. Accumulating this evidence requires careful study design to identify the separate effects of expected travel time and reliability on individuals' willingness to pay. It is clear enough how to measure the travel time and to assume that travelers can form expectations of its mean. Reliability is more problematic, both in determining travelers' expectations and in calculating a plausible proxy of this aspect of dispersion of travel time. Small and colleagues[9] have produced what appear to be the most compelling results about the value of time and the value of reliability from studies of auto travel in southern California. These studies are facilitated by the presence of two toll systems. One of the toll systems offers drivers a choice between a congested public road and a less congested but more costly private toll road. The toll road has lower expected travel time and greater reliability. Differences between the roads permit the separate identification of the value of time and value of reliability. For example, Brownstone and Small (2005) find that for east–west travel in southern California, reliability is valued at approximately one-third of the value of the travel time.

The broad notion that reliability in travel time is valuable seems reasonable. The connection between reliability for auto travel and many of the kinds of time requirements potentially affected by the Department of Homeland Security proposals, rulemaking and regulations appears weaker. Travelers on non-commuting trips may accept different deviations from expected travel, or may have less informative subjective distributions over travel time. So the research that has been conducted on freeways that are familiar to drivers may help highlight issues that need to be addressed, but not necessarily provide empirical findings that can be applied directly to the Department of Homeland Security situations. In the case of reliability, we know that travelers do not like delays, and delays are essentially unexpected increases in travel time.

PRACTICE

Valuing time is a significant research issue because of the large number of expensive transportation projects that must be subjected to some form of benefit–cost scrutiny. It is therefore not surprising that the US Department of Transportation (USDOT) has sponsored a significant amount of research on the value of time, and maintains guidelines of the values of time for use in benefit–cost analysis. States also must also decide whether and where to spend on transportation projects and have their own guidelines, typically modeled after the USDOT guidelines.

It is instructive to examine the USDOT guidelines.[10] These guidelines are condensed in Table 9.1. The guidelines must provide clarity for users and consistency across uses. Hence numerous compromises have been made. Two types of values are given: recommended and plausible. The guidelines give two figures: the appropriate percentage of the wage rate and the appropriate wage rate.

The recommended values as a percentage of the wage rate are stated for: two modes, surface and air; two trip lengths, local and intercity; and three types of trips, personal, business and truck drivers. The surface mode includes any transportation-related activity on the ground, such as waiting, walking and so on. The differences among these different trips make intuitive sense, based on the value of time models. The value of business travel is higher than the value of personal travel, which reflects the gap between the effective wage received by the worker and the effective wage paid by the employer. The value of personal time for intercity travel, 70 percent of the wage, is greater than the value of personal time for local travel, 50 percent of the wage, reflecting the declining marginal utility for longer trips. The lower value of local travel is also consistent with the work of Palmquist et al. (2010), who show that the value of a unit of time is larger when the block of time is longer. The value of business travel, 100 percent of wage, does not vary by mode or length of trip. This is reasonable because the value of the production foregone does not depend on the type of trip taken. The time of truck drivers is taken at 100 percent of their wage.

Table 9.1 *US Department of Transportation guidelines for valuing an hour of travel time (in 2000 price levels)*

Category	Surface modes			Air travel			Truck drivers	
	% of earnings (plausible range)	Hourly earnings	VOT (plausible range)	% of earnings (plausible range)	Hourly earnings	VOT (plausible range)	Hourly earnings	VOT
Local								
Personal	50% (35–60)	$21.10	$10.60 (7.40–12.70)					
Business	100% (80–120)	$21.20	$21.20 (17–25.40)				$18.10	
All Purposes			$11.20 (7.90–13.40)					
Intercity								
Personal	70% (60–90)	$21.10	$14.80 (12.70–19)	70% (60–90)	$33.30	$23.30 (20–30)		
Business	100% (80–120)	$21.20	$21.20 (17–25.40)	100% (80–120)	$40.1 0	$40.10 (32.10–48.10)	$18.10	
All purposes			$15.60 (13.20–19.80)			$28.60 (23.80–35.60)		

The actual wages used here depend on whether the travel is air or surface, based on the distribution of travelers within the mode, hence the higher value of intercity travel for the air mode. For travel that is associated with commuting back and forth to work, the wage would seem a reasonable measure of the opportunity cost of the time. For travel associated with specific business tasks, 100 percent of the cost of compensation for the person traveling seems appropriate. This could include the wage plus fringe benefits. Personal travel receives 70 percent of the cost of compensation. As an approximation, a personal time of 70 percent seems reasonable, especially when the employer's cost of compensation is not greatly above the wage rate.

The guidelines focus on the mode of travel and purpose of the trip; they do not consider activities associated with the trip such as screening at airports prior to boarding the plane or extra time required in entering secure locations or crossing borders by truck. The added time and its reliability may have more to do with the context of these activities than the mode of travel. The guidelines also implicitly assume the time changes involved are small so that differences in the value of time due to the heterogeneity of the travelers are not likely to be as important as the volume of traffic.

Thus, in the end, the guidelines are a useful device for calculating the *ex ante* gains or losses for a large number of travelers with unknown characteristics. The values are more generous than in those used in estimating the demand for recreation, where the standard practice is to use one-third of the wage rate. The value of travel time on any surface mode is recommended to be $21.10, regardless of purpose or duration. For intercity air travel, the values are set at $33.30 for personal travel and $40.10 for business travel. These estimates would be applied uniformly across different projects in different parts of the country.[11]

One important aspect of the new activities that add time to trips is adaptation to the new time requirements. For air travel, increased time at airports is required to assure time for security screening, but most airports have Wi-Fi facilities so for business travelers the time can be used to accomplish other job-related objectives. As a result, the cost of the added time is likely less than would be implied by applying the DOT guidelines directly to the added time, including excess waiting time due to unreliable screening times. It is not clear whether the same applies for personal travel. It does appear that airports are increasingly adding retail shopping facilities and upgrading the restaurant options. These changes may be in response to everyone spending more time in airport terminals, and with adequate advance planning on the part of the traveler they may offer the opportunity to accomplish multiple tasks while waiting. As a result, we would expect these adaptations to reduce the implicit cost of the waiting time. It is not 'wasted' to the extent that it can be used to accomplish other tasks that also would need to be completed using other time intervals. This more nuanced view of the opportunity costs of time also implies that policy design could incorporate mechanisms that allow easier adaptation.

SOME SALIENT RESEARCH ISSUES

Within a dynamic economy, the value of time for whatever purpose should not remain constant. Many forces bear on this. Here I address two issues that could have an impact the value of travel time.

Activities during Travel

Robinson (2007) has discussed how technical change could influence the value of time. As already noted in several of my examples, the evolution of wireless communication devices has made it possible to work practically anywhere that wireless networks are available. These networks have been available in many airports for a number of years. Recently wireless has arrived on planes, buses and trains. The expanded opportunities provided by better communication provide some utility for personal travel and some added productivity for business travel. Evidence of this is apparent to any one walking down the aisle of a plane for any but the shortest trips. Small and ultra-light laptops show movies, computer solitaire games, expense accounts and business-related spreadsheets. There is no doubt that the travel is less onerous for some travelers, and that other travelers are racking up billable hours that would not have been available without the technical changes.

What are the impacts of these changes? We can use Figure 9.1 to parse the effects of technical changes. To begin, for those trips and waiting times where multiple activities are feasible, we can reasonable assume that the opportunity cost of travel time declines, and with that decline the VOT goes down. Then, all else constant, we can use the relationship developed in connection with Figure 9.1:

$$\Delta costs\ or\ benefits = (\Delta cost) \times (quantity) = (\Delta time) \times VOTx(quantity),$$

to argue that the cost of an increase in waiting or travel time would be lower with these technical changes. Each trip permits more work or more pleasure. However, if the change in time requirements is significant, we can imagine that the net opportunity cost of business travel declines, and the number of trips potentially increases, which would attenuate the first impact of reduced costs.

Inequality in Allocations of Time to Leisure

Access to the American Time Use Survey (ATUS) is changing our understanding of how Americans use their time. It has also allowed analysis in the changes in amount of leisure time. While the conclusions one draws on the changes in leisure time since 1965 depend, in part, on how one classifies time uses,[12] there is consistent evidence that those with college degrees or higher have smaller increases or even losses in the time they allocate to leisure. By contrast, those with high school education as their highest degree have had larger increases in their time allocated to leisure. This may suggest increased heterogeneity in the valuation of time across these groups. It may also reflect greater investment of current time to work for the college graduates, anticipating greater financial returns in the future than would be possible for those with a high school education.

Business Cycles and the Value of Time

As noted at the outset of this section, the value of time should change over time and with aggregate economic conditions that affect employment opportunities. Aguiar et al. (2011) found, based on the ATUS, that about 40 percent of the foregone work time was allocated to home production. Market work for men fell by about 11 percent between 2008 and 2010. Using linear trends to compute the foregone work, they estimate for their aggregate sample that about 45 percent of the 2.09 hours shock to market work has been allocated to non-market work and 51 percent to leisure. We cannot gauge how these shocks affected the opportunity cost of leisure, but one would expect that the effects could be large and certainly worthy of further study.

The Value of Children's Travel

A large number of children travel, and the increased cost of their travel time apparently goes unaccounted for in most transportation studies. One issue here is the appropriate age for valuing children's time as adults. There is perhaps no really good economic principle to help, so an administrative decision will carry the day. The challenging research issue is the value or cost of the travel time for small children. The starting point for this research would be a model of household resource allocation. Although there may not be significant allocation issues between adult partners, there are clearly group travel issues. Interest would lie with the differences in the value of personal travel time as family composition changes. The difficulty with revealed preference valuation for this kind of difference is that there is a selection of travel modes and trip lengths based in part on family composition. Hence the valuation of travel time with children is a subject more suitably addressed with stated preference data, which has a long history[13] and is an active area of research.

CLOSING COMMENTS

The pressures to assess resource allocation will likely increase as efforts to reduce budget deficits at all levels of government grow. Since the cost of time will feature significantly in any measure of benefits and costs, researchers will no doubt return to the values of time. Given the interest in these values, it seems prudent to pursue all the means available for valuing time. There is a significant data resource available through the American Time Use Survey. There are opportunities to greatly enhance our understanding of how Americans used their time during a period of substantial change in security systems affecting all citizens. These opportunities seem largely untouched in the published literature. By considering the time profile of new rules and the activities they would impact, it may be possible to get better estimates of the time requirement due to these changes. Equally importantly, using geographic differences in performance of airports, state-level security-related activities and the patterns of time use it may be possible to design quasi-experiments to test specific aspects of the differences in rulemaking. Such estimates will not allow measurement of the opportunity cost of time in these other tasks. However, what is learned from these analyses could be used in the design of both stated preference approaches and field experiments for use in valuing travel, and especially travel attributes. The Department of Homeland Security has ample opportunity for experimentation, both for stated preferences and for true field experiments, with hundreds of waiting areas of potential willing experimental subjects.[14]

There are some insights into the potential for research by the Department of Homeland Security in valuing time. To begin with, the work by the Department of Transportation as well as many transportation economists has provided reasonably sharp estimates of travel time. While there are still refinements to be made, for example in the valuing of uncertainty, more important issues remain in other areas of time. There are significant gains that are available, especially with the use of stated choice and field experiments.

One area of particular interest is the value of waiting time. For small amounts of time, such as minor traffic tie-ups, this does not matter a great deal. But for longer waits, the nature and location of the wait may matter a lot. This is contrary to the basic Becker model of valuing time, which provides implicitly for a pure value of time. However, the value of waiting for a passport versus waiting for a plane may be quite different. It is appropriate to consider choice experiments for this research.

A second area that can be suitably addressed with choice experiments is the value of waiting time for families, or individuals traveling with small children. Is it appropriate to value the travel time of these children similarly to adults? Or should children be viewed as having zero travel time, but the costs associated with an accompanying adult? This is part of the larger issue of valuation within a household.

A final issue concerns the cost of waiting and efficiency in queues. Here there is an opportunity for field experiments. In large airports the security lines are often quite long. If the opportunity for arbitrage were present, then queues could be made more efficient. That is, an appropriately designed local market would let people buy or sell locations in line. A study of this would be supported by some conceptual work as well as field experiments

NOTES

1. President Obama, for example, in his version of the Executive Order requiring benefit–cost analysis, now EO 13563, added a requirement for an assessment of the implications of new rules for 'values' that are difficult or impossible to quantify, including equity, human dignity, fairness and distributive impacts. It also charged agencies to consider how to promote retrospective analysis of old rules. See Smith (2012), for a brief history of these executive orders
2. See for example Just et al. (2005).
3. A good deal of the material covered here is provided in greater depth in Robinson (2007).
4. This assumes non-essentiality; the firm's production can take place without these workers under consideration.
5. See Industrial Economics, Inc. (2008, Exhibit 3–2, pp. 3–4).
6. The US Department of Transportation has guidelines for the value of time that use median income divided by 2000 for personal travel. See http://regs.dot.gov/docs/VOT_Guidance_Revision_1.pdf, Table 3, footnote 1.
7. This graph is taken from Bockstael and McConnell (2006, Ch. 4).
8. See for example Smith et al. (1983).
9. These studies include Brownstone and Small (2005), Lam and Small (2001), Small et al. (2005), and many others.
10. The guidelines are available online at http://regs.dot.gov/docs/VOT_Guidance_Revision_1.pdf (accessed January 26, 2011).
11. Whatever else may be said about the DOT guidelines, they are far higher than the estimates of the value of commuting time from Calfee and Winston (1998), which were in the neighborhood of $5.

12. See the difference in estimates of the increase in leisure time between Aguiar and Hurst (2008) and Ramey (2007). Ramey argues that in comparing 1965 to 2003, Aguiar and Hurst were inconsistent in their treatment of some time allocations for the early year coding them as work and later as leisure and also included activities as leisure which are not rated as very satisfying.
13. An early survey by Hensher et al. (1988) and recent work by Hensher (2001) describe stated choice approaches to valuing travel time. This seems like a case where choice experiments would provide good insights, taking the composition of the traveling group as a travel attribute.
14. Group interactions make congestion effects difficult to perform experiments on. One example of such work is Anderson et al. (2006).

REFERENCES

Aguiar, M. and E. Hurst (2007). 'Measuring trends in leisure: allocation of time over five decades', *Quarterly Journal of Economics*, **122** (3), 969–1006.

Aguiar, M. and E. Hurst (2008). 'The increase in leisure inequality', NBER Working Paper # 13837, August.

Aguiar, M., E. Hurst and L. Karabarbounis (2011). 'Time use during recessions', NBER Working Paper # 17259, July.

Anderson, L., C. Holt and D. Reiley (2006). 'Congestion pricing and welfare; an entry experiment', available at http://www.u.arizona.edu/~dreiley/papers/CongestionPricing.pdf.

Becker, G.S. (1965). 'A theory of the allocation of time', *Economic Journal*, **75** (299), 493–517.

Bockstael, N.E. and K.E. McConnell (2006). *Environmental and Resource Valuation with Revealed Preferences*, New York City: Springer Publishing.

Brownstone, D. and K. Small (2005). 'Valuing time and reliability: assessing the evidence from road pricing demonstrations', *Transportation Research Part A: Policy and Practice*, **39** (4), 279–293.

Calfee, J. and C. Winston (1998). 'The value of automobile travel time: implications for congestion policy', *Journal of Public Economics*, **69** (1), 83–102.

Deacon, R. and J. Sonstelie (1985). 'Rationing by waiting and the value of time: results from a natural experiment', *Journal of Political Economy*, **93** (4), 627–647.

Hensher, D. (2001). 'The valuation of commuter travel time savings for car drivers: evaluating alternative model specification', *Transportation*, **28** (2), 101–118.

Hensher, D.A., P.O. Barnard and T.P. Truong (1988). 'The role of stated preference methods in studies of travel choice', *Journal of Transport Economics and Policy*, **22** (1), 45–58.

Industrial Economics, Inc. (2008). 'The Western Hemisphere Travel Initiative implemented in the land environment', Regulatory Impact Assessment for US Department of Homeland Security.

Just, R., D. Hueth and A. Schmitz (2004). *The Welfare Economics of Public Policy*, Cheltenham, UK and Northampton, MA, USA: Edward Elgar Publishing.

Lam, T.C. and K.A. Small (2001). 'The value of time and reliability: measurement from a value pricing experiment', *Transportation Research*, **37** (2–3), 231–251.

Palmquist, R.B., D.J. Phaneuf and V.K. Smith (2010). 'Short run constraints and the increasing marginal value of time in recreation', *Environmental and Resource Economics*, **46** (1), 19–41.

Ramey, V.A. (2007). *How Much Has Leisure Time Really Increased Since 1965?* Unpublished paper, Department of Economics, University of California San Diego, January.

Robinson, L. (2007). 'Valuing travelers' time for border crossings and related activities', Report prepared for US Customs and Border Protection, Department of Homeland Security, under subcontract to Industrial Economics, Inc., February.

Small, K., C. Winston and J. Yan (2005). 'Uncovering the distribution of motorists' preferences for travel time and reliability', *Econometrica*, **73** (4), 1367–1382.

Smith, V.K., W.H. Desvousges and M.P. McGivney (1983). 'The opportunity cost of travel time in recreational demand functions', *Land Economics*, **59** (3), 259–278.

10. Applicability of benefit transfers for evaluation of homeland security counterterrorism measures[1]

Kevin Boyle, Sapna Kaul, Ali Hashemi and Xiaoshu Li[2]

INTRODUCTION

Hobijn and Sager (2007) estimate that spending on homeland security in the United States increased by $44 billion from 2001 to 2005. They further estimate that 34 percent of this increase was dedicated to 'protection of critical infrastructure and key assets' and 11 percent to 'emergency preparedness and response'. Although no one disputes the Department of Homeland Security and the security actions it promulgates, questions have been raised about the economic efficiency of specific protection activities. Shapiro (2008) argues that there is a need to know whether the benefits of homeland security actions exceed costs, but the costs of homeland security measures have been underestimated and the benefits left uncalculated (see also Farrow and Shapiro, 2009). Farrow (2007) has proposed several approaches to investigating the cost-effectiveness of specific homeland security policies. Smith et al. (2009) go one step further to estimate United States households' willingness to pay (WTP) to prevent a shoulder-mounted missile attack on a commercial airline.

Estimating the benefits of homeland security policies goes beyond reporting the simple measure of people's WTP to reduce the probability of an attack. It requires identifying the expected consequences of the attack(s) in terms of morbidity, mortality, and other effects on the public. For example, a policy such as the Transportation Security Administration's (TSAs) checks of people boarding airlines reduces the probability of attacks, not just an attack, and there could be different types of attacks such as a bombing of a single plane or using a plane as a weapon of mass destruction. Thus, the protection policy prevents multiple attacks of terrorism and these different attacks can have different consequences that must be predicted to estimate benefits. This airline security example has a defined point of contact for providing security from terror attacks by those boarding an airline and has widespread consequences that are prevented. Attacks on the food supply or public water supplies, however, could occur at multiple points in the distribution systems, but generally will have well-defined spatial delineations of morbidity and mortality consequences. Thus, the processes of defining and measuring benefits associated with homeland security policies are complex, but for efficient resource allocation benefit analyses must proceed.

Presidential Executive Order 12866 (US Executive Office of the President, 1993) requires federal agencies to design 'cost-effective' regulations and to assess 'costs and benefits' of these regulations that are based on 'the best reasonably obtainable scientific, technical, economic, and other information'. There are many elements of antiterrorism policy that may warrant benefit analyses, ranging from intelligence gathering to preventative policies, to warning systems, to education programs, and more (Clinton, 1988). Benefit transfers are one economic approach used to estimate these benefits and costs. Estimating the benefits of homeland security policies can be challenging because they may require timely implementation and there may not be sufficient time to implement an original valuation study. Also the nature of the homeland security policies may make it challenging to implement an objective original study. Benefit transfer is one valuation approach that may provide an avenue for timely estimates of the benefits that accrue to homeland security policies. A benefit transfer generally involves adapting estimated values from existing original studies, the study sites, to a new application, the policy site.

In this chapter we explain the benefit-transfer method and explore the applicability of this valuation method to evaluate the monetary benefits of homeland security policies. The applicability of benefit transfers is considered in the context of three areas where original valuation data are readily available. Two applications involve pathways to effects on human health – water-supply contamination and food contamination – and the third application involves reductions in the health impacts of a terrorist attack. Homeland security policies can be designed to prevent terrorist attacks such as contamination of water and food supplies, or, given that an attack occurs, policies can be designed to reduce the health consequences of the attack. Since other chapters of this book address mortality effects and the value of a statistical life, here we restrict the discussion to applications considering the benefits of reducing morbidity effects from terrorist attacks.

Three messages arise from the information provided in this chapter. First, a credible benefit transfer, just like an original valuation study, requires careful analysis. Second, data for benefit transfers are limited and require careful selection and manipulation to conduct a credible benefit transfer. Third, the errors associated with benefit transfers are similar to those associated with an original study. These messages suggest that a research program be designed to estimate original values for antiterrorism policies and investigate the transferability of existing value estimates to new antiterrorism policies.

BENEFIT TRANSFERS IN CONTEXT

Benefit estimates can be transferred through time or space; the key feature is that study-site values are used to estimate a value for a policy that is different from the original policy objective. There are two types of benefit transfers: value transfers and function transfers. A value transfer uses a single value from a study site or a mean from multiple study sites to provide a policy-site value estimate. A function transfer uses an estimated valuation equation to compute a transfer estimate that is calibrated to policy-site conditions based on the values assigned to the independent variables. A function transfer may be an estimated preference function from a single study site or a meta-analysis of results from multiple study sites.

The benefit-transfer approach was developed in the field of environmental economics (Boyle and Bergstrom, 1992; Brouwer, 2000; Desvousges et al., 1992; Rosenberger and Loomis, 2003). However, the use of existing economic information to predict the effects of new policies is well established. Transfers are often conducted to predict the benefits and costs of future policies, although the process is rarely called 'benefit transfer' outside environmental economics. Hines (1999) notes that 'to quantify the economic costs of (taxes, regulations, externalities, monopolistic practices, etc.) . . . it is standard practice – and has been since the 1960s – to use a small number of assumptions and selected elasticities to estimate areas of the relevant "Harberger triangles"' (p. 167).[3] In fact, the transfer of existing information to new applications is not unique to economics. Engineers use steam tables to predict pressure and flow in power facilities, architects use weight-load tables to predict weight-holding capacity of floors and roofs, and the United States government publishes an actuarial table of the probability of death.[4] Additional examples of data transfers include dose-response functions developed by physical scientists that have been used to identify changes in quality for use in original valuation study sites (Spash and Vatn, 2006). A typical appraisal uses sale prices of three nearby and similar properties to develop a calibrated appraisal value for the subject property on the basis of an appraiser's professional judgment of differences between sold properties and the appraised property. Each type of transfer avoids the need to conduct a potentially time-consuming and expensive original study, or provides information where an original valuation study could not be conducted; past results to predict future outcomes. Property appraisals are a specific example of transfers of monetary values.

The United States Environmental Protection Agency (US EPA) *Guidelines for Preparing Economic Analyses* (2000, pp. 86–87) provides basic recommendations for conducting benefit transfers that include:

- describing the policy case;
- identifying existing, relevant studies;
- reviewing available studies for quality and applicability (basic commodities must be essentially equivalent, baseline and extent of change should be similar, and affected populations should be similar);
- transferring the benefit estimates; and
- addressing uncertainty.

The US Office of Management and Budget (2003) benefit-transfer guidelines are similar to the EPA guidelines and also advocate for benefit-function transfers over value transfers.

Benefit transfers are now common practice, but even a cursory review of the academic literature on this topic displays a wide variety of implementation procedures, with limited consensus on what procedures result in the lowest transfer error beyond two general principles: (1) study sites and policy sites should be similar; and (2) function transfers are more accurate than value transfers. These principles are related because functions can be used to predict welfare estimates that are calibrated to policy-site conditions, which is one approach to imposing similarity.

CONCEPTUAL FOUNDATION FOR BENEFIT TRANSFERS

Using the example of food contamination, let us assume for purposes of exposition that a person's (i) utility function can be defined as:

$$v_i(P, Q, I_i; D_i) \tag{10.1}$$

where $v(\cdot)$ is an indirect utility function, P is a vector of food prices, Q is a vector of food quality attributes that includes contamination, I is income and D is a vector of demographic characteristics. For expositional convenience we assume that v is separable in food and other arguments.

Person *i*'s WTP to avoid contamination from a terrorist attack that contaminates some element of the food supply (q_j) is:

$$v_i(P^\circ, Q^\circ, I_i - wtp_{i,j}; D_i) = \pi(R) * v_i(P^\circ, Q^\circ, I_i; D_i) + (1 - \pi(R))v_i(P', Q', I_i; D_i) \quad (10.2)$$

where $\pi(R)$ is a vector of probabilities associated with food quality and one element of R (r_j) is the risk of contamination of q_j from a terrorist attack such that $q_j^\circ > q'_j$. As noted above, we are just considering morbidity and assume that $\pi(R)$ only includes the probability of sickness.[5] Note, we allow P to vary such that a terrorist event, if large enough, could have both pecuniary and non-pecuniary effects and $p_j^\circ < p'_j$. Thus, $wtp_{i,j}$ is the individual's WTP to avoid the consequences of a contamination event. This framework could also be applied to drinking water assuming that water is a component of food consumption, and a modified framework would need to be applied for a health-consequences reduction application.

Estimated WTP also depends on the demographic characteristics of potentially affected individuals, and predicting policy-site values requires information on the income (I_{ps}) and population characteristics (D_{ps}) at the policy site (*ps*) in addition to information on the predicted change in food quality. Thus:

$$\widehat{wtp}_{i,j,ps} = f(\Delta p_{j,ps}, \Delta q_{j,ps}, \Delta\pi_{j,ps}, I_{ps}, D_{ps}; \hat{\beta}_{ss}) \quad (10.3)$$

where policy-site $\widehat{wtp}$ is based on policy-site data for p, q, π, I and D, and preference parameter estimates ($\hat{\beta}_{ss}$) are based on data from one or more study sites (*ss*).

Value Transfers

A value transfer uses a single statistic (usually an average from one or more study sites) to estimate a policy-site value; changes in p, q, π and I are implicit in the study-site mean, and demographic characteristics are assumed to be similar between the study site(s) and the policy site. For value transfers (*vt*) the aggregate benefit (AB_{ps}) at the policy site for quality change *j* is predicted as:

$$\widehat{AB}^{vt}_{j,ps} = M \times (\widehat{wtp}_{j,ss}) \quad (10.4)$$

where $\widehat{wtp}_{j,ss}$ is a mean from a single study site or the average of means from several study sites and M is the affected population at the policy site. This approach is appealing in simplicity, but value transfers do not allow predicted policy-site values to be calibrated to policy-site conditions; they simply rely on the assumed similarity between study-site and policy-site conditions.

Function Transfers

Function transfers (*ft*) use an econometric model such as equation (10.3) to predict a calibrated value for a new policy as a function of variables describing characteristics of the policy site and the population at the policy site. In this case, aggregate benefits for the policy site are predicted as:

$$\widehat{AB}^{ft}_{j,ps} = \sum_{i=1}^{M} f(\Delta p_{j,ps}, \Delta q_{j,ps}, \Delta \pi_{j,ps}, I_{ps}, D_{ps}; \hat{\beta}_{ss}) \tag{10.5}$$

where all terms are defined above. It is this calibration to policy-site conditions that supports the findings that function transfers are more accurate than value transfers, and this is an empirical approach to addressing the equivalence and similarity conditions required by the US EPA guidelines. Function transfers can be based on equations estimated in individual contingent valuation, choice modeling, hedonic or averting behavior studies or an equation estimated in a meta-analysis that statistically summarizes results from multiple original studies.

Types of Function Transfers

Four types of preference functions can be used in benefit transfers: reduced-form and structural meta-analyses, and reduced-form and structural preference functions estimated from original study data. The literature does not provide evidence as to which type of function transfer provides the most accurate benefit transfers.

Reduced-form meta-analysis is a statistical approach to summarizing valuation results across a number of studies. This approach typically is accomplished by regressing study-site value estimates on variables that describe the original studies in terms of the items valued, the population the value estimates apply to, and study design characteristics (Bergstrom and Taylor, 2006; Nelson and Kennedy, 2009). The first two sets of variables allow policy-site value predictions to be calibrated to policy-site conditions, but the investigator is left to decide how study design characteristics should be coded. This approach likely contains more variation in the quality change to be valued than would occur in a single-study case and typically has the implicit assumption that the average effects of the study sites represented by the meta-equation parameter estimates will represent preferences at the policy site.

Structural meta-analysis for benefit transfers have been labeled as preference calibrations (Smith et al., 2000; Smith et al., 2006). The process of preference calibration begins by choosing a parametric specification for the preference function, which may be a utility function or a demand function. Then the analyst derives the parameters of that function from study-site data. Like reduced-form meta-analyses, preference-calibration transfers can calibrate policy-site value predictions to the change in quality and the characteristics of the affected population at the study site. Unlike the reduced-form approach to meta-analysis, preference calibration requires the estimated function to be consistent with economic theory and generally does not require the analyst to make decisions regarding the methodological variables in the equation. Preference calibrations also force the analyst to be explicit in the assumptions that they make about how to specify the utility function, which original studies to select and how to translate the information from different studies into common units of measurement.

Original valuation studies may use stated-preference or revealed-preference applications to estimate equations. Stated-preference approaches, such as contingent valuation (Bateman et al., 2002; Boyle, 2003) and choice modeling (Bennett and Blamey, 2001; Holmes and Adamowicz, 2003), are the common approaches used to estimate $wtp_{i,j}$. Hedonic models (Taylor, 2003; Baranzini et al., 2008), travel-cost models (Parsons, 2003) and averting behavior (cost) (Dickie, 2003) are revealed-preference approaches to estimating $wtp_{i,j}$ Choice modeling and hedonic modeling always involve the estimation of equations that can facilitate calibrated predictions of policy-case values assuming that the estimated parameters are the same at the study and policy cases. Contingent valuation, travel cost models and averting studies may report solely value estimates or estimated equations to facilitate calibrated benefit-transfer predictions.

Original valuation studies may present reduced form or structural equation estimates. Like the reduced-form and structural meta-analyses, original study case valuation equations allow policy-site predictions to be calibrated to policy-site conditions. Unlike meta-analyses, these equations are based on the assumption that policy-site and study-site preferences are similar, which is in contrast to the general meta-analysis assumption that the policy-site preferences are similar to the average preferences from multiple study sites. Thus, here the analyst must pick the original study that best matches policy-site conditions through the information available in the estimated valuation function.

A Unified Conceptual Framework for Benefit-Function Transfers

The choice among function transfer methods has not been explicitly studied. Although the literature supports the inference that function transfers are more accurate than value transfers (Kirchhoff et al., 1997; Vandenberg et al., 2001), there is no consensus on which type of function transfer provides the most accurate predictions. However, a common set of assumptions is required for all function transfers to ensure that the transfer process will yield a consistent measure of value at the policy site (Boyle et al., 2009). Four key assumptions, when satisfied, provide a sound foundation for a benefit-function transfer. The four 'S' necessary conditions are: (1) utility must be separable in unobserved characteristics that are not included in the transfer function; (2) the transfer function must be specified correctly; (3) people must not be sorted according to unobserved features of their preferences; and (4) data used to estimate and implement the transfer function must be free of selection problems. The four 'S' assumptions are necessary for the consistency of all benefit transfers and sufficient to establish the consistency of benefit-function transfers.

This does not, however, guarantee that there will be no error associated with benefit transfer. The four 'S' conditions simply ensure a sound econometric foundation for implementing a benefit transfer. For example, the 'separable' assumption has different implications for the study site(s) and the policy site. If unobserved characteristics are not separable at the study site, then the estimated valuation function will have biased coefficient estimates and will result in biased value predictions at the policy site. If unobserved characteristics at the policy site are not separable and are not represented in the transfer function, value predictions will be biased even if the estimated transfer-function coefficients are unbiased.

POTENTIAL BENEFIT-TRANSFER APPLICATIONS

In the following sections we review three areas where original valuation studies might be applied to estimate the benefits of a homeland security policy. The first two, food safety and water quality, would be applicable to policies that prevent incidents to pathways where human health could be affected. A food safety violation could affect people over a broad geographic area depending on the quantity of food affected and the geographic extent of the supply distribution to final consumers. The second, water quality, could have a large effect on a localized community by an act that disrupts a public water supply. The third approach, valuation of health consequences, would be applicable to policies that minimize the morbidity effects after a terrorist incident has occurred.

For each area we have assembled tables of original valuation studies published in peer-reviewed journals between 1990 and 2010. In doing this we have not tried to be comprehensive and exhaustive in our search for studies. The purpose here is to provide the reader with perspective on the types of studies that might be available to conduct a benefit transfer for specific homeland security policies and, given these studies, what might be some of the challenges to conducting a benefit transfer in the face of limited original data.

Two protocols were followed when reporting empirical estimates of value below. First, if the authors of the study report multiple values for the same health risk (or consequence) due to different methodological manipulations in study implementation procedures, then a range of values is reported. Second, if a study reports values for multiple health risks (or consequences), then each of these value estimates are reported separately. Thus, multiple values might be reported for each study citation, and for each citation either a range or a single value estimate might be reported.

Food Supply Risk Valuation

Roberts (2007) quotes former Secretary of the Department of Health and Human Services, Tommy Thompson, as stating that he 'cannot understand why the terrorists have not . . . attacked our food supply because it is so easy to do' (p. 199). Protecting the nation's food supply is challenging because of the geographically extensive and interconnected production and supply systems that extend globally (see Lukas, 2004).

Terrorist attacks to the food supply could occur at several key steps in the food production process including farm inputs, on-farm production, processing, distribution and retail sales. An incident at a large food processing plant or wholesale distribution center could have substantial impacts as the food products are delivered spatially and through time. The consequences could be interruptions in food supply, illness and even death. The effects of food supply contamination can be demonstrated by outbreaks of pathogens, such as *Salmonella*, where hundreds of thousands of people can be sickened. According to the Government Accounting Office (2005) the cost of terrorist 'introduction of animal and plant diseases at the farm level would cause severe economic disruption given that agriculture accounts for 13 percent of the United States' gross domestic product and 18 percent of domestic employment' (p. 10). Actions that are being taken to ensure the safety of the nation's food supply include transferring the US Department of Agriculture's inspectors to the Department of Homeland Security, identifying agricultural products that are most vulnerable to terrorist attacks, and enhancing diagnostic and monitoring technologies (US Government Accounting Office, 2005).

Numerous empirical studies have investigated consumer WTP for food quality attributes, but most of these studies have not investigated food safety issues specifically. These studies have investigated WTP to obtain or avoid attributes such as beef tenderness and genetically modified foods and organic foods. In addition, a number of these studies have been conducted in experimental settings with students to test valuation methodologies and do not necessarily provide policy-relevant value estimates. We have excluded these types of studies from the discussion here.

Eight of the 15 study values reported in Table 10.1 were conducted in the United States. These studies are usually valuing a reduction in a mix of food-borne pathogens, and the changes in probabilities of sickness or the presence of pathogens. The challenge in using these estimates in a benefit-transfer context is that it would be necessary to match the pathogens and the probability of sickness with what might occur in a specific attack on the food system. For example, Teisl and Roe (2010) estimate WTP to avoid food-borne pathogens as 13–30¢ per package. To expand such unit values to a population estimate requires data on consumption and the extent of population that could be potentially affected. When we discuss a water incident below, the effects would in most cases be limited to a municipal water system that was a terrorist target, but here the food distribution system could have resulted in an affected population over a large geographic region.

Water Supply Risk Valuation

Damage to public water supply systems was a major concern prior to the 2001 terrorist attacks. In 1998 the Clinton administration identified large community water supply systems as one of the eight areas of critical infrastructure to protect from intentional acts of harm. A terrorist act at a strategic location in a public water supply could sicken hundreds of thousands of people in a small geographic region in a short period of time. Jeong et al. (2009) considered the risks of an attack on drinking water supplies from radioactive materials. They estimated that risks from a cesium-137 contamination event in the Seoul metropolitan area with a population of over 20 million could range from 4.77×10^{-7} to 6.92×10^{-7} in terms of morbidity and mortality effects. One action that could be taken to protect public water supplies is the placement of electronic sensors at strategic points in the systems to detect contaminants (Watson et al., 2009). Copeland and Cody (2007) noted that there has been progress

Table 10.1 Food supply risk valuation studies (selected journal articles, 1990–2010)

Author(s) (date)	Country	Cause of risk	Method*	Probability change (sickness or pathogens)	Mean value(s)	Units
Teisl and Roe (2010)	US	Pathogens	CE	5–10%	\$0.13–0.33	Package
Tonsor et al. (2009)	Canada	NA	CV	40 and 80%	\$3–5	Pound
	Japan	NA	CV	40 and 80%	\$1–24	Pound
	Mexico	NA	CV	40 and 80%	\$2–23	Pound
	US	NA	CV	40 and 80%	−\$0.75–1.78	Pound
Goldberg and	Germany	*Salmonella*	CV and CE	40 and 80%	€0.54–2.60	Kilogram
Roosen (2007)	Germany	*Campylobacteriosis*	CV and CE	40 and 80%	−€0.16–2.31	Kilogram
	Germany	*Salmonella* and *Campylobacteriosis*	CV and CE	40 and 80%	€2–6	Kilogram
Hammitt and Haninger (2007)	US	Pathogens	CV	3/10 000–1/10 000	\$8300–16 400**	Case
Nayga et al. (2006)	US	Pathogens	CE	99.9%	\$0.77	Pound
Fu et al. (1999)	Taiwan	Pesticide residues	CV	25–90%	NT\$12–19	Kilogram
Buzby et al. (1998)	US	Pesticide residues	CV	0.5/1 million	\$0.57	Household per week
Buzby et al. (1995)	US	Pesticide residues	CV	99/1 million	\$0.10–0.28	Grapefruit
Wessells and Anderson (1995)	US (Rhode Island)	NA	CV	NA	\$0.30	Pound
Eom (1994)	US (North Carolina)	Pesticide residues	CV	0.3/10 000–1/50 000	\$0.74–0.80	NA***

Note: * CV = contingent valuation and CE = choice experiment; ** Medians; *** NA = Not available.

in enhancing the protection of major water supply systems in the United States since 2001, but there is still more to do.

A terrorist event could interrupt water supply, make the water unpalatable or introduce contamination with morbidity and mortality effects. Even if disruption of service in a large metropolitan area did not result in morbidity effects, it could have substantial economic consequences. i

Thus, we consider supply reliability as well as drinking water quality valuation studies. Six of the 19 studies cited in Table 10.2 were conducted in the United States. One study addresses supply reliability and five address water quality. None of the five studies that value changes in water quality address contamination that would make the water unpalatable or have immediate morbidity or mortality consequences. Two of the international studies, conducted in Bangladesh (Ahmad et al., 2005) and Korea (Um et al., 2002), investigate quality changes that could have immediate health impacts, but their transferability to a United States application is questionable, even after adjustments for purchasing power parity.

The value estimates reported in Table 10.2 do suggest that households might be willing to pay hundreds of dollars to protect reliability and quality.[6] For example, Howe and Smith's (1994) upper-bound estimate for reliability is $84 per year in 1990 dollars, which exceeds $140 in current dollars.[7] Their study was conducted in Boulder County, Colorado. With a population of about 115 000 households, the aggregate benefits of avoiding a reduction in water reliability could be as much as $16 million per year.[8] Depending on the severity and duration of the shortage, household WTP could be more or less than this amount.

Jordan and Elnagheeb's (1993) upper-bound estimate for avoiding nitrates in public water supplies is $144 per year, which exceeds $232 per year in current dollars. No morbidity or immediate health effects of nitrate contamination were mentioned in the Jordan and Elnagheeb survey. Thus, one might infer that consumers would be willing to pay more to avoid a contamination event that has immediate morbidity effects. A lower-bound estimate for protecting the residents of Atlanta, for example, from a drinking water contamination event might be as much as $39 million per year.[9]

Thus, although the available drinking-water valuation data are limited in terms of relevance for a specific homeland security policy evaluation, they might be useful in scoping out the potential magnitude of benefits from a specific protection action, which could then be confirmed with an original valuation study to investigate the specific magnitude of benefits if these quick calculations indicate that benefits are not substantially less than or substantially exceed costs.

Table 10.2 Sample drinking water valuation studies (selected journal articles, 1990–2010)

Author(s) (date)	Country	Supply	Cause of risk	Method*	Mean value(s)	Units
Polyzou et al. (2010)	Greece	Public	Quality	CV	€10	Bi-monthly
Vásquez et al. (2009)	Mexico	Public	Microbes, bacteria, heavy metal	CV	Mex$55–230**	Monthly
	Mexico	Public	Supply reliability	CV	Mex$23–55**	Monthly
Genius et al. (2008)	Greece	Public	Quality	CV	€11	Monthly
Casey et al. (2006)	Brazil	Public	Supply reliability	CV	R$11–17	Monthly
Genius and Tsagarakis (2006)	Greece	Public	Supply reliability	CV	€9–14	Quarterly
Cho et al. (2005)	US (Minnesota)	Public	Iron, sulphates	CV	$3–4	Monthly
Hensher et al. (2005)	Australia	Public	Supply reliability	CE	AU$ 4–55	Annual
Ahmad et al. (2005)	Bangladesh	Public	Arsenic	CV	Tk9–11	Monthly
Whittington et al. (2002)	Nepal	Public	Improved supply	CV	Rp230–1030	Monthly
Kim and Cho (2002)	US (Minnesota)	Public	Copper	CV	$30–57	Annual
Um et al. (2002)	Korea	Public	Suspended solids	AB	$1–$6	Monthly
Abrahams et al. (2000)	US (Georgia)	Public	Quality	AB	$47	Annual
Howe and Smith (1994)	US (Colorado)	Public	Supply reliability	CV	$5–7	Monthly
Jordan and Elnagheeb (1993)	US (Georgia)	Public/ private	Nitrates	CV	$10–22	Monthly
Seip and Strand (1992)	Norway	NA*	NA	CV	kr232	Annual
Whittington et al. (1991)	Nigeria	Private	Supply reliability	CV	₦0–2	Per 45 gallons
Whittington et al. (1990)	Haiti	Public	Supply reliability	CV	G6–7	Monthly

Note: * NA = not available; ** CV = contingent valuation, CE = choice experiment and AB = averting behavior; *** medians.

Health Consequence Valuation

Engel et al. (2007) note that although the media focuses on the immediate injuries and mortality associated with a terrorist attack, there is need for longitudinal treatment of long-term morbidity and persistent idiopathic symptoms. Landrigan et al. (2004) reports that dust from the World Trade Center consisted 'predominantly (95 percent) of coarse particles and contained pulverized cement, glass fibers, asbestos, lead, polycyclic aromatic hydrocarbons (PAHs), polychlorinated biphenyls (PCBs), and polychlorinated furans and dioxins' (p. 731). Firefighters and clean-up workers showed subsequent increases in cough, bronchial hyperactivity, wheezing and shortness of breath. These types of persistent health effects reduce the utility of people directly affected by terrorist attacks and individuals in the nearby area who might experience secondary effects. Thus, while some homeland security actions are targeted at preventing terrorist attacks, other policies are designed to minimize the collateral damage when a terrorist attack occurs.

The health consequence valuation literature appears promising for estimating the morbidity costs of a terrorist attack such as the World Trade Center attack. Eleven of the 23 studies cited in Table 10.3 were conducted in the United States, and four of these studies value respiratory issues (albeit asthma in three cases). The Centers for Disease Control and Prevention (see http://www.ncbi.nlm.nih.gov/pubmed/16601667) reports that 'more than half (56.6%) of survivors reported experiencing new or worsening respiratory symptoms after the attacks'. Using Blumenschein and Johannesson's (1998) estimate for the United States for asthma of about $1330, which exceeds $1749 in current dollars, results in a potential annual benefit of minimizing the respiratory effects of the survivors of the World Trade Center event of about $71 million per year. This number may underestimate or overestimate benefits depending on the severity of the attack symptoms vis-à-vis the asthma symptoms valued, and the difference between the affected population and the population that was sampled for the original valuation study. However, the data presented in Table 10.3 suggest that information may be sufficient to infer benefits of homeland security policies that would reduce the morbidity consequences of a terrorist attack.

Insights from Example Study-site Applications

The three potential applications of benefit transfer for evaluating homeland security policies present important insights:

Table 10.3 Sample health consequence valuation studies (selected journal articles, 1990–2010)

Author(s) (date)	Country	Cause of risk	Method*	Mean value(s)	Units
Blomquist et al. (2010)	US (Mississippi and Kentucky)	Asthma	CV	$1700–$4000	Annually
Chestnut et al. (2006)	US (California)	Respiratory and cardiovascular hospitalization	CV	$2,400	5 days
Dickie and Messman (2004)	US (Mississippi)	Acute symptoms	CV	$53–$218	1–30 days
Ready et al. (2004)	Norway, Netherlands, Portugal, Spain, England	Acute symptoms	CV	£14–426	1–8 days
Lee et al. (2002)	US (North Carolina)	Influenza	CV	$15	Daily
	US (North Carolina)	Nausea	CV	$62	Daily
	US (North Carolina)	Dizziness	CV	$56	Daily
	US	Hepatitis A	CV	$3011	Per cure
Zillich et al. (2002)	US (Kentucky)	Asthma	CV	$48–$331	Monthly
Ready et al. (2001)	Norway	Cough	CV	kr93–143	1 day
	Norway	Flu	CV	kr380–629	3 days
	Norway	Respiratory symptoms	CV	kr1016–1086	8 days
Navrud (2001)	Norway	Asthma	CV	kr99–1772	Daily
Johnson et al. (2000)	Canada	Respiratory and cardiovascular	CE	C$3–1002	1–10 days
Liu et al. (2000)	Taiwan	Cold	CV	$37–57**	6–7 days
Torrance et al. (1999)	Canada	Acute bronchitis	CV	C$868–1,235	Annually

Table 10.3 (continued)

Author(s) (date)	Country	Cause of risk	Method*	Mean value(s)	Units
Lundberg et al. (1999)	Sweden	Psoriasis and eczema	CV	kr960–1956	Monthly
Alberini and Krupnick (1998)	Taiwan	Acute respiratory symptoms	CV	$26–54	1–10 days
Bala et al. (1998)	US (Florida)	Pain from shingles	CV	$379–1198**	2–8 weeks
Blumenschein and Johannesson (1998)	US	Asthma	CV	$189–$343	Monthly
Alberini et al. (1997)	Taiwan	Acute respiratory symptoms	CV	$20–52	1 and 5 days
Chestnut et al. (1996)	US (California)	Angina attacks	CV	$203–218	4–8 episodes
Kartman et al. (1996)	Sweden	Angina attack	CV	kr1145–3350	Weekly

Note: * CV – contingent valuation and CE – choice experiment; **Medians.

- All three applications indicate that limited numbers of studies are available to support benefit transfers. Although we did not attempt to identify all studies published between 1990 and 2010, we do believe that we have identified the major studies. A limited number of studies does not preclude or limit the potential for benefit transfers. The key issue, referring back to the US EPA benefit-transfer guidelines, is whether individual studies or groups of studies, via a meta-analysis, can approximate the benefits that would occur from a homeland security policy.
- Less than half of the studies were conducted in the United States. If international value estimates are to be used, adjustments for purchasing power parity across countries are needed. Having done this, it is necessary to assume that preferences are otherwise comparable across countries with different baseline levels of risk and institutional structures for addressing risks.
- Since terrorist attacks are probabilistic events and the long-term health effects of attacks also have probabilistic dimensions, knowledge of values related to probabilities is desirable for *ex ante* analyses.
- The units that value estimate apply to may vary substantially for each study case and must be converted to the units of the outcomes from the homeland security policy to be evaluated.

These issues indicate that conducting a credible benefit transfer requires careful evaluation of the available literature on study-site values and careful attention to detail in manipulating study-site values to predict the benefits of a homeland security policy. Not surprisingly, these issues are no different from those encountered in benefit transfer in any application.

There are some unique aspects to consider in benefit transfer to policies directed to address terrorist acts. Are the benefits different between preventing a terrorist act and minimizing the collateral effects in the wake of a terrorist act? For example, while the attacks on the World Trade Center resulted in many deaths, first responders and others nearby continue to experience chronic health problems (Brackbill et al., 2006). Will the public pay more to avoid a terrorist act than they would for an event with similar consequences that was caused by nature or human error? Answers to these questions will tell us whether the preferences underlying existing studies, individually or collectively, provide unbiased estimates of the benefits of terror policies or, perhaps, if they might provide a lower bound if people are willing to pay more to prevent a terror attack.

Of the three types of valuation applications we discussed above, over three-quarters of the public thinks a terror attack on our food system is

Table 10.4 Example benefit-transfer function

Variable	Definition	Benefit-transfer coding
*WTP*ACUTE	Mean willingness to pay (2000 $s)	Dependent variable
Independent variables		
ln(Δ*DAYS*)	Reduction in days with health problem	Policy-site estimate
QWBSYSCORE	Symptom score (27 symptoms)	Policy-site estimate
QWBMOBCORE	Mobility score (3 levels)	Policy-site estimate
QWBSACSCORE	Social activity score (3 levels)	Policy-site estimate
QWBPACSCORE	Physical activity score (3 levels)	Policy-site estimate
ln(*INCOME*)	Mean household income (2000 $s)	Census data
ln(*AGE*)	Mean age	Census data
%MALE	% male	Census data
US	Study conducted in the US	US
WTPAVOID	Avoid decrease in health problem	Avoid
JOURNAL	Published in a journal	Journal

Source: Van Houtven et al. (2006, Table 6, p. 788).

likely in their lifetime, and they assign the highest share of antiterrorism spending on this category (Gosh et al., 2007). This suggests that from a public perspective focusing on valuation estimation of food safety to support benefit estimation of antiterrorism policies might be an appropriate place to start in a research program to refine original benefit estimation and benefit transfers for these types of applications.

Function-Transfer Example

We present some simple estimates above to provide an idea of the potential magnitude of benefits of homeland security policies.[10] The benefit-transfer literature indicates that simply using these values for transfers is less accurate than function transfers.

Van Houtven et al. (2006) conducted a meta-analysis of values estimated for health consequences. Information from this study can be used to demonstrate how study-site information can be used to develop a function-transfer estimate that is calibrated to policy-site conditions. Variables from the Van Houtven meta-equations are replicated in Table 10.4. Before any data are applied to the benefit-transfer function, it is necessary to decide if the values are to be estimated for the average affected person or perhaps the average person in different groups, where each group experiences a different type of health effect or differs in some important characteristic that is delineated by one of the explanatory variables in the equation. Let us assume, for expositional simplicity, that all people will experience the same type of health effect and we want to predict the value for the average affected person.

Using the Van Houtven information to conduct a benefit-function transfer would require collecting some data for the policy-site days of sickness and each of the illness characteristic scores. These are not data that are always readily available and may require some primary data collection; policy-site data are needed to characterize the duration and severity of the health consequences. Socio-demographic characteristics could be obtained from census data. Finally, the analyst must make careful judgments in coding the remaining variables and may choose to code for a study conducted in the United States that estimates WTP to avoid a health consequence and, perhaps, published in a journal so that the estimates would include the advantages of a study subject to peer review. This process provides a benefit-transfer estimate that is calibrated to the specific effects of the homeland security policy and the population that is the beneficiary of the policy.

ACCURACY OF BENEFIT TRANSFERS

Some degree of error is unavoidable in any information transfer. Fisher et al. (1999) found an average error in United States commercial real estate appraisals between 1980 and 1998 of 11 percent, with 89 percent of the prediction errors falling between 0 percent and 25 percent. Hausman (1981) showed that for a single price change, which is similar to many benefit-transfer applications, it is possible to derive estimates of Hicksian consumer surplus and that the error associated with using Marshallian elasticities can be small for compensating variation (3.2 percent) and much larger for deadweight loss (32 percent).

Research on the validity of benefit transfers has largely focused on convergent validity (Carmines and Zellner, 1979). Convergent validity asks whether parallel studies, one conducted at the study site and one conducted at the policy site, provide statistically similar estimates of value or if study-site data can be used to predict a calibrated policy-site value, the policy-site estimate being the validity criterion. A benefit transfer is deemed valid in this context if one fails to reject the null hypothesis of no difference between the policy-site value estimate and the predicted value obtained by calibrating the study-site estimate(s) to policy-site conditions.

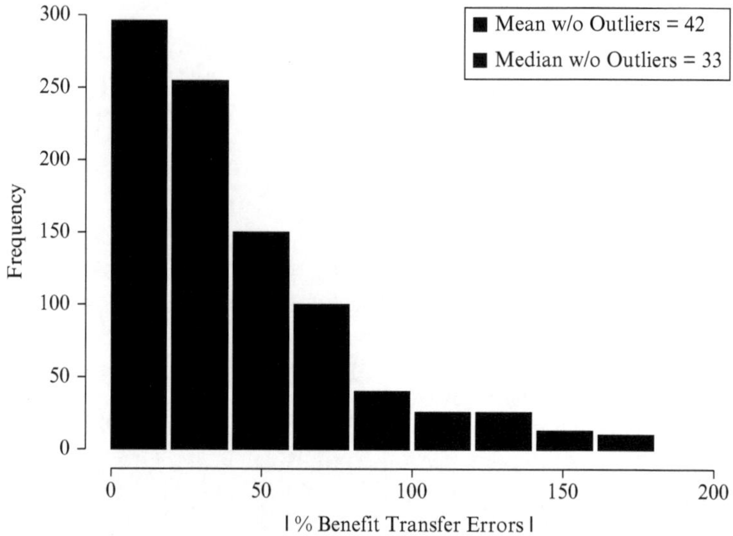

Note: Histogram is drawn for |%*BTE*| without outliers. Of 1071 observations 13.63% are outliers according to the interquartile range criterion.

Figure 10.1 Benefit-transfer errors (N = 925)

Here we will address the accuracy of benefit transfer by considering prediction errors from convergent-validity studies. Prediction errors (PE) are computed as:

$$PE = \left(\frac{\widehat{wtp}_{ss} - \widehat{wtp}_{ps}}{\widehat{wtp}_{ps}}\right) \tag{10.6}$$

where both the study-site (*ss*) and policy-site (*ps*) WTP are denoted by 'hats' because they are estimates from original studies at the respective sites.

We reviewed 34 studies that investigated the convergent validity of benefit transfers. A preliminary look at the data provides two insights: (1) a small number of benefit transfers provide underestimates ($PE < 0$), but most benefit transfers provide overestimates (PE > 0); and (2) transfer errors can be large, but the majority of errors are less than 50 percent (Figure 10.1). In reviewing the benefit transfer, convergent validity studies, we found that five studies contributed very large errors and the convergent validity comparisons were made perhaps because of data availability instead of cases one would logically consider appropriate for a benefit-transfer application. After removing data for outliers the mean absolute error is 42 percent and the corresponding median is 33 percent.

The validity criterion at the policy site is an estimate in convergent validity studies, not a known value. For example, the information in Tables 10.1, 10.2 and 10.3 indicate that most original studies have used contingent valuation to estimate values. Murphy et al. (2005) report a median error in original study-site values, compared with cash transactions, of 35 percent when stated-preference methods are used. If we assume that the policy-site value is overestimated by 35 percent, then a non-negative benefit-transfer error will add to the overestimation, and the converse would occur if the benefit-transfer error were negative.

The simple computations we reported above of $39 million per year for protecting water quality and $71 million per year for health effects of the World Trade Center attack could be associated with transfer errors of ±$13 million and ±$23 million, respectively. These potential errors are a caution that any benefit transfer should not proceed without careful implementation of the transfer. However, we do think that the transfer errors reported overestimate what the error would be in a well-designed and well-conducted benefit transfer. Many of the validity studies appear to have been conducted when there were two conveniently available studies to investigate the accuracy of transfers, and the investigators either did not apply or did not report applying conditions such as those proposed by the US EPA guidelines.

CONCLUDING COMMENTS

In this chapter we have provided an overview of how benefit transfers should be conducted, we have considered three areas where existing studies might be used for evaluating homeland security policies via benefit transfers, and discussed the accuracy of benefit transfers. The general insights developed from this chapter apply to all types of benefit transfer applications for homeland security policies. A credible benefit transfer requires the following:

1. a sound theoretical foundation of the value(s) to be estimated via benefit transfers;
2. careful selection of original studies (or meta-analysis) that matches policy-site conditions;
3. careful attention to detail, preferably using a transfer function to calibrate prediction values to policy-site conditions, when conducting the transfer;

4. the need to think ahead to identify data needed to calibrate benefit-transfer predictions with an eye towards identifying available data sources and developing plans to collect types of needed data; and
5. an investigation of uncertainty in the transfer process that could lead to error, with particular emphasis on overestimation.

Adherence to these insights can provide benefit-transfer estimates of homeland security policies that will inform public decision-making. As we note above, these considerations are important for any benefit transfer and valuating antiterrorism policies is no exception.

We suggest that a research agenda is needed to better understand public preferences for terrorism prevention policies and policies that minimize the consequences of a realized terror attack. This includes original studies that address whether benefits associated with terror policies are any different from benefits of policies with similar outcomes, which are caused by human error, nature or another source. Paramount in this research is a consideration of whether benefits are overstated, in both revealed-preference and stated-preference studies, from overreaction to low-probability events with high social consequences such as has occurred with major terror attacks (Cass and Zeckhauser, 2011). Such a research agenda will establish the foundation of a literature that provides valid estimates of benefits for homeland security policies through original studies and benefit transfers. The government is made up of people and there is no reason to believe that leaders are immune to the 'overreaction to fearsome risks' that is observed in the general public. Thus, such a research agenda is needed to ensure that public funds are efficiently allocated between antiterrorism activities and the many other government programs.

In the absence of such a research agenda, benefit transfers using existing data, at a minimum, are useful for making several types of decisions. First, a benefit transfer can indicate whether the benefits of a homeland security policy are large enough to warrant an original valuation study to estimate benefits; that is, are the benefits large enough that a careful original study is warranted to confirm the preliminary benefit-transfer estimate? Second, given that benefit transfers generally overestimate policy values, an aggregate benefit estimate based on a benefit transfer that is substantially less than costs would likely indicate that the policy is not feasible and should not be implemented from an economic perspective. Third, if estimated aggregate policy benefits are small and similar to costs, decision criteria other than net benefit analysis may warrant consideration such as the cost-efficiency approaches recommended by Farrow (2007). If the estimate of aggregate policy benefits is very large and similar to aggregate costs, this outcome may suggest that an original study is warranted, such as the study reported by Smith et al. (2009). Given the overestimation bias that has been documented, uncertainty analysis is crucial if benefits are close to costs in magnitude or exceed costs.

NOTES

1. This research was supported in part by a grant from the US EPA STAR Program.
2. The authors thank Carol Mansfield, Kerry Smith and Robert Paterson for their comments on an earlier draft of this chapter and comments by participants in the workshop on 'Estimating the Benefits of Homeland Security Policies'.
3. Harberger (1964, 1971) triangles are based on elasticities from Marshallian demand functions that are estimated using choices people make in markets.
4. For links to tables for steam, weight-load and probability of death, see http://www.engineeringtoolbox.com/saturated-steam-properties-d_101.html (accessed September 17, 2010), http://www.awc.org/technical/spantables/tutorial.htm (accessed September 17, 2010) and http://www.ssa.gov/OACT/STATS/table4c6.html (accessed September 17, 2010).
5. It is important to recognize that outcomes of some terrorist events could result in short-term or long-term sickness prior to death. In such a case, with careful analytical procedures, WTP to avoid morbidity consequences could be added to a value of statistical life estimates to obtain an estimate of total benefits of a homeland security policy. In practice, depending on the level of contamination and the effects on human health, estimates of WTP may include both morbidity and mortality considerations, which could lead to double counting if WTP and value of a statistical life estimates are added to obtain a total benefit estimate. This would be true for both the food and water risk applications discussed here.
6. The citations in this section do not include studies that have investigated the price elasticity of drinking water demand (Espey et al., 1997). These citations are excluded because they do not address shifts in demand that would arise from a quality shock, and any terrorist shock to supply reliability may have an effect on the water market beyond that which would be predicted from regulated water pricing.
7. http://www.bls.gov/cpi/cpid1007.pdf (accessed September 20, 2010).
8. http://quickfacts.census.gov/qfd/states/08/08013.html (accessed September 20, 2010).
9. http://quickfacts.census.gov/qfd/states/13/1304000.html (accessed September 20, 2010).
10. Robinson et al. (2010) report a homeland security benefit transfer using the value of statistical life estimates. We do not discuss this paper here because our focus is on morbidity, not mortality.

REFERENCES

General

Baranzini, A., J. Ramirez, C. Schaerer and P. Thalman (eds) (2008). *Hedonic Methods in Housing Markets: Pricing Environmental Amenities and Segregation*, New York: Springer.

Bateman, I.J., R.T. Carson, B.W. Day, M. Hanemann, N. Hanley, et al. (2002). *Economic Valuation with Stated Preference Techniques: A Manual*, Cheltenham, UK and Northampton, MA, USA: Edward Elgar.

Bennett, J. and R. Blamey (2001). *The Choice Modeling Approach to Environmental Valuation*, Cheltenham, UK and Northampton, MA, USA: Edward Elgar.

Bergstrom, J.C. and L.O. Taylor (2006). 'Using meta-analysis for benefits transfer: theory and practice', *Ecological Economics*, **60**, 351–360.

Boyle, K.J. (2003). 'Contingent valuation in practice', in P.A. Champ, K.J. Boyle and T.C. Brown (eds), *A Primer on Nonmarket Valuation*, Dordrecht: Kluwer Academic Publishers, pp. 111–170.

Boyle, K.J. and J.C. Bergstrom (1992). 'Benefit transfer studies: myths, pragmatism and idealism', *Water Resources Research*, **28**, 657–663.

Boyle, K.J., N.V. Kuminoff, C.F. Parmeter and J.C. Pope (2009). 'Necessary conditions for valid benefit transfers', *American Journal of Agricultural Economics*, **91**, 1328–1334.

Brackbill, R.M., L.E. Thorpe, L. DiGrande, M. Perrin, J.H. Sapp II, D. Wu, S. Campolucci, D.J. Walker, J. Cone, P. Pulliam, L. Thalji, M.R. Farfel and P. Thomas (2006). 'Surveillance for World Trade Center disaster health effects among survivors of collapsed and damaged buildings', *Surveillance Summaries*, **55**, 1–18.

Brouwer, R. (2000). 'Environmental value transfer: state of the art and future prospects', *Ecological Economics*, **32**, 137–152.

Carmines, E.G. and R.A. Zellner (1979). *Reliability and Validity Assessment*, Beverly Hills, CA: Sage Publications.

Cass, R.S. and R. Zeckhauser (2011). 'Overreaction to fearsome risks', *Environmental and Resource Economics*, **48**, 435–439.

Clinton, W. (1988). 'Critical infrastructure protection', Presidential Decision Directive, 63, http://www.fas.org/irp/offdocs/pdd/pdd-63.htm (accessed September 9, 2010).

Copeland, C. and B.A. Cody (2007). 'Terrorism and security issues facing the water infrastructure sector', in E.V. Linden (ed.), *Focus on Terrorism*, Vol. 9, New York: Nova Science Publishers, pp. 257–272.

Desvousges, W.H., M.C. Naughton and G.R. Parsons (1992). 'Benefits transfer: conceptual problems in estimating water quality benefits using existing studies', *Water Resources Research*, **28**, 675–683.

Dickie, M.A. (2003). 'Defensive behavior and damage cost methods', in P.A. Champ, K.J. Boyle and T.C. Brown (eds), *A Primer on Nonmarket Valuation*, Dordrecht: Kluwer Academic Publishers, pp. 395–444.

Engel, C.C., S. Locke, D.B. Reissman, R. DeMartino, I. Kuts, M. McDonald and A.J. Barsky (2007). 'Biosecurity and bioterrorism; biodefense strategy, practice, and science', *Practice and Science*, **5**, 155–163.

Espey, M., J. Espey and W.D. Shaw (1997). 'Price elasticity for residential demand of water: a meta-analysis', *Water Resource Research*, **33**, 1369–1374.

Farrow, S. (2007). 'The economics of homeland security expenditures: foundational expected cost-effectiveness approaches', *Contemporary Economic Policy*, **25**, 14–26.

Farrow, S. and S. Shapiro (2009). 'The benefit-cost analysis of security focused regulations', *Journal of Homeland Security and Emergency Management*, **6**, 1–19.

Fisher, J.D., M.E. Miles and R.B. Webb (1999). 'How reliable are commercial appraisals? Another look', *Real Estate Finance*, **16**, 9–15.

Gosh, K., D. Degeneffe, J. Kinsey and T. Stinson (2007). 'How would Americans

allocate anti-terrorism spending? Findings from a national survey of attitudes about terrorism', *Homeland Security Affairs*, **3**, 1–17.
Harberger, A.C. (1964). 'The measurement of waste', *American Economic Review*, **54**, 58–76.
Harberger, A.C. (1971). 'Three basic postulates for applied welfare analysis', *Journal of Economic Literature*, **9**, 785–797.
Hausman, J.A. (1981). 'Exact consumer surplus and deadweight loss', *American Economic Review*, **71**, 662–676.
Hines, J.R. (1999). 'Three sides of Harberger triangles', *Journal of Economic Perspectives*, **13**, 167–188.
Hobijn, B. and E. Sager (2007). 'What has homeland security cost? An assessment: 2001–2005', *Current Issues in Economics and Finance*, **13**, 1–7.
Holmes, T.P. and W.L. Adamowicz (2003). 'Attribute based methods', in P.A. Champ, K.J. Boyle and T.C. Brown (eds), *A Primer on Nonmarket Valuation*, Dordrecht: Kluwer Academic Publishers, pp. 171–220.
Jeong, H.J., W.T. Hwang, E.H. Kim and M.H. Han (2009). 'Radiological risk assessment for an urban area: focusing on a drinking water contamination', *Annals of Nuclear Energy*, **36**, 1313–1318.
Kirchhoff, S., B.G. Colby and J.T. LaFrance (1997). 'Evaluating the performance of benefit transfer: an empirical inquiry', *Journal of Environmental Economics and Management*, **33**, 75–93.
Landrigan, P.J., P.J. Lioy, G. Thurston, G. Berkowitz, L.C. Chen, S.N. Chilrud, S.H. Gavett, P.G. Georgopoulos, A.S. Geyh, S. Levin, F. Perera, S.M. Rappaport, C. Small and the NIEHS World Trade Center Working Croup (2004). 'Health and environmental consequences of the World Trade Center disaster', *Environmental Heath Perspectives*, **112**, 731–739.
Lukas, A. (2004). 'Protection without protectionism: reconciling trade and homeland security', *Trade Policy Analysis*, **27**, September 8, http://www.cato.org/pub_display.php?pub_id=3629.
Murphy, J.J., P.G. Allen, T.H. Stevens and D. Weatherhead (2005). 'A meta-analysis of hypothetical bias in stated preference valuation', *Environmental and Resource Economics*, **30**, 313–325.
Nelson, J.P. and P.E. Kennedy (2009). 'The use (and abuse) of meta-analysis in environmental and natural resource economics: an assessment', *Environmental and Resource Economics*, **42**, 345–377.
Parsons, G.P. (2003). 'The travel cost model', in P.A. Champ, K.J. Boyle and T.C. Brown (eds), *A Primer on Nonmarket Valuation*, Dordrecht: Kluwer Academic Publishers, pp. 269–330.
Roberts, M.T. (2007). 'Role of regulation in minimizing terrorist threats against the food supply: information, incentives, and penalties', *Minnesota Journal of Law, Science and Technology*, **8**, 199–224.
Robinson, L.A., J.K. Hammitt, J.E. Aldy, A. Krupnick and J. Baxter (2010). 'Valuing the risk of death from terrorist attacks', *Journal of Homeland Security and Emergency Management*, **7**, 1–25.
Rosenberger, R.S. and J.B. Loomis (2003). 'Benefit transfer', in P.A. Champ, K.J. Boyle and T.C. Brown (eds), *A Primer on Nonmarket Valuation*, Dordrecht: Kluwer Academic Publishers, pp. 445–482.
Shapiro, S. (2008). 'Analysis of Homeland Security regulations, small steps forward, giant leaps to go', *Regulatory Analyses*, September 8, http://regulation2point0.org/wp-content/uploads/downloads/2010/04/RA08–03_topost.pdf.

Smith, V.K., C. Mansfield and L. Clayton (2009). 'Valuing a Homeland Security policy: countermeasures for the threats from shoulder mounted missiles', *Journal of Risk and Uncertainty*, **38**, 215–243.
Smith, V.K., S.K. Pattanayak and G.V. Van Houtven (2006). 'Structural benefits transfer: an example using VSL estimation', *Ecological Economics*, **60**, 361–371.
Smith, V.K., G. Van Houtven and S.K. Pattanayak (2000). 'Benefit transfer via preference calibration: "prudential algebra" for policy', *Land Economics*, **78**, 132–152.
Spash, C.L. and A. Vatn (2006). 'Transferring environmental value estimates: issues and alternatives', *Ecological Economics*, **60**, 379–388.
Taylor, L.O. (2003). 'The hedonic method', in P.A. Champ, K.J. Boyle and T.C. Brown (eds), *A Primer on Nonmarket Valuation*, Dordrecht: Kluwer Academic Publishers, pp. 331–394.
US Environmental Protection Agency (EPA) (2000). *Guidelines for Preparing Economic Analyses*, EPA 240-R-00–003, Washington, DC: EPA.
US Executive Office of the President (1993). 'Executive Order 12866: regulatory planning and review', *Federal Register*, **58**, http://www.reginfo.gov/public/jsp/Utilities/EO_Redirect.jsp.
US Government Accounting Office (2005). 'Homeland Security: much is being done to protect agriculture from a terrorist attack, but important challenges remain', GAO-05–214, Washington, DC: GAO.
US Office of Management and Budget (2003). *Circular A-4: Regulatory Analysis*, September 17, http://www.whitehouse.gov/omb/circulars_a004_a-4/.
Van Houtven, G., J. Powers, A. Jessup and J.-C. Yang (2006). 'Valuing avoided morbidity using meta-regression analysis: what can health status measures and QALYs tell us about WTP?' *Health Economics*, **15**, 775–795.
Vandenberg, T.P., G.L. Poe and J.R. Powell (2001). 'Assessing the accuracy of benefits transfers: evidence from a multi-site contingent valuation study of ground water quality', in J.C. Bergstrom, K.J. Boyle and G.L. Poe (eds), *The Economic Value of Water Quality*, Cheltenham, UK and Northampton, MA, USA: Edward Elgar, pp. 100–120.
Watson, J.P., R. Murray and W.E. Hart (2009). 'Formulation and optimization of robust sensor placement problems for drinking water contamination warning systems', *Journal of Infrastructure Systems*, **15**, 330–339.

Food Safety Valuation

Buzby, J.C., J.A. Fox, R.C. Ready and S.R. Crutchfield (1998). 'Measuring consumer benefits of food safety risk reductions', *Journal of Agricultural and Applied Economics*, **30**, 69–82.
Buzby, J.C., R.C. Ready and J.R. Skees (1995). 'Contingent valuation in food policy analysis: a case study of a pesticide-residue risk reduction', *Journal of Agricultural and Applied Economics*, **27**, 613–625.
Eom, Y.S. (1994). 'Pesticide residue risk and food safety valuation: a random utility approach', *American Journal of Agricultural Economics*, **76**, 760–771.
Fu, T.-T., J.-T. Liu and J.K. Hammitt (1999). 'Consumer willingness to pay for low-pesticide fresh produce in Taiwan', *Journal of Agricultural Economics*, **50**, 220–233.
Goldberg, I. and J. Roosen (2007). 'Scope insensitivity in health risk reduction

studies: a comparison of choice experiments and the contingent valuation method for valuing safer food', *Journal of Risk and Uncertainty*, **34**, 123–144.
Hammitt, J.K. and K. Haninger (2007). 'Willingness to pay for food safety: sensitivity to duration and severity of illness', *American Journal of Agricultural Economics*, **89**, 1170–1175.
Nayga, R.M., R. Woodward and W. Aiew (2006). 'Willingness to pay for reduced risk of foodborne illness: a nonhypothetical field experiment', *Canadian Journal of Agricultural Economics*, **54**, 461–475.
Teisl, M.F. and B.E. Roe (2010). 'Consumer willingness-to-pay to reduce the probability of retail foodborne pathogen contamination', *Food Policy*, **35**, 521–530.
Tonsor, G.T., T.C. Schroeder, J.M.E. Pennings and J. Mintert (2009). 'Consumer valuations of beef steak food safety enhancement in Canada, Japan, Mexico, and the United States', *Canadian Journal of Agricultural Economics*, **57**, 395–416.
Wessells, C.R. and J.G. Anderson (1995). 'Consumer willingness to pay for seafood safety assurances', *Journal of Consumer Affairs*, **29**, 85–107.

Drinking Water Quality Valuation

Abrahams, N.A., B.J. Hubbell and J.L. Jordan (2000). 'Joint production and averting expenditure measures of willingness to pay: do water expenditures really measure avoidance costs?' *American Journal of Agricultural Economics*, **82**, 427–437.
Ahmad, J., B. Goldar and S. Misra (2005). 'Value of arsenic-free drinking water to rural households in Bangladesh', *Journal of Environmental Management*, **74**, 173–185.
Casey, J.F., J.R. Kahn and A. Rivas (2006). 'Willingness to pay for improved water service in Manaus, Amazonas, Brazil', *Ecological Economics*, **58**, 365–372.
Cho, Y., K.W. Easter, L.M.J. McCann and F. Homans (2005). 'Are rural residents willing to pay enough to improve drinking water quality?' *Journal of the American Water Resources Association*, **41**, 729–740.
Genius, M., E. Hatzaki, E.M. Kouromichelaki, G. Kouvakis, S. Nikiforaki and K.P. Tsagarakis (2008). 'Evaluating consumers' willingness to pay for improved potable water quality and quantity', *Water Resources Management*, **22**, 1825–1834.
Genius, M. and K.P. Tsagarakis (2006). 'Water shortages and implied water quality: a contingent valuation study', *Water Resources Research*, **42**, n.p.
Hensher, D., N. Shore and K. Train (2005). 'Households' willingness to pay for water service attributes', *Environmental and Resource Economics*, **32**, 509–531.
Howe, C.W. and M.G. Smith (1994). 'The value of water supply reliability in urban water systems', *Journal of Environmental Economics and Management*, **26**, 19–30.
Jordan, J.L. and A.H. Elnagheeb (1993). 'Willingness to pay for improvements in drinking water quality', *Water Resources Research*, **29**, 237–246.
Kim, H.J. and Y. Cho (2002). 'Estimating willingness to pay for reduced copper contamination in southwestern Minnesota', *Journal of Agricultural and Resource Economics*, **27**, 450–463.
Polyzou, E., N. Jones, K.I. Evangelinos and C.P. Halvadakis (2010). 'Willingness to pay for drinking water quality improvement and the influence of social capital', *Journal of Socio-Economics*, **40**, 74–80.

Seip, K. and J. Strand (1992). 'Willingness to pay for environmental goods in Norway: a contingent valuation study with real payment', *Environmental and Resource Economics*, **2**, 91–106.

Um, M.J., S.J. Kwak and T.Y. Kim (2002). 'Estimating willingness to pay for improved drinking water quality using averting behavior method with perception measure', *Environmental and Resource Economics*, **21**, 285–300.

Vásquez, W.F., P. Mozumder, J. Hernández-Arce and R.P. Berrens (2009). 'Willingness to pay for safe drinking water: evidence from Parral, Mexico', *Journal of Environmental Management*, **90**, 3391–4000.

Whittington, D., J. Briscoe, X. Mu and W. Barron (1990). 'Estimating the willingness to pay for water services in developing countries: a case study of the use of contingent valuation surveys in southern Haiti', *Economic Development and Cultural Change*, **38**, 293–311.

Whittington, D., D.T. Lauria and X. Mu (1991). 'A study of water vending and willingness to pay for water in Onistha, Nigeria', *World Development*, **19**, 179–198.

Whittington, D., S.K. Pattanayak, J. Yang and K.C. Bal Kumar (2002). 'Household demand for improved piped water services: evidence from Kathmandu, Nepal', *Water Policy*, **4**, 531–556.

Health Consequence Valuation

Alberini, A., M. Cropper, A. Krupnick, D. Shaw and W. Harrington (1997). 'Valuing health effects of air pollution in developing countries: the case of Taiwan', *Journal of Environmental Economics and Management*, **34**, 107–126.

Alberini, A. and A. Krupnick (1998). 'Air quality and episodes of acute respiratory illness in Taiwan cities: evidence from survey data', *Journal of Urban Economics*, **44**, 68–92.

Bala, M.V., L.L. Wood, G.A. Zarkin, E.C. Norton, A. Gafni and B.O. Brien (1998). 'Valuing outcomes in health care: a comparison of willingness to pay and quality-adjusted life-years', *Journal of Clinical Epidemiology*, **51**, 667–676.

Blomquist, G.C., M. Dickie and R.M.O. Conor (2010). 'Willingness to pay for improving fatality risks and asthma symptoms: values for children and adults of all ages', *Resource and Energy Economics*, **33**, 410–425.

Blumenschein, K. and M. Johannesson (1998). 'Relationship between quality of life instruments, health state utilities, and willingness to pay in patients with asthma', *Annals of Allergy, Asthma and Immunology*, **80**, 189–194.

Chestnut, L.G., L.R. Keller, W.A. Lambert and R.D. Rowe (1996). Measuring heart patients' willingness to pay for charges in angina symptoms', *Medical Decision Making*, **16**, 65–76.

Chestnut, L.G., M.A. Thayer, J.K. Lazo and S.K.V.D. Eeden (2006). 'The economic value of preventing respiratory and cardiovascular hospitalizations', *Contemporary Economic Policy*, **24**, 127–143.

Dickie, M. and V.L. Messman (2004). 'Parental altruism and the value of avoiding acute illness: are lids worth more than parents?' *Journal of Environmental Economics and Management*, **48**, 1146–1174.

Johnson, F.R., M. Ruby and W.H. Desvousges (2000). 'Willingness to pay for improved respiratory and cardiovascular health: a multiple-format, stated-preference approach', *Health Economics*, **4**, 295–317.

Kartman, B., F. Andersson, and M. Johannesson (1996). 'Willingness to pay for reductions in angina pectoris attacks', *Medical Decision Making*, **16**, 248–253.

Lee, P.Y., D.B. Matchar, D.A. Clements, J. Huber and J.D. Hamilton (2002). 'Economic analysis of influenza vaccination and antiviral treatment for healthy working adults', *Annals of Internal Medicine*, **37**, 225–231.

Liu, J.T., J.K. Hammitt, J.D. Wang and J.L. Liu (2000). 'Mother's willingness to pay for her own and her child's health: a contingent valuation study in Taiwan', *Health Economics*, **9**, 319–326.

Lundberg, L., M. Johannesson and M. Silverdahl (1999). 'Quality of life, health-state utilities and willingness to pay in patients with psoriasis and atopic eczema', *British Journal of Dermatology*, **141**, 1067–1075.

Navrud, S. (2001). 'Valuing health impacts from air pollution in Europe', *Environmental and Resource Economics*, **20**, 305–329.

Ready, R., S. Navrud, B. Day, R. Dubourg, F. Machado, S. Mourato, F. Spanninks and M. Rodriquez (2004). 'Benefit transfer in Europe: how reliable are transfers between countries?', *Environmental and Resource Economics*, **29**, 67–82.

Ready, R.C., E. Navrud and W.R. Dubourg (2001). 'How do respondents with uncertain willingness to pay answer contingent valuation questions?' *Land Economics*, **77**, 315–326.

Torrance, G., V. Walker, R. Grossman, J. Mukherjee, D. Vaughan, J.L. Forge and N. Lampron (1999). 'Economic evaluation of ciprofloxacin compared with usual antibacterial care for the treatment of acute exacerbations of chronic bronchitis in patients followed for 1 year', *PharmacoEconomics*, **16**, 499–520.

Zillich, A.J., K. Blumenschein, M. Johannesson and P. Freeman (2002). 'Assessment of the relationship between measures of disease severity, quality of life, and willingness to pay in asthma', *PharmacoEconomics*, **20**, 257–265.

11. What we know and what we need to learn

Carol Mansfield and V. Kerry Smith

Economic information derived from the analysis of proposed policies can have important effects on decision processes. This is especially true when agencies are making rules that restrict private behavior. In these situations, there are implications for both public and private resource allocations. The Office of Management and Budget and congressional committees exercise oversight on commitment of public resources. The implicit commitment of private resources to comply with new rules, however, lacked a specific mandate for scrutiny until Executive Order (EO) 12291 in 1981. After that, all United States (US) presidents have reauthorized comparable orders, extending the types of information assembled but retaining the basic requirement that, where feasible, there should be measures of the net economic benefits of the proposed policies. For example, EO 12866, Section 1(b) (6) states that to the extent permitted by law and where applicable, '[e]ach agency shall assess both the costs and the benefits[1] of the intended regulation and, recognizing that some costs and benefits are difficult to quantify, propose or adopt a regulation only upon a reasoned determination that the benefits of the intended regulation justify its costs'.

As we noted in Chapter 1, this volume resulted from a conference and follow-up research sponsored by the United States Department of Homeland Security (DHS) through the National Center for Risk and Economic Analysis of Terrorist Events (CREATE), at the University of Southern California. For the most part, the authors have used experience outside the realm of security-related rules to describe the issues and empirical findings relevant to the evaluation challenges DHS policy analysts face in assessing the benefits and costs of their major rules. In this chapter, we discuss the main themes and suggestions from the research discussed in Chapters 2–10. Then we consider practical steps that can be taken to develop what we have called (in Chapter 2) the architecture of a platform for policy analysis. We close the chapter with a discussion of some new research challenges that extend beyond security issues, but share common elements with the analysis of security threats from terrorism.

LESSONS FROM THE PRACTICE OF POLICY ANALYSIS

Five of the chapters in this volume adopted an *ex ante* perspective in describing the challenges in measuring the trade-offs people would make for security-related policies. They focused on how people respond to different types of risk. The US Environmental Protection Agency's (EPA) risk assessment and risk valuation efforts provide a useful starting point for consideration of how these issues can be addressed.

The first lesson from the EPA stems from the risk assessment logic developed over several decades by EPA analysts and the research community. By combining public-health data that have improved over time with more extensive records of the ambient concentrations of air pollutants, and greater resolution in the nature of the health effect being measured, analysts have developed reasonably well-accepted estimates of the relationship between ambient concentrations and health outcomes, most notably premature mortality. This research has led to a set of spatially delineated baseline estimates for the risks of health effects at current levels of air pollutants. Moreover, it has provided the basis for estimating the risk changes that would be associated with changes in ambient concentrations of the pollutants. Both types of estimates are important in evaluating new environmental rules with benefit–cost analysis.

Comparable information is simply not available for security-related risks. The set of events at risk is diverse. As with environmental policies, mortality and morbidity risks are important. However, the channels linking the sources of these risks to the actual risk changes that might arise from policy are exceptionally large. Threats can arise through transportation infrastructure, food and water supply systems, public spaces, and in residential and workplace environments. Equally important are some key differences in the mechanisms giving rise to the risks. Dockins and Wheeler's description (Chapter 3) implicitly suggests that the process of exposure to environmental contaminants, especially air pollutants, is a continuous one. People can undertake averting behaviors to reduce their exposure, but the atmospheric channel conveys pollutants as long as the sources of emissions are active. These sources are usually power generation, manufacturing, and transportation systems in the communities where people live, but sources can be in distant areas if they are linked through an air-diffusion system with the local area. It is therefore not surprising that we would observe regular 'doses' of pollution. In contrast, the sources of security risks may be continuously present, but the magnitude of the threat is largely unobserved until the events take place.

Monitoring systems that detect evidence of threats compromise individual privacy and thus can constitute another type of threat to freedom, as the activities since Edward Snowden leaked National Security Agency records have suggested. It seems unlikely that we can expect to be able to structure analysis strategies around data gathered at the expense of individual privacy. But we can use the EPA risk assessment structure as a template for organizing research to inform the structure of the risk assessment methods that underlie current security decisions. For example, we could adapt Posner's (2004) suggestion for 'inverse benefit–cost analysis'. He describes the process as follows:

> Analogous to extracting probability estimates from insurance premiums, it involves dividing what the government is spending to prevent a particular catastrophic risk from materializing by what the social cost of the catastrophe would be if it did materialize. (p. 177)

Posner's logic assumes that expected social cost, C, is the product of the loss, L, and the probability, p. Estimates for C and L then allow for computing the p implied by past policies. More specifically, if equation (11.1) defines the expected social cost, then equation (11.2) reverses the logic by describing how large the perceived probability of a threat would need to be in order to motivate an action:

$$C = p \cdot L \tag{11.1}$$

$$\hat{p} = \frac{C}{L} \tag{11.2}$$

For specific policies, the details are a bit more complex than this example.[2] To illustrate what we have in mind, suppose we assume that before a security policy is introduced, the expected loss due to terrorist action is given in equation (11.3):

$$C^0 = p^0 \cdot L \tag{11.3}$$

When a policy is introduced that affects only the probability, the expected loss is given by (11.4), where a is the cost (public and private) of the policy:

$$C^1 = p^1 \cdot L + a \tag{11.4}$$

Subtracting equation (11.4) from (11.3), we have (11.5):

$$L(p^0 - p^1) = C^0 - C^1 + \mathrm{a} \tag{11.5}$$

Thus, the incremental probability reduction is defined by the expected social cost saving plus the policy cost divided by the loss due to the action, as in equation (11.6):

$$p^0 - p^1 = \frac{C^0 - C^1 + a}{L} \tag{11.6}$$

Filling in the unknowns in (11.6) is a tall order. Nonetheless, it does offer a first step in quantifying the implicit risk assessments underlying past decisions.

Consider as an example, a Transportation Security Agency policy to screen air passengers. Assume that the likely targets of terrorist actions would be high-profile flights, such as on the anniversary of 9/11, in the time since the screening was introduced. L would then be the set of flights on this date from major US and international airports. For the sake of argument, suppose a string of three attacks in successive years would be sufficient to cripple air travel. Then $C^0 - C^1$ is the expected social loss due to these attacks. Valuing the lives lost as 'statistical lives' in L and $C^0 - C^1$, plus the costs of screening, including time costs, would allow us to gauge the implied $p^0 - p^1$.

There are a multitude of judgments embedded in these simple computations. However, comparing the results across several *ex post* policy choices begins to fill in the matrix of implied risk assessments associated with these security decisions and the policies involved. We could debate the assumptions about exactly what the population at risk would be, as well as what the targeted events would be. The value of the exercise is not as a critique of past decisions, but rather as a window into the risk assessments that might be associated with proposed policies. To the extent that policies are associated with eliminating some sources of risk, the strategy recovers an estimate of baseline risks.

This reverse logic is only a beginning. It provides a template for organizing the information we have from past policy decisions. It allows analysts to construct 'what if' benefit–cost assessments for new policies associated with similar channels for security threats. Even when past policies were not based on benefit–cost analyses in quantitative terms, they can still be used as a database for risk assessment matrices by computing what their costs (direct and implicit) and estimates of avoided losses imply for the risk changes they must have provided to warrant action. The goal should not be *ex post* rationalization, but rather systematizing the information on risk assessments implied by these past choices.

Chapters 4 and 5 described the reasons for heterogeneity in estimates of the value of a statistical life (VSL), and the arguments for adopting a single value for the purposes of policy evaluation. We agree that a single value is likely to be best for *ex ante* analyses of future policies. However, it is important to recognize that this decision does not preclude using different values for the VSL based on the specific circumstances of past policies in the process of filling in the different *ex post* risk assessment matrices that we described earlier. Using a variety of assumptions can help in identifying the important features of security problems that will influence how risk assessment is done for future security decisions.

The discussion of natural hazards in Chapter 6 indicates that it may be possible to estimate environmental risk reductions for policies for some natural hazards. We could infer implied values for components of infrastructure that might also be subject to terrorist threat. Chapter 9, which discussed the value of time, offers another dimension for variation in the *ex post* template; the potential estimates for the shadow value of time that enter into the indirect costs of policy.

A second set of lessons from EPA arises from recognition that substitution within household and firm production activities can mitigate the effects of security-related disruptions. The consequences of closing transportation routes or banning foods due to threats depend on substitution. Chapter 8 shows how computable general equilibrium (CGE) models can be adapted for use in economic-impact analyses of threats and policies. The sensitivity analyses associated with these economic analyses offer a menu of research questions about the parameters that are especially influential.

There are at least three further ways in which economic impact analyses can be linked to policy evaluation. Firstly, using a CGE framework to evaluate the consequences of past policies can enhance the information available for the reverse-logic approach we propose to construct risk assessments. This is especially true when the effects of a policy are associated with non-human health risks and extend across sectors.

Secondly, the logic used to match security disruptions to the simple multiple-market setting for most CGE models requires a specific display of what the analyst believes will be the channels of influence to the economy. Would disruption shut down access to some resources, be equivalent to an added 'shadow price' for resources, or alter the patterns of substitution in production for consumption? How would effects confined to a few key regions influence the whole economy? Chapter 8 describes the connection to past analysis of natural disasters in framing an adaptation to conventional CGE models. It also highlights the generic similarities in considerations of how disasters that have regional-scale impacts can be linked to the economy-wide models used to evaluate security policies.

Recent empirical research on the effect of natural disasters on economic growth and income highlights the importance of many of the issues raised in Chapter 8. We will return to them in our discussion of future research, below. For now, four insights from this empirical research should be noted. First, the spatial scale, sector, and timing of an exogenous shock influence the path of per capita growth in response to disaster. Second, some of the methods that these empirical studies have used select specific economies as 'control observations' to match the 'treated economies'. This strategy usually selects specific economic activities in developing economies as features that would define the key attributes of an economy. They provide the basis for arguing that the treated and control economies are similar aside from the treatment. In this example the treatment is the natural disaster. In the end it is difficult to separate the assumptions each analyst is making in selecting the activities judged to be important in specifying comparable economies. We believe there should be greater focus on these decisions, because they serve to identify what are actually comparable economic conditions for the statistical evidence of disruptions due to natural hazards from the perspective of the analysts involved. The insights derived from such a closer focus would assist those analysts involved in modifying the CGE models to reflect adjustments in response to hazards. Adam Rose's research reported in Chapter 8 is an example where these types of adjustments had to be made to estimate the economic impacts of terrorism. More specifically, the features that are associated with comparable economic conditions should match the changes that are relevant to economies at different stages of development.

Third, empirical research on the effect of natural disasters on economic growth has found that shortcomings in governance and the public institutions associated with responses to hazards can compound the effects of an exogenous shock. While the natural hazard itself may not impact growth, it can precipitate transformations in governance that have permanent growth impacts. Fourth and finally, there is a growing set of research suggesting that terrorist activities can influence both economic and non-economic outcomes. Abadie and Gardeazabal (2003), for example, found that the Basque civil war negatively impacted economic activity in Spain. Later, and also in Spain, Montalvo (2011) reported evidence that terrorist bombings affected elections, noting that before the election (and the terrorist bombings) opinion polls suggested that conservative politicians had a clear advantage. After the attacks when the actual election was held, the socialist party won in the congressional election.

This evidence indicates that market effects alone are insufficient to capture the full effect of terrorist actions. Attitudes expressed through elections and, in some cases, through more extreme political actions, can affect economic outcomes.

A final lesson to be learned from EPA is that private adaptation always needs to be considered. As Chapter 7 suggests, the persistent threat of terrorism influences private responses. Responses can take the form of relatively low-cost averting behaviors that are small: backup generators, extra inventories of food and/or medical supplies, and so forth. More significant changes in urbanization patterns and in large, discretionary social or entertainment venues can result from persistent threats. The extreme precautions for the recent Winter Olympics offer a vivid example. When such changes occur, those creating the threat may respond by selecting a different set of targets. In contrast to the case of environmental hazards, the agents who are the source of terrorism threats can respond to the security changes by altering their targets. Thus we do not necessarily avoid the threats; we displace them to other areas or activities.

All of these issues imply a need to distinguish between short-term and long-term analysis of policy. Adaptations to urban form are not likely to be relevant concerns in short-term analysis. Over the longer term, anticipated policies and threats are likely to affect behaviors in ways that cannot be reflected in the evaluation of rules. But the potential for adaptation implies that rules themselves should be designed to be adaptive to new circumstances.

SOME PRACTICAL FIRST STEPS

There are a number of steps that DHS can take to improve the analysis of homeland security policy. One of the key suggestions made in the CREATE workshop was for DHS to establish an Economic Analysis Advisory Committee of outside experts. Much like the Science Advisory Board at EPA does, the Economic Analysis Advisory Committee would provide direction for long-term research, guidance on methods and data, and review of past analyses. By establishing the committee, DHS would commit to being guided by experts in the fields that are essential to conducting a high-quality benefit–cost analysis. DHS should commit to preparing draft guidance for the Advisory Committee. Such guidance could begin by defining practices for risk assessment and strategy for benefit analysis. The strategy development would be a shared, involving effort on the part of DHS and the Advisory Committee. It would also signal to the research community the areas where assistance is needed.

The retrospective analyses mandated under EO 13563 (and described in Chapter 1) suggest another practical step. DHS's plan to improve policy analysis calls for systematic reviews of past rules. Why not use these reviews to assemble the information for a pilot evaluation of our proposed 'reverse benefit–cost' logic to fill out implied risk assessment matrices?

It would be productive for DHS to engage with the academic community in several different ways. The challenges posed by the evaluation of DHS rules will require long-term research activity. The Advisory Committee is a first step towards acquiring the research information essential to policy evaluation. Involvement of DHS policy staff in professional meetings, DHS sponsorship of graduate student interns, and programs for postdoctoral visiting appointments to the policy staff are all ways to develop the expertise necessary to produce high-quality policy evaluation procedures.

EPA's National Center for Environmental Economics is an outgrowth of over a decade of consistent involvement of professional staff in the theory and practice of regulatory design and evaluation. Current staff members were, in some cases, visitors to the center at an earlier stage in their careers, or were supported as graduate students. The center's commitment to research that improves evaluation methods attracted them to stay. Center staff members are active in professional organizations. This activity contributes to processes that highlight the agency's key questions for researchers, and facilitates the use of emerging research on policy evaluation.

RESEARCH QUESTIONS

Small Steps

Extensive research has been done on the trade-offs people are willing to make to enhance a variety of environmental services. Researchers also have several decades of experience in estimating the physical relationships between health outcomes and various air pollutants. Both literatures have been subject to multiple meta-analyses. Indeed, we are at the stage where comparative meta-analyses of important valuation concepts, such as the VSL, serve to frame policy debates and research design.

But what do we know about the trade-offs people would make for security from different types of threats: from natural hazards, crime, terrorism, and similar risks? To our knowledge, comparative reviews of these literatures have not been undertaken. Comparative reviews were the first steps leading to the meta-analyses that are now undertaken routinely in the environmental literature. Before such analyses were possible, commissioned literature reviews served to organize the empirical record and to highlight consistencies and differences. In Chapter 2 we discussed the features of three different stated preference studies that we developed under the CREATE research program. There is now sufficient research to assemble literature reviews that would answer the following questions:

1. What do we know about the trade-offs people would make to avoid risks due to natural hazards, crime, and security? In developing this review, we should consider how stated and revealed preference estimates compare.
2. What have we learned about people's risk perceptions from the literature, since Slovic's (1987) classic paper, and how do events and information change these perceptions?
3. What do we know, at a fine-grained level, about the spatial distribution of damage from natural hazards and other unpredictable events, such as large fires or industrial accidents, and the pattern of regional economic recovery? Which groups move back after a disaster and which ones do not?

There is no reason, aside from support (and encouragement to the research community), that these literature reviews could not be completed and used to inform the design of policy evaluation strategies.

We might expect to realize short-term pay-offs from research by following the playbook for EPA's early efforts to develop risk assessment methods. Before the development and cross-validation (through replication) of statistical concentration-response functions for major air pollutants, the Office of Air Quality Planning and Standards invested resources in encoding expert assessments of risk relationships. A similar effort could be made for security risks, and used in conjunction with *ex post* analyses of rules as a source of the implied risk assessment. A comparison of encoded risk assessments with those implied by a variation on Posner's (2004) reverse benefit–cost logic would help to fill in the elements important to distinguishing implicit risk assessments.

The final small step we suggest involves a bit more effort than the others. In October 2011, the Transportation Security Administration introduced the Trusted Traveler pre-screening program, in which travelers apply to be admitted to the TSA pre-screen for a fixed fee. Members of selected airlines' frequent-flyer programs may also apply to be pre-screened. An option for pre-screening is also available to military personnel. Pre-screening occurs at randomly assigned times, according to the TSA web page. This program is described as one that will not be as frequent or consistent for travelers who have joined the Trusted Traveler program.

These programs offer opportunities to evaluate several dimensions of the screening program. For example:

1. How does the pre-screening program affect screening times at different airports for peak and off peak times?
2. Who incurs the time and application costs for these programs? What would be the implicit values for the time savings?

DHS could consider varying the cost of pre-screening applications to learn about travelers' willingness to provide the data required to qualify and to pay for membership in the program so that they received the anticipated future time savings. These estimates would be useful for a wide array of policy evaluations.

Larger Steps

A major theme of Chapters 1 and 2 is that DHS needs to commit to organizing the analyses it is currently undertaking, both for new rules and as part of the retrospective program, in a way that helps to build an 'analysis platform'. Such a platform provides an organized set of practices for DHS risk assessments and benefit–cost analyses. It would also need to be framed in a way that is consistent with the call from the United States Office of Management and Budget (OMB), the Office of Science and Technology Policy (OSTP), and the Council of Economic Advisers (see Burwell et al., 2013 for an evidence- and innovation-based approach to rulemaking). Our introductory chapter highlighted features of security policy that create unique challenges. Nonetheless, the risk assessment and economic-valuation logic used for environmental regulations can be modified to start the platform-building process. Modification and learning by doing will no doubt lead to amendments that create a more nuanced and tailored set of activities to fit the unique dimensions of benefit–cost analyses for new security policy. The CREATE workshop, which led to this volume and subsequent research, identified longer-term research needs. Two of them deserve special attention.

The first need is connected to the problem of the general insecurity that arises from a non-specific perception of threats to private activity. We describe this as ambiguity, inability to specifically quantify risks, or the effects of a set of risks that all lead to a perception of worry about safety when undertaking certain activities. Chapter 6 described several ways that non-specific perception of threats influences non-expected utility models. In Chapter 2, we discussed how these perceptions motivate strategies that would treat the outcomes of programs to reduce specific risks as yielding a bonus outcome if overall perceptions of safety were enhanced.

For the most part, the discussions of bonus outcomes in this book are based on either theoretical analyses of non-expected utility models, with specific assumptions to describe how ambiguity affects well-being, or on attitudinal surveys that evaluate how individuals perceive some sources of risk and why they might evaluate them differently. We do not know of any studies that have considered the 'bonus' from multiple actions, or the mechanisms that give rise to worry or reduce it. We need research that links applied theorists to two other groups: social scientists and psychologists doing surveys of risk perceptions, and economists exploring opportunities for field experiments (see Harrison and List, 2004). Moving beyond 'vague stories' requires a systematic program of research.

We need, also, to consider the links between non-market and market outcomes in a general equilibrium setting. Carbone and Smith (2008, 2013) have proposed strategies for introducing non-market effects as alternatives that make non-separable contributions to preferences or production in a generalization to conventional CGE models. These are largely technical linkages, outside markets, between activities or choices and consequences for non-market services. We need to extend this kind of strategy to security-related threats that could disrupt infrastructure, reduce safety (and willingness to undertake some activities), impose external effects, and have other, similar consequences. This activity could begin with the template described in Chapter 8, but it must move beyond exogenously imposed parameter changes that mimic a policy, to changes in a technical set of linkages that allow a general equilibrium set of responses similar to the logic described in Carbone and Smith's discussion of ecosystem services. Strategy development is a long-term initiative that requires dedicated research programs. It can inform and be informed by the short-term initiatives we have described.

We began this volume by citing Samuelson's description of national defense as the prototypical example of a pure public good, both in terms of its attributes and in the seeming impossibility of measuring its value to people. We hope that the discussions in this volume have shown that this description is no longer relevant. We are producing enhanced security and making direct expenditures and implicit expenditures of time and other resources for it. Applied economists have learned a great deal in the nearly four decades since Samuelson described national defense as the prototypical public good. We *can* make progress in the measurement of how separate activities contribute to security, and of how that security enhances aggregate outputs and society's well-being.

NOTES

1. 'Costs and benefits shall be understood to include both quantifiable measures (to the fullest extent that these can be usefully estimated) and qualitative measures of costs and benefits that are difficult to quantify, but nevertheless essential to consider' (EO 12866).
2. The example extends and clarifies the effort to implement Posner's logic in Akhtar et al. (2010).

REFERENCES

Abadie, Alberto and Javier Gardeazabal (2003). 'The economic costs of conflict: a case study of the Basque Country', *American Economic Review*, **93**, 113–132.

Akhtar, Juned, Torkel Bjornskau and Knut Veisten (2010). 'Assessing security measures reducing terrorist risk: invers ex post cost–benefit and costs-effectiveness analyses of Norwegian airports and seaports', *Journal of Transportation Security*, **3** (3), 179–195.

Burwell, S.M., C. Muñoz, J. Holdren and A. Krueger (2013). *Memorandum to the Heads of Departments and Agencies, Subject: Next Steps in the Evidence and Innovation Agenda*, July 26, Executive Office of the President, Office of Management and Budget.

Carbone, Jared C. and V. Kerry Smith (2008). 'Evaluating policy interventions with general equilibrium externalities', *Journal of Public Economics*, **92**, 1254–1274.

Carbone, Jared C. and V. Kerry Smith (2013). 'Valuing nature in a general equilibrium', *Journal of Environmental Economics and Management*, **66**, 72–89.

Harrison, Glenn W. and John A. List (2004). 'Field experiments', *Journal of Economic Literature*, **42**, 1009–1055.

Montalvo, José G. (2011). 'Voting after the bombings: a natural experiment on the effect of terrorist attacks on democratic elections', *Review of Economics and Statistics*, **93**, 1146–1154.

Posner, Richard A. (2004). *Catastrophe: Risk and Response*, New York: Oxford University Press.

Slovic, Paul (1987). 'Perception of risk', *Science*, **236** (4799), 280–285.

Index

9/11 attacks, impact of 108–11, 146, 158, 175, 193

Abadie, A. 158, 259
adaptation, need for 260
adaptive resilience 184
advantages of cities
  trading 159–60
aggregated willingness to pay (AWTP) 33, 34, 120–21, 133
Aguiar et al. 220
aid for terrorism victims 109, 110
air pollution 132, 255
  policies 80–81
  rules 55
air quality standards 67
Air/Sea Biometric Exit Project (Exit) 10, 11, 12–16
air travel 213–14, 217, 218, 257
  airport scanners 167
    fatalities 94
    safety 8, 81, 94, 225–6
    terrorist threat 39, 40–44, 175, 178
ALARP ('as low as reasonably practicable') 127, 129, 130, 131
Aldy, J.E. 78, 83, 88, 90, 91, 94, 96, 98
American Time Use Survey (ATUS) 220, 221
arithmetic mean 120, 121, 125
Arrow et al. 36
Arrow, K. 148
Arzaghi, M. 162
auto travel 213, 215–16
  accident risks 105, 204
  fatalities 94, 108, 113, 122
  non-fatal injuries 131
Axelrad et al. 71

Baker et al. 120
baseline conditions/risk 11, 17, 33, 124, 125, 126, 241
Basque civil war 259
Becker, G.S. 165
Becker model 208–10, 222
behavior
  averting behavior studies 231
    economic 185–6, 193, 194
    irresponsible and risk 113
behavioral linkages 175, 177, 178
benefit–cost analysis
  inverse benefit–cost analysis 256
  reverse benefit–cost logic 262
benefit-function transfers 232, 243
benefit transfers 226–47
Benzene Study 103–4
Bier, V. 149
bioterrorism 177–9
bladder cancer cases 73
Blomberg, S.B. 193
BLS (Bureau of Labor Statistics) 99, 101
Blumenschein, K. 238
Boisvert, R. 180
bombs 48–54, 174, 175, 186
bounded rationality 181, 194
Boxer, Senator Barbara 93
breakeven analysis 73
Brookshire, D. 180
Brownstone, D. 215
Burwell et al. 263
business interruption (BI) 178, 181, 190, 192
business travel 216, 218, 219

cameras, security 51
Canada 93
cancer 72, 73
  risk 52, 103–5, 126
Carbone, J. 188, 264
Carmines, E.G. 243
Carson et al. 36
Carter, D.A. 125

Carthy et al. 123, 131
car travel *see* auto travel
catastrophic events 135, 137–8
Caves et al. 186
CBD (central business district) 161–2
Centers for Disease Control and Prevention 238
CFOI (Census of Fatal Occupational Injuries) 88, 91, 99, 102, 103, 106
CGE (computable general equilibrium) analysis 173, 178, 179–90, 258, 259
chained approach 123, 131
chemical, toxic 71
Chicago 158
children and travel 220–21, 222
Chilton et al. 124, 125
choice experiments 222
choice model 41, 51, 231
choice panels 41, 49–50
choice set 32–3, 34–5, 44, 68, 70
city centers 157–70
  consumer city center 163
Clean Air Act 67, 101, 102, 103
Clear Skies Initiative 93
climate change 159, 166–8, 180
Clinton administration 234
closure rules 188, 189
Cobb–Douglas production functions 180
Cody, B.A. 234, 236
collateral effects of terrorism 238, 241
commuting, reverse 163
compensation 91, 105–7
compensation test 120, 136
complementarities 4
Connecticut 162
constant elasticity of substitution (CES) production function 181, 184, 185
contamination of water system 190–93, 234, 236–7
consumer surplus (Hicksian) 143
contingent valuation (CV) 36, 121, 130, 231
convergent validity 243, 244
Copeland, C. 234, 236
Costa, D.L. 169
cost–risk trade-off 105
Council of Economic Advisers 263
Covey et al. 113, 123, 125, 132
CPS (Current Population Survey) 86, 90
CREATE (National Center for Risk and Economic Analysis of Terrorist Events) 5, 263
crime, falling 163, 169
Cropper et al. 126
crowd-out effect 168
Customs and Border Protection (CBP)/US 30

Dalvi, M.Q. 131
damage 91, 105–7, 143, 144, 145, 146, 147, 150, 151, 168
  natural disasters 36, 167
damage function approach 67
death
  premature 124, 126, 131
  risks 108–13
Defra (Department for Environment, Food and Rural Affairs)/UK 132
demand shocks 160
Dermisi, S. 158
DHS (Department of Homeland Security)/US 6–18, 28, 55, 57, 63–4, 149, 167, 168, 170, 225, 260–61, 263
  budget for 6, 8
  and events the size of September 11, 2001 146
dirty bombs 48–54, 174, 175, 186
disequilibria 188–90
disinfection byproducts (DBPs) 72–3
disproportion 129
Dixon et al. 183, 184
DOT (Department of Transportation)/US 39
dread effect 124–5, 126
drinking water program/regulations 72
Duchin, F. 182

earthquake 180, 181
econometric models 181, 183, 184
economic analysis 64, 66, 67, 68, 69, 70
Economic Analysis Advisory Committee 260, 261
economic consequence analysis 174–6
economic disequilibria 182
economic losses 183
economic resilience 182, 188–90

economic valuation 69
education, effect on leisure time 220
Edwards v National Coal Board (1949) 127
elections, effect of terrorist bombings 259
electricity outages 186–7
Elnagheeb, A.H. 236
employment
  effect of time 220
  and labor pooling 160, 162
  and pay 210–12
endogenous probability 147–52
endpoints, health 71–2
Engel et al. 238
environmental risk reduction 104
EPA (Environmental Protection Agency) 54, 63–75, 80–81, 99, 101, 103, 228, 255–7, 258, 259–60
  National Center for Environmental Economics 261
  risk management strategy 36
  and senior discount controversy 93
  and valuation of life controversy 96
European Commission 93
evacuations 50–51, 52, 190
Evans, M.F. 37
ex ante analyses 107, 141, 142–3, 144–6, 147, 149, 151, 172–3, 218, 241, 255, 258
Executive Order (EO) 12291 80, 254
Executive Order (EO) 12866 226, 254
Executive Order (EO) 13563 8–9, 10
Exit (Air/Sea Biometric Exit Project) 10, 11, 12–16
exogenous risk 147–51
exogenous shock 259
ex post analyses 141–2, 143, 144, 145, 148, 151, 173, 258, 262
ex post policy choices 257

FAA (Federal Aviation Administration) 94
fairness 93, 94
families and travel 220–21, 222
Farrow, S. 141, 142, 145, 146, 147, 149, 150, 225, 246
fatalities 135–6
  auto 94, 113, 122
  rail 131, 132
fatality risk 36, 82–3, 86, 90, 91, 98, 99, 101, 102, 103, 104, 108
  and HSE 127
FDA (Food and Drug Administration)/US 46
fear as public bad 5
fear factor 175, 178, 190, 193
federal income taxes 44–5
Federal Reserve 193–4
FEMA (Federal Emergency Management Agency) 8, 146
fiscal and monetary policy 193–4
Fischhoff et al. 185
Fisher et al. 243
floods 145–6, 147–8, 167
food-borne illness 44, 47
food security 44–8
  home test kit 44, 45, 47
  test kit for food-borne contaminants 44, 45, 47
food supply attacks 226, 228–9, 232, 233, 241–2
food supply risk valuation 233–4, 235
foot and mouth disease attack 178
Freeman, A.M. 27, 141, 142, 143, 144, 145, 146
freeways 215–16
function transfers 227, 230–31, 232, 242–3

game theory 149
Gardeazabal, J. 259
gasoline tax 41, 43
GDP (gross domestic product) 8
general equilibrium effects 186–8
geographic information system (GIS) 181
Giesecke et al. 175, 184, 186, 194
Gollier, C. 27
Google 162
  Google Insights 165–6
  Google Trends 165
Gordon et al. 175, 184
government relief for terrorism victims 109, 110
Greenstone, M. 26
Greenwich 162
gross disproportion 129, 130
gross output approach 117
ground-to-air missiles 42

Guha, G. 180
Guidelines for Preparing Economic Analyses (EPA) 66, 67, 228

Hammerton et al. 130
Hammitt, J.K. 126
Harberger triangles 227
harmonic mean 120–21
Harrison, Glenn W. 264
Hausman, J.A. 243
hazard quotient 70
hazards 140–52, 185, 186, 258–9
Hazus model 146
HCT (hypothetical compensation test) 120, 136
Health and Safety at Work Act 1974 (HSWA)/UK 127
Health and Safety Executive (HSE)/ UK 125, 126, 127–30
health consequence valuation 238, 239–40
health endpoints 71–2
hedonic model
  hedonic damages 105
  hedonic labor market model 82–3, 84
  hedonic labor market studies 101, 112–13
  hedonic modeling 231
  hedonic pricing 121
  hedonic wage studies 98–9
Henderson, V. 162
Hersch, J. 84, 85, 86
heterogeneity 79, 83–4, 87–9, 107, 114
hijacking 42
hindsight bias 109
Hines, J.R. 227
Hirst, I.L. 125
HMRI (Her Majesty's Railway Inspectorate)/UK 128–9, 131
Hobijn, B. 8, 225
Homeland Security Act (2002)/US 6
Howe, C.W. 236
human health risk assessment 75
hurricanes 147–8, 149, 168
hypothyroidism 72

immigration 86–7
improvised explosive devices (IEDs) 174
income 91, 94–5, 96, 168, 208, 209–10, 212
income elasticity 91, 94
income tax 41, 43, 44–5, 50
India 83
indirect effects of policy 55–6
intelligent adversaries 147–51
intercity travel 216, 217, 218
interview methods 123
investor premia 185, 186
I-O models 181, 182, 183, 184, 187, 188
Iraq War 194
Israel 168

Jacobs, Jane 160, 162
jamming device 43, 44
Jeong et al. 236–7
Johannesson, M. 238
Jones-Lee et al. 122, 130, 131
Jones-Lee, M.W. 122, 125, 126
Jordan, J.L. 236

Kahn, M.E. 169
Kasperson et al. 185
Katrina, hurricane 147–8
Klaiber, H.A. 173, 176, 193
Kniesner et al. 88, 91
Knowledge Networks 108
  panelists 45, 48
Kokoski, M. 180
Krugman, Paul 158

labor markets 84–7
labor pooling 160, 162
labor productivity 8
Lady Gaga 166
Landrigan et al. 238
Lange, G. 182
latency 104, 105, 126
leave time, paid 50, 51
Lee et al. 177
leisure time 208, 209, 211, 220
lettuce crop attack 178
leukemia risk 103–4, 105
Liao, S. 180, 184–5, 190, 194
life expectancy 94, 132, 133
Lind, R. 148
List, John A. 264
Liu, J.T. 126
local travel 216, 217

location and CGE 183
London, risk of terrorism 169
Loomes, G. 125
Los Angeles 175
loss of life 178
Lukas, A. 233

macroeconomic indicator approach 173
macroeconomic repercussions 183
Magat et al. 105
Management of Health and Safety at Work Regulations 1992 (MHSW)/ UK 127
Managing Risks to the Public: Appraisal Guidance (HM Treasury) 129–30
Manhattan 169
man-portable air-defense systems (MANPADS) 175
marginal social utility of income 120
marginal utility of income 41, 208, 209, 212
marginal utility of leisure 208
marginal WTP 36, 45
market
  behavior 181
  feedback effects 188
  resilience 182
  work 220
Markusen, J.R. 188
Marshallian elasticities 243
Marshall v Gotham Co Ltd (1954) 128
Mason et al. 133
May et al. 55, 56
Mayne, Thom 167
MCDA (multi-criteria decision analysis) 134–5
McKee, M. 180
media, coverage of terrorism 165
medicine 44, 45, 47
meta-analyses 91, 241, 242, 261
metropolitan areas 157–70
Mexican immigrants 86–7
Microsoft 162
military response, US 194
minimizing regrets analysis 73–4
minimizing social losses 73
missiles 42, 43
mitigation 176
monetary policy 193–4
money–risk trade-offs 81, 84, 101, 112
monitoring devices 51
Montalvo, José G. 259
Moore, Michael 88, 89
moral hazard 113
morbidity 236, 238, 255
mortality risk 37, 39, 101–2, 236, 238, 255
motor-vehicle accident deaths 94, 108, 113, 122
Mrozek, J.R. 96
multi-criteria decision analysis 137
multiple-fatality accidents 125, 131, 132, 136, 137
murder rate 163
Murphy et al. 245

National Center for Environmental Economics (US) 71, 261
National Center for Risk and Economic Analysis of Terrorist Events (CREATE)/US 5
National Flood Insurance Program (US) 145, 146
National Institute of Occupational Safety and Health (US) 99
National Oceanic and Atmospheric Administration (NOAA/US) panel 36
National Research Council (NRC)/US 63–5
National Traumatic Occupational Fatality (NTOF/US) data 99
natural hazards/disasters 36, 108, 111, 112, 113, 137, 140–52, 166–8, 180, 258–9
Navarro, P. 8
net benefits, measuring 68
Network Rail (UK) 131
New Immigrant Survey (NIS) 87
New Orleans 168
New York City 163, 169, 175
NICE (National Institute for Health and Clinical Excellence)/UK 132–3
non-cancer health effects 70
non-cancer risk assessments 64
non-fatal injury risks 86
non-fatal road injuries, prevention 130

non-fungibility of time 213
non-homeland security 6, 8
non-linear dose-response function 72
non-market effects 182, 264
non-smokers 86
non-work income 208, 210

OAQPS (Office of Air Quality Planning and Standards) 54, 96
objects of choice 31–3, 34, 39, 68, 70
Office of Air Quality Planning and Standards 262
Office of Rail Regulation (ORR)/UK 131
Office of Research and Development, EPA 75
Okrent, D. 125
Oladosu, G. 182, 193
OMB (Office of Management and Budget)/US 92, 228, 263
opportunity cost of time 38, 39, 45, 205, 210, 219, 221
opportunity cost of travel 209, 219
OSHA (Occupational Safety and Health Administration)/US 92
OSTP (Office of Science and Technology Policy)/US 263
outages, cost 186–8
outcomes 28, 32, 34
  probabilities of 67
output-based values 130
overtime wage 211–12

paid leave time 50, 51
Palmquist et al. 212–13, 216
Panel Studies of Income Dynamics 91
passengers, airline 81
  information 28, 30, 31
  screening 257
patrols 43, 44
policy analysis architecture 80
policy site 226, 228, 229, 232, 244
  days of sickness 243
  value 245
  value estimate 227
  value predictions 230, 231
pollution 132, 255
  policies, air 80–81
  rules, air 55
Posner, E. 106, 107, 256, 262
prediction errors (PE) 244
preference calibrations 231
preference elicitation 122, 123
premature death 124, 126, 131
preparedness 53, 55, 56
pre-screening 262–3
prevention 53, 55, 56, 57
probabilities of outcomes 67
production disruption 180
production function, CES 181, 184, 185
production recapture 185
productivity 192–3
  advantages of metropolitan areas 159–60, 161, 169
property appraisals 227–8
property damage 178, 180, 181
protection 53, 55, 56, 57, 192
proximity, productivity advantages 160
public good 33, 264
public water supplies 236–7
  attack 226, 234

quality of life improvements and terrorism 163
queues, cost of waiting and efficiency 222

rail accidents 113, 125
  single-fatality rail accidents 125, 126, 131, 136, 137
rail industry, UK 126
Rail Safety and Standards Board (RSSB)/UK 128–9, 131–2
Railways (Safety Case) Regulations 1994 (UK) 127
RDDs (radiological dispersion devices) 48–54, 174, 175, 186
real estate, effect of terrorism 164, 192
'Reckonings: an injured city' (Krugman) 158
recollection bias 109
recovery 53, 55, 56, 182
Red Book 65, 66
reduced form
  equation estimates 231
  meta-analysis 230
Reducing Risks, Protecting People (HSE) 128, 129

regulatory option 74
relative to a reference dose (RfD) 70
reliability
  and travel 214–15
  of water supply 236
relocation 190
remediation 175–6, 192
Republicans 112
resilience 174, 175, 177, 178, 180–81, 184–5, 190, 192, 193
response 53, 55, 56
revealed preference methods 34–5, 36–9, 121, 231, 246
  revealed preference valuation 221
reverse commuting 163
RIAs (regulatory impact analyses) 10–17, 92
risk 36, 63–4, 75, 81, 84–6, 241, 255
  ambiguity of 4, 5, 17
    analysis 63–4, 66, 71, 74–5
    assessment 54, 64–70, 71–5
  baseline 11, 17, 124, 125
  of being killed in an automobile accident 122
  of cancer/leukemia 52, 103–5, 126
  change 38
  changes in 78
  and hazards 185
  irresponsible behavior and 113
  job fatality risk 82–3
  lifetime 104
  management 36, 54, 55, 63, 66, 68–9
    mortality 39
    non-incremental changes 100–102
    non-specific perception of 263
    orientation 55
    personal responsibility 113
    personal risks 113
    'protective' risk management decision 68–9
    reduction 11, 17, 32, 37, 46, 55, 57, 73, 79, 81, 94, 133
    risk–money trade-offs 81, 84, 101, 112
    risk–wage combinations 82–3, 97
    risk–wage trade-offs 81, 89, 94, 98, 100–101, 106–7, 121
    risk–wealth trade-offs 121–2, 123, 131
  from terrorism 108–13, 161
  and trade-offs 97
  in the workplace 99
Risk Assessment for Benefits Analysis (RABA) 71–2
Risk Assessment in the Federal Government: Managing the Process (NRC) 65, 66
road safety 94, 112, 130
Roberts, M.T. 233
Robinson et al. 137
Robinson, L. 219
Robson, A.J. 188
Roe, B.E. 234
Rose, A. 174–6, 180, 183, 184–5, 190, 193, 194
Rose et al. 173, 175, 177, 184, 187, 188, 190
Rosen, S. 83

SAB (Science Advisory Board) 66, 75
safety
  adequate margin of 54, 67
  airline 81, 94
  food 48, 232, 233, 234, 242
  highway 94, 112, 130
  job market 113
  perception of 4, 8
  and public sector appraisal 117–38
  regulation 81
Sager, E. 8, 225
Samuelson, Paul 3, 264
Sandy, hurricane 147–8
San Jose, California 162
scanners, airport 167
Schelling, Thomas 161
Science and Decisions (NRC) 66
scope insensitivity 122, 123–4
Scott, M. 141, 145, 146, 147
screening 110–11, 257, 262–3
Secure Flight rule 28, 30, 32, 33, 38
security cameras 51
segmentation of labor markets 85–7
selection effect 159, 161
September 11, 2001 attacks, impact of 108–11, 146, 158, 175, 193
SFAIRP ('so far as is reasonably practicable') 127
shadow value of time 258
Shapiro, S. 142, 225

shelter 50–51, 52
Shepard, D.S. 88
Shoven, J. 178
slackness conditions 188–9, 190
Slovic et al. 124
Slovic, P. 17, 185
Small et al. 214
Small, K. 215
Smith, Adam 82
Smith et al. 137, 149, 225, 247
Smith, M.G. 236
Smith, V.K. 37, 173, 176, 180, 188, 193, 212, 264
smokers 85–6, 109, 110
social capital 169
social cost 141, 205
social losses 73–4
societal concern 129
societal risk 129
Sohn et al. 184
space 183
Spencer, A. 8
spillover effects 56, 160, 161
stadium attack 178
Stage 1 Disinfectants and Disinfection Byproducts Rule (DBPR) 73–4
stated choice experiments 35–6, 213, 222
stated preference methods 35–6, 38, 39–54, 97, 104, 107, 121–3, 221, 231, 246
  and non-fatal road injuries 131
  on terrorism risks 111, 113, 137
statistical fatality 118
stock and flow losses 181
structural
  equation estimates 231
  meta-analysis 231
suburbs 157, 160–61, 162
Sunstein, C. 26, 106, 107, 124
Superfund program 70
surface mode travel 216, 217, 218
surface-to-air missiles (SAMs) 42
swing weighting 134

targeting passengers for airport screening 110–11
taxes 41, 43, 44–5, 46, 47, 50, 209–10
tax revenues 46
Taylor, L.O. 96
technical change
  and effect on time 219
  technological change 185
Teisl, M.F. 234
television, coverage of terrorism 165
terrorism 44, 55–6, 137, 140, 141, 143–4, 145–6
  baseline probability of successful attack 11, 17
  commercial aircraft, threat to 40–44
  compared with natural hazards 148–52
  deaths from 107–13
  effect on elections 259
  macroeconomic consequences of 172–94
  reduced risk 32
  risk in city centers 157–70
  threats 39, 64
  and VSL 147
Thaler, R.H. 83
Thompson, Tommy 233
thyroid cancer 72
time
  opportunity cost 38, 39, 45, 205, 210, 219, 221
  preference 104
  value 203–22
The Tolerability of Risk from Nuclear Power Stations (HSE) 129
toll roads 215
tort damages 79
TOR (risk tolerance) 127
tourism 163, 169
toxic chemical 71
trade-offs 33, 37–8, 54, 68, 97, 100–101, 118–19, 261–2
  between civil liberties and risk 109
  between civil liberties and waiting time 110
  cost–risk 105
  ex ante 11
  injury–risk of death 123
  and labor markets 86
  measuring individual 34–6
  and revealed preference measures 39
  and risk of automobile injury 204
  and VSL 81
  wage–risk 83

wealth–risk 121–2, 123, 131
weighting 134
trading, advantages of cities 159–60
traffic accidents 111, 113, 137
transportation 204
Transportation, Department (USDOT) 94–5, 221
guidelines 216–19
Transportation Security Administration (TSA)/US 28, 30, 225, 262–3
Transport Department (UK) 117, 119, 121, 123, 130–31
travel 204–8, 209, 212, 213–19, 220–22
personal 216, 218, 219, 220–21
see also air travel; auto travel
travel cost models 231
treatment effect 159, 161
truck drivers 216, 217
Trusted Traveler pre-screening program 262–3

UK
Department for/of Transport 117, 119, 121, 123, 125, 130–31
railway accidents 113, 125, 126
uncertainty 73, 247
unemployment
and labor pooling 160, 162
and negative demand shock 160
United States (US)
best cities 164
budget for 'non-homeland security' 6, 8
National Flood Insurance Program 145, 146
natural disasters 111, 112, 113
Office of Air Quality Planning and Standards 262
OMB 92, 228, 263
protection of water supplies 236
terrorist attacks 108–11, 112, 113
VSL 83, 92–3, 94–6, 99, 101–3, 137–8
see also DHS (Department of Homeland Security); EPA (Environmental Protection Agency)
urban center attack 178
USDOT (Department of Transportation) 216–19, 221
US Government Accounting Office 233–4
utility functions 123, 173, 194
utility service disruption 180

validity criterion 245
valuation study 246
value estimates 227, 231, 241, 242
value of life's pleasures 107
value predictions 230, 231, 232
value transfers 227, 228, 229–30, 232
Van Houtven et al. 105, 242, 243
Viscusi et al. 104
Viscusi, W.K. 78, 84, 85, 86, 90, 96, 113
and terrorist risks 108, 109, 111, 137
and VSL 83, 88, 89, 91, 94, 98, 147
VOLY (value of a life year) 132, 133
VSL (value of a statistical life) 36, 37, 39, 73, 78–114, 118, 119, 120, 133, 136, 147
adopting single 124–6, 257–8
age 87–9, 93, 94
demographic adjustments, banning 93
government number for VSL 106
and RSSB 131–2
senior discount 93
for single- and multiple-fatality accidents 137
valuation of life controversy 95–6
VSLY (value of a statistical life year) 89–90, 93–4

wage
compensation 104
differentials 81–2, 85
premia 185, 186
rate 208, 209–10, 211, 212, 214, 216, 218
wage–risk combinations 82–3, 97
wage–risk trade-offs 81, 89, 94, 98, 100–101, 106–7, 121
waiting time 8, 38, 39, 110–11, 204–5, 218–19, 221–2
watch lists 30, 31, 32
water quality 236
regulations 55
water supply risk valuation 234, 236–7
water system attack 178, 181, 190–93, 226

wealth–risk trade-off 121–2, 123, 131
welfare measures 176
Western Hemisphere Travel Initiative (WHTI) 10–11, 206–7
Whalley, J. 178
Wing et al. 188
wireless networks 219
women and support for government relief for terrorist victims 109, 110
Wooldridge, J. 150
World Trade Center 238, 241
wrongful death cases, compensation 105–7
WTA (willingness to accept) 97, 98, 99
  and magnitude of risk change 100–102
WTP (willingness-to-pay) 11, 17, 35, 36, 41–2, 95, 98, 99, 122
  and age 94
  aggregated 33, 34, 120–21, 133
  and Department of Transport (UK) 130, 131
  and dirty bombs 50, 51, 52, 54
  and *ex post*/*ex ante* approaches 142–3, 145, 146, 149
  and food safety plans 45, 48, 229, 234
  and income 91
  for large risk decreases 99
  and magnitude of risk change 100–102
  and NICE 133
  for reducing cancer risks 104
  and safety 118–19
  for security of commercial airlines 43, 225
  and VSL 88
  for water 236

Zeckhauser, R.J. 88, 108, 109, 113
Zellner, R.A. 243
Zhuang, J. 149